Edible Wild Plants

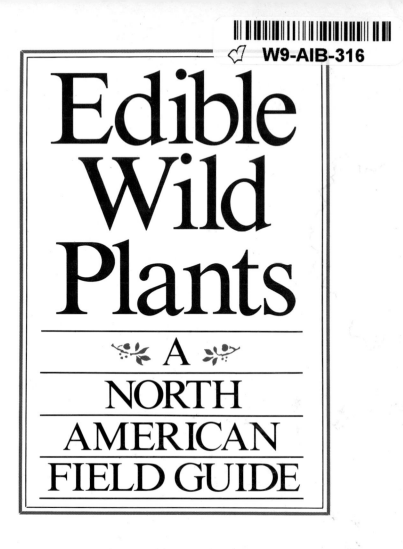

A

NORTH AMERICAN FIELD GUIDE

Thomas S. Elias & Peter A. Dykeman

AN
OUTDOOR
LIFE BOOK

Sterling Publishing Co., Inc.   New York

Library of Congress Cataloging-in-Publication Data

Elias, Thomas S.
　　Edible wild plants : a North American field guide / Thomas S.
　　Elias & Peter A. Dykeman.
　　　　p.　　cm.
　　Includes index.
　　Reprint. Originally published: New York : Outdoor Life
　　Books, c1982.
　　　1. Wild plants, Edible—United States—Identification.　2. Wild
　　plants, Edible—Canada—Identification.　3. Cookery (Wild foods)
　　I. Dykeman, Peter A., 1935–　　　II. Title.
　　QK98.5.U6E35　1990
　　581.6′32′0973—dc20　　　　　　　　　　　　　　90-39506
　　　　　　　　　　　　　　　　　　　　　　　　　　　　CIP

10

Published 1990 by Sterling Publishing Company, Inc.
387 Park Avenue South, New York, N.Y. 10016
Originally published as *Field Guide to North American Edible Wild Plants*
by Outdoor Life Books © 1982 by Thomas S. Elias and Peter A. Dykeman
Distributed in Canada by Sterling Publishing
% Canadian Manda Group, P.O. Box 920, Station U
Toronto, Ontario, Canada M8Z 5P9
Distributed in Great Britain and Europe by Cassell PLC
Villiers House, 41/47 Strand, London WC2N 5JE, England
Distributed in Australia by Capricorn Ltd.
P.O. Box 704, Windsor, NSW 2756 Australia
Printed in China

Sterling ISBN 0-8069-7488-5

Contents

Acknowledgments

This book is a compendium of information we gathered over many years of study. Of course, any work on edible wild plants builds upon the experiences of others, beginning with the accounts of the American Indians and early European settlers, and continuing to the present.

Many people assisted us in the preparation of this book. Central to the entire effort was Neil Soderstrom, who served as editor and friend. His ideas helped make the book more useable and his encouragement and prodding brought it to fruition. Jeff Fitschen designed the pages and created the maps. Lloyd Birmingham drew the edible symbols. Helen Dykeman helped with typing, and Brian Elias assisted in some of the photo sessions. We are also grateful to the New York Botanical Garden for use of its botanical library resources, among the finest in North America.

While the majority of the photographs here are our own, many came from other sources. We are grateful to friends, colleagues, and institutions that supplied color transparencies. We've listed full names of photo sources below, alphabetically. Credits by last name or institutional abbreviation appear in parentheses in photo captions.

Dr. Loran C. Anderson
Nelson T. Bernard Jr.
Frank P. Bogel
James Clawson
Bill Cramer
Dr. Garrett Crow
Desert Botanical Garden, Phoenix, AZ
Dr. Peter A. Dykeman
Dr. Thomas S. Elias
Osbra L. Eye
Dr. Albert Feldman
Dr. George W. Folkerts
Dr. James Hardin
Jepson Herbarium, University of California, Berkeley
Bob Hutchins
Berrie Kavasch
Arthur R. Kruckenberg

Dr. Dale McNeal
John Mathisen
Dr. Robert H. Mohlenbrock
Helen Mulligan
New York Botanical Garden (NYBG), Bronx, NY
Dr. Robert Ornduff
John Pawloski
Robert A. Ross
James R. Shevock
Neil Soderstrom
Robert Speas
James Stevenson
University of California, Davis
U.S. Dept. of Agriculture (USDA)
C. S. Webber
Dr. William A. Weber
Kay Young

T.S.E. and P.A.D.

Introduction

How to use this book

This is a season-by-season guide to identification, harvest, and preparation of over 200 of the most popular and common edible wild plants of the U.S. and Canada. Hundreds of related edible species are also noted. In addition, the book covers identification of 20 poisonous plants and notes many other poisonous ones. Neither edible nor poisonous mushrooms are included.

Detailed texts, maps, drawings, and nearly 400 photos (mostly in color) allow easy identification. But since there are over 20,000 species of plants to choose from in North America, excluding Mexico, it's important to make identifications with care and caution. The trick is to carefully compare features of the plant at hand against those here. Remember this rule: *When in doubt, leave the plant out.*

We have included edible plants for each season from every major region of the U.S. and Canada, except for the subtropical areas of southern Florida. We have excluded obscure plants and plants that are only marginally edible. Likewise, we have omitted plants that occur in limited numbers or are threatened. Two such plants are the Joshua tree *(Yucca brevifolia)* and the Saguaro cactus *(Cereus giganteus),* both slow-growing trees of the southwestern U.S. Rare or threatened species should never be gathered.

The book's plant-seeking and identification systems are simple and versatile. In most cases, you'll probably want to begin by consulting the "Seasonal Key to Plants," beginning on page 30. This Key groups plants by *primary* "edible season," with other edible seasons noted there as well. Within the Key, you can easily hunt up plants in various ways: whether by common or scientific name, by distribution range, by general plant type, by habitat, or by edible options — whether you have an urge for something boiled, baked, raw, and so on. The more you use the Key, the more you'll like it.

On the other hand, you may know a plant's scientific or common name and simply want to learn more about it. In this case, just find its page reference in the Index in the back of the book. *Caution:* Often, unrelated plants share a common name — from region to region, and from guidebook to guidebook. Thus, it is wise to learn or at least check the scientific names.

At other times, you might prefer to browse a seasonal section in the body of this book itself to see what kinds of plants you might encounter on your next outing. There you'll find plants arranged as they are in the Key, by edible season. Within each of these seasonal sections, plants are arranged by type. That is, ferns appear first. Then come monocots such as the lilies and grasses. Last come the largest group, the dicots, which include herbs (most soft-stemmed plants), then vines and shrubs, and finally trees. Within the herb groupings themselves, the plants are arranged according to flower color and leaf arrangement.

The following table gives contrasting features of monocots and dicots.

Monocots	Dicots
(such as onions, wild rice, cattail, corn lily, sweet flag, reed, camass lily)	*(such as amaranth, mustard, blackberries, strawberries, sunflower, plums, cherries, blueberries)*
Narrow leaves with parallel veins	Broader leaves with netlike veins
Flower parts in 3s or multiples of 3	Flower parts in 5s, sometimes 4s
Vascular strands (bundles) scattered throughout a nonwoody stem	Vascular strands (bundles) arranged in a ring on stem that may be woody
One seed leaf per seed	Two seed leaves per seed

Common names and scientific names.   Common names are useful, especially so if they are descriptive, but they often vary from region to region. Adding to the disadvantage of using only common names, several plant species may be known by the same common name. In this book, we've preferred to use a single common name but may list a second or even third common name when the names are widely used. But you'd be wise to confirm scientific names when consulting other plant guides or when using common names in everyday discussions.

The scientific name, in Latin, is important because it is the universally accepted name. Scientific names for all plants and animals adhere to a binomial (two-word) system and are always italicized. The first word designates the genus and begins with a capital letter. A genus is a group of closely related species. The second word indicates the species and begins with a small letter. A species is a group (or groups) of individuals that look similar and can freely interbreed. Hybrids between species do occur though.

Typographical tipoffs.   The texts covering each plant in this book employ typographic variations that highlight categories for quick reference and announce whether a mentioned plant is covered elsewhere in this book. As in the example shown two paragraphs below, each species text begins with the common name or names, beneath which are listed additional seasons in which the plant is edible. Then comes the scientific name, always in *italics,* which may be followed by an italicized synonym in parentheses. This synonym is the outdated scientific name under which you may find the plant listed in older plant guides.

Bold face type draws your eyes to the sequence of descriptive categories. ***Bold face italic*** announces primary identifying features. SMALL CAPITAL LETTERS are used for common names of plants covered in detail elsewhere in the book and located by means of the Index. For mentioned plants not covered in detail, both the common and the scientific names are given. To look up these plants in other guides, use the scientific name.

Utah juniper   *Juniperus osteosperma*
Also edible autumn, winter   (synonym: *J. utahensis*)

Habitat: mesas, mountain slopes, high plains, principally from 1,000–2,650 m (3,300–8,700 ft) elevation in dry rocky or gravelly soils. **Identification:** large *shrub* or small *bushy tree* to 8 m (26 ft) high with *furrowed ash-gray bark that shreds in long, loosely attached strips. Leaves* tiny, *scalelike, opposite and overlapping one another in 2s, closely pressed against branchlets*, 3–4 mm (0.1–0.2 in) long, usually gland-dotted on back, *sharp-pointed at tip, yellowish-green.* Male and female flowering cones usually produced in spring on separate trees, inconspicuous and usually overlooked. *Fruits small, leathery berries 6–9 mm (0.2–0.4 in) in diameter, nearly globe-shaped, reddish-brown, resinous, sweet,* with mealy texture, containing 1, rarely 2, seeds. **Harvest and preparation:** same as for ROCKY MOUNTAIN JUNIPER. **Related edible species:** CALIFORNIA JUNIPER and ROCKY MOUNTAIN JUNIPER (preceding). **Poisonous look-alikes:** same as for ROCKY MOUNTAIN JUNIPER.

Nature's diversity

Some plants taste good and are easy to digest, while others are marginally so. Many others are unpalatable or even poisonous. Why? Plants, like animals, are products of millions of years of evolution and adaptation. Through all this time and even today, they are subject to many influences, including changes in climate, soil, and water; competition from other plants; and the scores of plant-eating animals, ranging from insects to mammals. Some animals, particularly the insects, have gradually specialized by feeding on and laying eggs on specific plant species and groups. If a plant fails to adapt to these external influences, the result can be serious depletion or even extinction of its species.

Plants, like animals, have developed a myriad of defense mechanisms to counter the continuing attacks by animals. But, unlike animals, plants cannot pick up their roots and race for safety. Nor have many plants taken the offensive and become predators; the parasitic and insectivorous plants are remarkable exceptions. So to defend themselves or ensure survival of their species, most plants have developed elaborate mechanical, chemical, and reproductive characteristics.

Reproduction.   Some plant species survive largely because of their high reproductive capacity. Here, the plants reach sexual maturity early, produce large quantities of seeds or other propagules, and may be adapted to a wide variety of habitats, especially on sites disturbed by man. In these ways, dandelions, chickweed, shepherd's purse, and other plants channel much of their resources into reproduction. With their rapid growth and early maturation, they outcompete many slower-growing plants. This phenomenon is easiest to observe in yards and on land reverting back to a wild state.

Armament.   Still other plants employ an arsenal of external structures (spines, thorns, stinging hairs) that can deter larger animals from browsing. These defensive structures often occur in conjunction with internal mechanisms such as tough fibers and bitter-tasting or even poisonous chemical compounds. Did you ever notice how many thistles remain uneaten in fields otherwise heavily browsed by deer or cattle?

External chemical defense.   Another defense is the production of tiny glands or glandular hairs on the plant surfaces. These structures may produce an array of chemical compounds that may even be secreted onto the surfaces of stems and leaves. Secreted substances usually glisten in direct light and are sticky. They may also emit a repulsive odor. Many members of the sunflower family have tiny glands on the leaves, stems, or outer surface of the flower clusters. As a test, place some fresh leaves and flowers of tarweed (*Grindelia* species) in a plastic bag for a few hours and then open the bag. You'll smell a heavy resinous odor from the glandular secretions. The secretion and odor are believed to repel leaf-eating animals.

Internal chemical defense.   Many plants produce chemical compounds within the leaves, flowers, and fruits, which make the plant taste bad or render it toxic.

The cholla's armament, below left, consists of spines that readily pierce flesh. Spine tips may break off when you attempt to remove them. Below right, the glistening, sticky coating on tarweed flowers is secreted by tiny flower glands. As a chemical defense, it renders the plants unappetizing to potential predators. (Elias photos)

This is why some recipes later in this book tell you to soak the plant parts in water first or to discard the water after the plants have been cooked. Other recipes recommend using only young leaves or stems because the young parts do not contain high levels of the undesirable chemical compounds. Also, young parts are tenderer because the vascular strands and fibers have not had enough time to enlarge and toughen. Even extended cooking won't render all plants edible. The poisonous components in such plants as irises, water hemlock, and others cannot be broken down, nor can they be leached out by water changes or cooking.

Appeal to animals. There are times when it is to a plant's advantage to be eaten. After plants have flowered and produced fruits, reproduction and, ultimately, survival of the species require that the seeds be dispersed to sites suitable for germination and growth. To achieve seed dispersal, plants use unwitting animals. Consider the tasty and nutritious flesh of wild berries. The tiny seeds inside many kinds of berries pass through animals unaffected by the digestive process and are so dispersed in excrement.

What determines the taste of wild plants?

Experienced foragers know that the taste of a particular species from one site may differ slightly from that of the same species at another site. This is due to genetic variation usually manifested in differing physical or chemical characteristics. Thus, the degree of bitterness or mildness in many members of the mustard and daisy families, for example, can be attributed to natural genetic variations. Chemical composition of the soil along with other substances added by man or animals can affect the taste of some plants, especially smaller herbs.

Then too, people themselves differ in their ability to taste and in their tolerance of certain plant compounds. Just as many foragers enjoy fresh dandelion greens and boiled cattail stalks, others may detest them. You might acquire a taste for certain wild edibles only after experimenting with harvest and preparation techniques.

Danger of overharvesting

Avoid overharvesting and thus eradication of a plant from a site. Try to make a note of the reproduction levels of wild edibles in your area. If you harvest native plants faster than they can reproduce, you'll have a detrimental impact on the environment. It's a good rule always to leave some mature plants to produce fruits and seeds.

Obviously, you won't cause serious ecological damage if you harvest plants introduced from other countries. Introduced plants are already alien to native habitats. The widespread invasions of these introduced plants in the wake of man's new settlements have permitted them to become established and in some

In summer, gravelly flood-scoured streambanks may be dominated by purple loosestrife, as shown left. Beneath the loosestrife, mature ostrich fern fronds are drying. Their brown plumes will remain until spring to help foragers find the fern's tasty young fiddleheads. Right, the density of this cattail "garden" on the edge of an artificial pond was annually increased by weeding. (Dykeman photos)

cases to overcome the natives. Examples of introduced species include dandelions, chickweed, mustard, and plantain.

Habitat guide

With the acquisition of this book, you have taken the first and easiest step toward a feast of wild edibles. Though good eating is a major goal here, don't overlook the potential fun in simply foraging for plants. With a little knowledge of plant ecology and field identification you can find an abundance of wild foods.

Except for nuts, acorns, and sap in season, forested areas have fewer edibles to offer than most unforested areas. Yet in northern deciduous forests you might find Indian cucumber and bunchberry, among many other plants. In hardwood forests early in the growing season, look for marsh marigold, toothwort, and several of the violets near small streams and adjacent mucky areas. In the rich,

Left, bulldozed two years prior to the photo at left, this "disturbed" site offers various edibles including dock (brown mature seed stalks), evening primrose (yellow-flowered stalks), and stinging nettle (dark green plants topped by long slender flower spikes). Right, desert habitats dominated by tall saguaro cacti, with edible fruits, may also offer edible prickly pear and mesquite. (Dykeman and Elias photos)

moist and neutral-soil woods you may find wild onions and leeks. Near the edge of the woods, you may see the broad leaves of garlic mustard. Here also dwell the greenbriers and catbrier.

In spring, along gravelly stream banks regularly scoured by floods, look for the delicious fiddleheads of the ostrich fern. The task is easier if you first notice the tall brown fern plumes from the previous year. Later this habitat may offer tender young nettles and one or both species of jewelweed, which, away from streams, may grow in moist, fairly open areas. Partially sunny areas in spring may reward you with mints and watercress.

Marshy pond edges often offer wild-food bonanzas. From the cattail ("Cossack asparagus") early in spring to the arrowhead tubers in the fall and winter, these sites provide continuous sources of foods. Among the providers are pickerel-weed, cattail, common reed, arrowhead, water lilies, great bulrush, and wild rice. It's often wise to start the spring harvest by checking for new sprouts on the cattail roots. Fortunately, none of us needs to complete the harvest season in December the way the Indian squaws did, according to Lewis and Clark, by standing in chest-deep ice water, loosening arrowhead tubers from the mud with their toes.

Sights disturbed by bulldozers or plows are always worth a close look. For a grand variety of greens, from early spring to summer, visit such disturbed areas frequently. Lawns provide dandelions, chicory, plantain, and other greens best gathered as early as possible. In recently disturbed sites such as last year's garden, mustard, winter cress, chickweed, and shepherd's purse are followed by lamb's quarters, amaranth, purslane, and many other edible "weeds." A year or so after being disturbed, these sites may then produce docks, pokeweed, evening prim-rose, salsify, milkweed, and many other edibles.

Roadsides offer bounty closely akin to bulldozed areas. Yet auto traffic and its pollutants often make roadside foraging unhealthy. In June along a lightly traveled dirt road, you may want to cut poke or asparagus shoots, or pick common day lily buds. In fall, you might dig for Jerusalem artichokes or common day lily tubers.

While foraging for spring greens, note locations of the flowers of blackberry, raspberry, blueberry, and elderberry. Most old fields and forest edges produce one or more species of berry plants during the succession toward a woodland plant community. Elderberry blossoms are edible, but be sure to leave plenty for fruit production. In the Northeast, raspberries and blueberries fruit first, followed by blackberries and elderberries. If you live in an area with heavily fruiting serviceberries, first locate their white flowers in spring against the leafless grays and browns of woods and river edges. Gather the serviceberries that the birds don't get first, during blackberry time in midsummer.

In summer throughout the rough lands of the West, look for currants, yuccas, prickly pears, and immature mesquite pods.

If you plan your vacation to the East Coast for late summer, look for ripe beach plums. They are frequently plentiful, though few people seem to pick them. If camping in national or state parks, of course, first obtain permission to pick.

In the East, September is a great month for sumac berries along the edges of woods and in old fields. The staghorn sumac is best then and the smooth sumac, which reaches its peak earlier, still has good flavor. In the West, squawbush fruits are harvested in September. As the first frost approaches, grapes and viburnums ripen along brushy fencerows and wood's edge. Early fall is also the time to drive the country roads looking for the first fallen nuts. The best-producing nut trees are in the open and along roads and old fences. Make note of the nut tree locations early and check them periodically in order to beat wildlife to the nuts when they begin to fall. In fact, you can gain the advantage over wildlife by climbing nut trees and shaking the nuts loose.

Through the fall, look in fields for hawthorn and rose fruits undergoing their post-frost sweetening. After that, you might sit back and relax until the following spring's maple sugar season.

Winter foraging serves almost exclusively for survival fare or for diversion during a January thaw. If the wild food fever strikes you in winter, you'd be best served in warmer southern climes.

Harvest and preparation

Shoots, leaves, and other aboveground parts.   For all aboveground tender parts, the time between harvest and eating is critical. Some plants lose much of their vitamin content in a few hours. So avoid saving them until they taste as flat as if they'd come from a supermarket!

It's also important to forage at correct times. Several greens, including chicory and winter cress, become bitter very early in the growing season. Pokeweed shoots increase in toxicity as they grow. And many other greens such as ostrich fern and plantain become tough or fibrous with age.

Even though the shoots lose palatability as they grow, new leaves and growing tips of many plants, such as miner's lettuce and lamb's quarters, remain tender and edible throughout the growing season. Plants such as milkweed, cattail, and common day lily also produce edible flower buds and flowers, and during the growing season are worth several foraging visits. As the years pass, you may want to develop your own regional calendar of the harvest dates for plant parts.

Some plants are best picked by hand—a leaf or tender tip at a time. Densely leaved plants such as sheep sorrel and chickweed are best pulled up whole before you use scissors to shear off the leaves. Since nettles, greenbrier, and some other edibles are armed in various ways, you'll need gloves and shears for harvesting.

Wash the freshly harvested plants with cold water. Then cook them with concern for their taste, tenderness, and nutritional value. With shoots, you can retain most vitamins by bundling and steaming them like asparagus. This works well with fern fiddleheads, cattail shoots, Japanese knotweed, and, of course, wild asparagus. Shoots with bitter sap like milkweed's or a toxic substance, as in pokeweed, may be bundled but must be submerged in changes of boiling water to render the plants safe to eat.

Normally you should avoid submerged boiling of tender, delicate leaves and

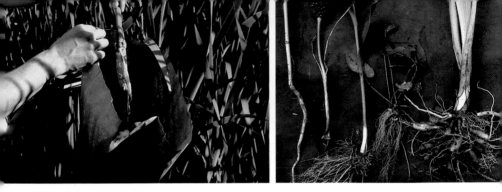

Left, for a nutritious flour additive, shake pollen from cattail male flower spikes. Plants at right (not all edible) illustrate terms used in this book to characterize underground plant parts: l. to r. are a wild carrot taproot, a jack-in-the-pulpit corm, a lily-of-the-valley bulb, violet rhizomes, and day lily tubers. (Dykeman photos)

growing tips. Here boiling has about the same effect as soaking your breakfast cereal in boiling water and then draining the water off: All the flavor and texture and much of the nutritional value are lost. For such plants, including lamb's quarters and chickweed, use just a few tablespoons of water beyond that which is left from washing. Within 1–3 minutes such greens are done to perfection.

Coarser greens such as dock and cleavers require longer cooking, barely covered with water. Cook until tender instead of just chewy. Plants with toxic or bitter substances must be boiled in changes of water, although the process reduces much of the vitamin content. A pinch of baking soda will help tenderize tough greens but promotes vitamin loss.

When possible, try to combine bland greens with those having a bitter or sour character. While coarse dry-textured greens are cooking, add a little bacon grease or butter. Season only *after* cooking.

Roots, tubers, and other underground parts.   Several plants produce taproots, tubers, or corms that are excellent substitutes for potatoes and root crops. These plants are usually best from fall through early spring when most other wild foods are scarce. The underground structures serve as storehouses of carbohydrates and are richest in starch at the end of the growing season. As the earth warms in early spring the starch is converted to sugars that may sweeten the underground structures. When the plants begin to grow and most of the starches have been converted, the underground structures generally become soft and unpalatable.

But there are disadvantages to using underground parts as food. The aboveground parts of many plants die in autumn and either shrivel greatly or break away from the root, making foraging very difficult. Then positive identification is a tough challenge since you nearly always need aboveground parts for reference. Mistaking a species such as death camass (*Zygadenus*) for the edible camass (*Camassia*) would be fatal. As with all wild food gathering, be certain of what you collect.

Once you have gathered a batch of fleshy roots or other underground parts, cook them like potatoes. Options include boiling, baking, and frying, as well as the pit-roasting method used by Indians in dry climates. For pit roasting, dig a hole at least 2 ft by 3 ft and about 2 ft deep. Line the bottom and sides with rocks. Build an intense fire inside the pit to heat the stones and adjacent earth. After several hours of burning, clean out the burning wood and coals and line the rocks with green grass or leafy twigs. Lay in the food to be roasted and cover it with more grass. Pour in a pint of hot water to produce steam. Top the pit with 5 cm (2 in) of soil and build a fire on it. For groundnuts and arrowhead tubers, maintain the fire for 3–4 hours. To reduce camass bulbs to a sweet blackish mass, Indians cooked them from up to 3 days. Whatever way you cook underground edibles, leave the skins on to preserve most of the vitamins.

Underground parts of some plants are excellent raw as trail nibbles or in salads. Examples include wild onions, Indian cucumber, and cattail root tips. You can experiment to determine which others are neither too tough nor too bitter for eating raw.

Tough roots of cattails and some other species can be crushed to release the starch, which can then be dried for use as flour. Other species may be dried whole or sliced and stored for long periods, a very valuable preparation for Indians, who relied on seasonally available foods. Drying also removes the toxicity of the roots of plants such as skunk cabbage and jack-in-the-pulpit, which are not included in this book because of their toxicity when fresh.

Beverages.   You can brew teas from a wide range of leaves, fruits, twigs, and even roots, many of them high in vitamin C. Most tea materials may be used fresh or dried; check the species texts in this book to learn which is best for each plant.

Pick leaves at their peak growth. Then dry them in a warm place out of direct sunlight. If you use a warm oven, remember that too much heat will drive off oils that give the beverage its flavor. Store dried leaves in a sealed container. The

Below, a berry scoop fashioned from a plastic container can greatly increase your harvest rate, but it won't distinguish between ripe and unripe berries. Right, you can use a fabric-covered board to bounce most hard, unripe berries beyond a collector box. (Dykeman photos)

same principles apply to the drying and storage of fragrant twigs and root bark and to flowers of such species as basswood and clover.

To prepare a cup of tea, 1 tsp of dried material or 2 tsp of fresh are usually enough. Steep the dried ingredients in boiling water, but do not boil the tea. Otherwise you'll drive off the fragrant oils. Like commercial teas, strong-flavored ingredients need only a few minutes of steeping. Delicately flavored strawberry leaves, birch twigs, and the like may require 15 minutes or more.

For flavor variations in teas, experiment with blends of ingredients. Since many plants make good teas, the combinations are limitless, as suggested by the labels on commercially packaged wild tea blends. *Caution:* Be certain that all of your ingredients are safe to use. In this book we've avoided mention of folk remedies and medicinal uses of plants. Some of these are unproven and even dangerous. And those that may have merit often depend on correct diagnosis of an ailment. You're better off using commercially prepared medicine. Still, a cup of birch tea for a queasy stomach won't hurt you.

Coffee substitutes are usually made from roasted, coarsely ground roots and tubers. Some, such as chicory and dandelion, are best harvested outside the growing season, while chufa tubers are firm and good to use anytime. Roast the material slowly, browning it all the way through. Too high a temperature will scorch it and give you a terrible cup of coffee. Store the prepared material in a sealed container. Generally use 2 tbsp of "coffee" per cup of water. Brew it like regular coffee but do not overbrew unless you have a cast-iron stomach.

Fruits and fruit juices.   You'll need to handpick many fruits because they'll be attached too firmly to be shaken loose. But the shake method works well for bushes or trees such as mulberry, cherry, and highbush blueberry. Any large sheet of plastic or fabric will suffice. Just spread it under a portion of the plant and shake the branches above. You may be amazed at the quantities you harvest. Large trees may require climbing. This method works well on nut trees, too, and helps you beat the squirrels to the nuts.

If shaking won't work but the fruits are large and firm like cranberries, improvise a toothed scoop from a plastic 2 liter (2 quart) jug. With practice, you can make this scoop a highly efficient gathering device.

Some clustered fruits such as grapes, mountain ash berries, and elderberries will not yield to shaking or scoops. Here you'll need to take the whole cluster with fingers, knife, or pruning shears. Then you can strip the fruits from their stems. Soft fruits like strawberries and raspberries have to be picked by hand.

If you strip firm fruits such as blueberries from the twigs, you'll usually wind up with many unripe fruits in the bucket. You can sort out unripe fruits tediously by hand, or you can rig up a bounce board, as shown in the accompanying photo.

Drying Fruits. Drying processes are described later in many of the texts on individual species or plant groups. But as a general rule, select only fully ripe fruits. Dry small fruits whole, pit the pitted ones, and cut large ones into pieces or slices.

For best results place the fruits in a single layer on a rack made with a nylon screen or thin cloth. If drying is done outside, place the rack out of direct sunlight. Turn the fruit once or twice daily and cover the rack or take it inside at night. You may find it more convenient to place the rack in an attic, which may be ideally warm and dry during the summer. Just be certain there are no mice or squirrels there. Attic and outdoors drying requires from a few days to two weeks, depending on the fruit and the weather.

If you are ambitious, make a solar dryer, which is basically a sun absorbing box with adjustable vents to allow air exchange while maintaining a temperature below 80°C (175°F). The effect is the same as from using a warm oven, but the energy is free. Drying time in a solar box or kitchen oven will be from 6 hours to 2 days. Remember to turn the fruit occasionally to promote uniform drying. The process is completed when no juice can be squeezed from the fruit. If you fail to dry the fruit enough, it will mold. Store it in sealed plastic or glass containers away from light.

Most dried fruits store well but a few, such as saguaro, may have insect eggs on them and will become wormy in time. Avoid worms by pulping and boiling the fruit, then drying it in a thin sheet to make fruit leather. This lightweight, nutritious fruit form is great for trail use. For cooking use ¾ cup of dried fruit per cup of fresh fruit called for in a recipe. But soak the dried fruit about 15 minutes beforehand.

Cold drinks can be made from the juices of many fruits. Extract the juices after crushing the fruits and cooking them over low heat. To finish the beverage, you usually need only add sweetening and perhaps a little water. Grapes, cranberries, and red mulberries are among the best fruits for juices. To extract the flavors of drier fruits such as the sumacs, soak them in hot water. Served cold or hot with or without sweetening, sumac juice is delicious.

Saps from maples, birches, and other trees, taken during sugaring season, make excellent drinks. Sap is best within a day or two of harvest. Try some in spring while you are making maple syrup.

Jellies.   Most jellies are made from fruits, but any leaves with fragrant oils can be used as a base, mints being the best example. For most preparations, select firm ripe fruit. Some fruits such as grapes produce better jelly from a mixture of ripe and unripe fruits.

Wash the fruits and remove blossom ends and stems. Cut up large fruits. Crush soft fruits to start the release of juice. Add water and cook until very soft or until all seeds are free from the pulp. Pour into a wet jelly bag and drain. Squeezing the bag increases quantity but reduces clarity of the juice.

Accompanying recipes are based on the use of commercial powdered pectin. But, depending on ripeness and type, some fruits may not need pectin. To determine the need for pectin, mix 1 tbsp each of juice and alcohol (grain or wood). If a solid mass forms, no additional pectin is needed. If flakes or a loose mass forms, add pectin. Slightly underripe fruits are generally richer in pectin than ripe ones.

Jelly Recipes

Note: All recipes except grape require pectin.

Fruit	Approx. amount (cups)	Water (cups)	Approx. simmer time (min)	Juice (cups)	Sugar (cups)	Lemon	Yield (cups)
Barberry/Apple	6/3	1	20	4	3	none	4
Blackberry, Dewberry	8	none	3	3½	5	none	6
Blueberry, all types	11	1	10	5½	7	¼ C	9
Buffaloberry	8	1	10	4	6	none	7
Cherry	7	½	10	3½	4½	none	5
Currant	14	1½	10	6	6	none	8
Grape (use no pectin)	8	½	10	4	4	none	6
Huckleberry	11	1	10	5½	7	¼ C	9
Indian Fig	6	2½	20	4	4	½ C	6
Mint	1½ *	3½	**	3	4	¾ C	5½
Mountain Ash	8	4	10	4	7	¼ C	7
Mulberry, Red	8	2	20	4	5½	none	6
Plum, American	8	1½	20	6	6	3 tbsp	8
Plum, Beach and Flatwood	8	1½	20	6	8	3 tbsp	8½
Prickly Pear	6	2½	20	4	4	½ C	6
Raspberry, Black	14	1	10	5	6½	none	7
Raspberry, Red; Wineberry; Thimbleberry	10	1	5	4	5½	none	6
Rose Hips	6	2	25	4	7	none	7
Salal	6	2	20	5	5	none	7
Serviceberry	6	4	20	4½	3	½ C	6
Thornapple	8	4	10	4	7	¼ C	7
Violet Blossom	4	†	‡	2	4	¼ C	4

*Chopped leaves   **Quick boil; let stand 10 min.   †3 C boiling water   ‡Infuse 24 hr.

You can substitute liquid pectin or apple juice for powdered pectin, or you can boil the juice down until the jelly temperature reaches 105°C (220°F).

Measure the specified volume of juice in a large kettle that will allow the rolling boil required for jelly making. Stir in pectin and lemon juice, if indicated in the recipe. Bring to a full boil with constant stirring. Stir in sugar and bring to a rolling boil. Boil hard for one minute, remove from heat, and skim off foam. Immediately pour into hot, sterilized jars. When jelly is set, cover the surface with at least ⅛ inch of hot, melted paraffin. Remove any bubbles and make certain a complete seal is formed with the jar.

For the recipes in the accompanying jelly table, amounts of water and sugar will vary according to the individual batch of fruit, desired consistency of the jelly, and your taste preferences.

Jams. Jams are made from whole fruits, cooked to a thick syrupy consistency. Select fully ripe fruits, and prepare no more than 3–4 quarts of fruit in one batch.

Wash and drain fruit. Remove pits, if present. Seeds of species such as black-

Jam Recipes

Fruit	Approx. amount	Special procedures	Fruit pulp (cups)	Sugar (cups)	Other	Yield (cups)
Barberry	5 C	Crush in 1 C water; cook 20–30 min; sieve seeds	3	3¼	none	4
Blackberry	2 qt	Crush; sieve seeds; no water	5	7	none	7½
Blueberry	1½ qt	Crush thoroughly; no water	4	4	2 tbsp lemon	5½
Gooseberry	2½ qt	Remove ends; grind; no water	5½	7	none	8½
Ground Cherry	1 qt	Halve and crush; 1 cup water	4	4½	¼ C lemon	5½
Grouseberry	1½ qt	Crush thoroughly; no water	4	4	2 tbsp lemon	5½
Huckleberry	1½ qt	Crush thoroughly; no water	4	4	2 tbsp lemon	5½

Fruit	Approx. amount	Special procedures	Fruit pulp (cups)	Sugar (cups)	Other	Yield (cups)
Mayapple	2 qt	Crush in ½ C water; cook gently 20 min; colander	4	4	⅛ tsp salt	5½
Mulberry, Red	2 qt	Crush; ½ C water	4	3	none	5
Persimmon	2 qt	Halve; colander; no water	4	3	none	5
Plum, Amer.	4 qt	Pit; chop fine; ½ C water	6	8	none	9½
Plum, Beach and Flatwood	4 qt	Pit; chop fine; ½ C water	6	10	none	10½
Raspberry, Wineberry, Thimbleberry (See Blackberry)						
Salal	1½ qt	Crush and sieve; no water	3¾	5	½ C lemon	6
Sea Grape	2 qt	Crush in 2 C water; cook 15 min; colander seeds	5	2	none	5
Serviceberry	1 qt	Chop with 2 oranges; grate orange peels; water to cover	4	3	5 tbsp lemon	5½
Strawberry	2 qt	Crush; sieve seeds; no water	5	7	none	7½

berries and grapes may be strained out during the process. Chop, grind, or crush the fruits as indicated in the accompanying jam recipe table. Put in a saucepan, add water (if called for), and simmer 8–10 minutes—longer if specified. Measure fruit pulp into a large saucepan and add pectin. Bring to a full boil with constant stirring. Stir in sugar and other ingredients. Boil hard for 1 minute. Skim off foam. Ladle the jam into hot, sterilized jars to within ¼ inch of top. Seal with paraffin or airtight lids. If you use canning jars with 2-piece lids, sterilize the filled, loosely capped jars in a canner after you fill them.

For jams without commercial pectin, boil prepared fruit pulp with an approximately equal volume of sugar for about 30 minutes. Pack and store as above.

Uncooked jam can easily be prepared from many fruits by grinding or blending 2 cups of fruit with 4 cups of sugar. Let stand 30 minutes. Bring to a boil one package of powdered pectin in 1 cup of water. Stir liquid into fruit and sugar. Pour into sterilized jars and cover. Leave at room temperature for one day before refrigerating or freezing. Use within 3 months.

Pies.   Pie fillings can be as simple as fruit and sugar, but usually additional ingredients will enhance the quality. If the fruit is bland, add lemon juice; if dry, add 2 or 3 tbsp water. Vary the amounts of flour and sugar according to juiciness and sweetness. Spices may add zest. Experiment with the extras. The accompanying pie recipe table gives general, not absolute, quantities.

Nine-inch pies will require 3–4 cups of fruit unless other ingredients add significantly to the volume of the filling. For most pies, pour the fruit into the pie shell. Then mix the flour, sugar, lemon juice, water, and salt as called for and pour over the fruit. Top with spices and butter. Fruits such as huckleberries make better fillings if floured before going into the pie shell. Once again, experience or a detailed recipe book will help you arrive at the best procedure.

Bake pies at 190–205°C (375–400°F) for 40–50 minutes, unless you partially cook the fruit and other ingredients before putting them into the pie shell. For baking next to a campfire the temperature is right if you can hold your hand for

Pie Recipes

Fruit	Amount (cups)	Sugar (cups)	Lemon juice	Flour	Other ingredients
Blackberry	4	1	none	3 tbsp	2 tbsp butter
Blueberry	4	1	1½ tbsp	3 tbsp	½ tsp nutmeg, 2 tbsp butter, mix berries with flour
Currant	2	2	none	2 tbsp	2 beaten eggs

Fruit	Amount (cups)	Sugar (cups)	Lemon juice	Flour	Other ingredients
Elderberry	3½	1½	4 tbsp	2 tbsp	2 tbsp butter
Ground Cherry	3	¾	3 tbsp	none	½ tbsp ground cloves, 2 tbsp butter
Huckleberry	4	1	1½ tbsp	3 tbsp	½ tsp nutmeg, 2 tbsp butter, mix berries with flour
Japanese Knotweed	4	1½	none	4 tbsp	3 beaten eggs, ¾ tsp nutmeg
Mayapple	3 (halves)	¾	6 tbsp	none	½ tsp each, ground cloves and cinnamon
Mountain Ash	3	1¼	1 tbsp	2 tbsp	½ tsp cinnamon, 2 tbsp butter
Mulberry, Red	3	1	none	4 tbsp	2 tbsp butter
Pawpaw	6 large, sliced fruits	1	4 tbsp	none	1 tsp cinnamon, ½ tsp allspice, 2 tbsp butter
Plum	1½ sliced	1½	none	4 tbsp	1½ C sliced peaches, 2 tbsp butter
Raspberry, all	4	1	none	2 tbsp	½ tsp cinnamon, 2 tbsp butter
Serviceberry	4	¾	1½ tbsp	3 tbsp	½ tsp cinnamon or nutmeg, 2 tbsp butter
Spanish Bayonet	3 pulp	¾	3 tbsp	none	½ tsp cinnamon, ¼ tsp ground cloves or nutmeg, 2 tbsp butter
Strawberry	4	¾	none	4 tbsp	
Wineberry	4	1	none	2 tbsp	½ tsp cinnamon, 2 tbsp butter

not more than 8–10 seconds where the pie will be placed. In situations where heat may be uneven, rotate the baking pie a part of a turn every few minutes. On a campout few diners will complain even if the pie isn't cooked to perfection.

Grains, nuts, and seeds.   These fruits, like the fleshy fruits, generally ripen late in the growing season. Grains, nuts, and seeds are usually high in proteins and oils, making them valuable wild foods. Oily seeds and nuts may be used in many ways: Chopped or sliced, they serve well in baked goods and preserves and with green vegetables. They can be eaten fresh or pressed for oil extracts. Most people have tried hickory nuts, walnuts, and—perhaps among westerners—pinyon nuts. But these few most popular nuts are just the beginnings of nature's grain, nut, and seed bounty.

If you forage close to civilization, abandoned and disturbed sites will provide seeds of common weeds such as lamb's quarters, amaranth, and purslane. Conduct experimental harvests after the seeds are fully formed but before they have fallen from the plants. Cut whole plants and dry them on a cloth. When dry, the seeds can be shaken out and separated from other plant parts. This is labor-intensive harvesting, but it can be fun.

With dozens of grasses, you can separate grains from their hulls by rubbing them between your hands or rolling or pounding them lightly with a rolling pin between two towels on a hard surface. Use either a natural breeze or an electric fan to blow the hulls away as you pour the mixture of hulls and grains from a height of several feet into a container. Here are two other winnowing methods: (1) Shake the seeds and chaff in a deep container or sack, causing the denser seeds to settle to the bottom while the hulls and other light debris rise to the top. (2) Also, you can shake the mixture in water, causing the seeds, which are heavier, to sink and other materials to float. Experimentation will yield the most effective process for the seeds you have at hand.

You can grind seeds into flour the old way with stones, but a modern blender or food mill makes the task much faster. Substitute your wild flour for some of the commercial flour in any recipe. You will soon concoct some favorite blends. Some ground-up seeds also make a pleasant boiled gruel.

Little need be said about the various nuts in addition to the comments you'll find on each species later in this book. But here are a few general tips: When collecting hickory nuts and walnuts, search out trees that produce large nuts because nut cracking is too much effort to make small nuts worthwhile. The husks of hickory nuts are easy to remove. Those of the walnut must be crushed and rubbed off. If you take the trouble to remove husks in the field, you'll eliminate a stain and mess at home. Drying the nuts for at least a month makes nutmeat extraction easier.

Plant foods of the Indians

As the big-game hunting phase of American Indian history evolved into the hunting/gathering phase, wild plants became an increasingly important part of the Indian diet. Inland tribes in particular could no longer sustain themselves almost wholly on game within tribal territory, and infringement on territory of competing tribes posed a more sudden threat to life than malnourishment did. The successful tribes learned to use the plants of their region in hundreds of ingenious ways. Overall, Indians used more than 250 species of wild fruits alone.

The first cultivated crop in the Southwest was probably sunflower. But well before that crop, several thousand years B.C., Mexican Indians began to cultivate upland vines and grasses that bore goodly quantities of edible fruits and seeds. From these efforts came many forms of squashes, pumpkins, and gourds and six species of Indian-cultivated corn with more than 150 varieties. Later, Indians domesticated beans that through the centuries became five species with many color varieties. Through sound agricultural practices, Indians developed bean varieties that thrived in the many climates from Mexico to Maine. In various parts of the country, Indians also began cultivating peanuts, white and sweet potatoes, chocolate, vanilla, sunflower, Jerusalem artichokes, and other plants.

Agriculture gave the Indians more reliable food sources and, therefore, more control over their lives. Yet many tribes continued to spend much of the year away from their summer settlements by taking advantage of a sophisticated system of wild food harvesting. For example, cultivated crops accounted for only about 25 percent of the Apaches' food.

Harvesting game and wild plants dictated a nomadic life with extensive knowledge of nature. The tribes learned to harvest crops such as berries and wild rice at very specific stages to minimize losses to wildlife and natural shedding.

In the dry Southwest, sparse vegetation resulted in intensive harvesting. And Indians naturally learned to favor high-calorie foods. Saguaro fruits provided the first succulent, sweet food of the summer for the Pimas and Papagos. In addition to high sugar content, the saguaro fruits offer high amounts of fat, protein, and vitamin C. Unfortunately, today as in early times, the dried fruits become infested with fly larvae and so can't be kept long. Thus, eating the fruits, like harvesting, is seasonal. Since harvesting does not destroy the saguaro and since plenty of seeds are left behind for reproduction, intensive use over the centuries has had little effect on the saguaro population.

Other desert plants including prickly pear, agave, Spanish bayonet, and the mesquite and screw beans provided important fleshy foods. A few plants such as pigweed, purslane, and tumbleweed provided greens. To the Sonoran desert Indians, mesquite and screw beans were nutritionally more important than corn. Generally, the edible seeds used by the desert tribes came from more than 50 species of grasses. Gathering them was extremely tedious. Several hours of work often provided only a cupful of seeds that served more as a flavoring than as a nutritional ingredient.

In arid regions, the Indians employed as little water as possible when preparing foods. Many foods were prepared from dried ingredients which were soaked and then baked or roasted. Early Indians boiled foods by placing hot stones in water-filled watertight baskets or hides. Later, ceramic pots came into use. Because of the mealy nature and bland taste of the major edibles in the Southwest, Indians supplemented the flavor with herbs, salt, sugar, onions, and chili.

In less arid regions, Indians made extensive use of hundreds of plants. Roots, shoots, and leafy foods were often cooked with oils from animals, nuts, acorns, and sunflowers. Most inland tribes lacked access to salt but employed flavor accents such as mints, bearberry, spicebush, onions, leeks, and partridgeberry. Sweets came from maple sugar and many fresh and dried fruits.

To help ensure good harvests, Indians gave special care to many native plants in their natural settings. These included rice, water lilies, blackberries, cherries, currants, mulberries, oaks, hickories, walnuts, beeches, and chestnuts.

By the time the Pilgrims landed, all northeastern tribes except those of eastern Maine employed agriculture. This involved burning and clearing land, followed by the planting of native and introduced crops. Native plants included strawberries, grapes, plums, Jerusalem artichokes, and milkweed. Large fields were planted with the "three sisters"—corn, beans, and squashes (including pumpkins) introduced from the Southwest.

For some northern tribes rice was the staple food, often served with maple sugar. Family groups staked out fields for harvesting one or two weeks before the grains ripened. They harvested most of the crop by boat or canoe using two sticks—one to bend the stalks over the canoe, the other to sweep the grains off the stalk. Skilled harvesters made only the ripe grains fall. The complete crop was taken in several harvests a few days apart. Yet Indians took care to leave enough grains to produce the next year's crop. A canoe full of grain was considered a good day's work. After gathering came a complex process of drying, parching, pounding, winnowing, and a final treading to remove the last bits of the hulls before storage in bags.

In the Northeast, maple sugaring was a family project. Each family had its own reserved woodland dominated by sugar maples (sugar bush) with a sugaring lodge and a smaller storage lodge. An average camp with 900 taps in trees would obtain several hundred pounds of sugar. Sugaring was especially difficult before the introduction of iron kettles. Till then the Indians boiled sap by immersing hot stones into hide or bark containers and then reheated the stones as they cooled. After three to four weeks of maple sugaring, the family returned to their village with all the sugar they could carry. They stored the rest underground.

Today, we still use many Indian food processing techniques. For example, the Indians parched or thoroughly sun-dried grains and then stored them until grinding them just before use. Stone grinding, touted by commercial bakeries today, was the only method available to the Indians. Beans, roots, and fruits were sun-dried. For an energy rich trail food, Indians made pemmican, consisting of dried berries, tallow, and meat. This combination was usually stuffed into a cleaned intestine of a large game animal and hung to dry. The Indians also gave us techniques of barbecuing, pit steaming, and baking, as well as dishes such as succotash, bannock, and hominy.

Colonists introduced many food plants to North America. Many came by intent. Others were unwittingly introduced in the soil ballast of ships. And many of these foreign plants established themselves quickly. Today's Pimas and Papagos of Arizona may include in their diets lamb's quarters, curly dock, and dandelion introduced in the East by the colonists.

Nutrition

Media advertisements give the impression that highly refined, vitamin enriched foods are the most nutritious. Vitamins are added to compensate for those lost in processing. Next come more additives to extend shelf life. Only the food companies know how it's all prepared. Certainly food additives have some merit in today's hurry-up lifestyle, but it's doubtful that they improve on nature.

Wild foods aren't advertised since they're free for the picking. Yet wild plants are just as tasty and nutritious as store-bought produce; often more so since they're fresh and unadulterated. Nutrition, the process of digestion and utilization of foods, is the same regardless of whether the food is wild or cultivated. The more we know about nutrition, the more assurance we have for balancing our diet.

You can think of food as body fuel. The energy produced by food is measured in calories. An adult male requires about 18 calories a day, per pound of body weight. Women require somewhat less; children and adolescents, somewhat more. Strenuous exercise can increase requirements upwards of 50 percent, and exposure to cold also increases caloric needs. Thus a 175-pound man might burn a little over 3,000 calories during a 24-hour period of normal activities and burn over 5,000 calories climbing a mountain in winter.

It's impossible for us to eat exactly the right amount of food at the rate we need it, so we all carry reserves of food energy in our bodies. The most readily available energy is stored in muscles and liver in the form of animal starch, or glycogen. When energy is needed, this starch can be quickly converted to sugar. Fat, the body's secondary energy reserve, takes longer to break down into a useable source of energy. But the fat reservoir is larger. Even slim people carry enough fat to sustain life for two weeks without additional food. Fat is the most concentrated form of food energy and contains about 3,500 calories per pound.

What we eat is just as important as how much. All food contains three primary nutritional building blocks in addition to water. These are protein, fats, and carbohydrates. The enzyme action of our digestive system requires a combination of these three substances in order to function properly. Thus a knowledge of them will help you practice good nutrition and supplement your diet with wild plants in the most beneficial way.

1. Protein.   This is the only substance that can supply the amino acids necessary for building and maintaining body tissue. Protein not needed for tissue is converted to sugar and used for energy, or further converted to fat and stored. Protein in its original form cannot be stored by the body, and neither sugar nor fat can be reconverted to protein. Thus our bodies need a constant protein supply. Nutritionists recommend that 15 to 20 percent of caloric intake come from protein.

Protein also promotes the oxidation (burning) of fats and sugars for energy. An adult needs roughly a half gram of protein a day per pound of body weight; more for growing youngsters and people who are sweating heavily. Most Americans eat more protein than they need.

Although all foods contain some protein, the most significant amounts are provided by animal sources such as meat, milk, eggs, fish, and poultry. Protein from these sources is complete and contains all amino acids necessary in the diet. This is not true of vegetable protein. Each plant species is unique in the amounts and types of amino acids it provides, and no single species supplies all of the essential ones. Incomplete proteins from two or more species, however, may be combined to form a complete protein. Beans and corn are complementary in this respect, and the combination is a popular one when cooked with tomatoes. Plant and animal protein combinations also complement nicely. In this case it doesn't take much meat to satisfy human requirements. Orientals have long used poultry and fish primarily as a condiment, combined with vegetables to provide complete and adequate protein.

2. Fats.   These should provide another 15 to 20 percent of your caloric intake. Eggs, nuts, milk, cheese, butter, and oils are important sources of fats. Most people feel that fatty foods "stick to your ribs" longer, which is just another way of saying that it takes longer to digest them. This is also true of protein, so the traditional breakfast of bacon and eggs, heavy on fats and protein, sticks to the ribs. A normal diet containing meat and milk usually provides a full quota of fat.

3. Carbohydrates.   About 65 percent of your caloric intake should come from carbohydrates. And wild plants are primarily valuable for their carbohydrates. For dietary purposes, carbohydrates fall into two groups: starches and sugars. Foods high in carbohydrates include grains, vegetables, and fruit. Of these, vegetables are especially important because they are a secondary source of protein. The traditional breakfast of bacon and eggs usually includes toast and jelly, the sugars from both providing a quick shot of energy. When that's used up, the fats and proteins will be ready to provide additional fuel. Since carbohydrates are digested faster than fats and proteins and are then burned up quickly, don't be surprised if snacks of cookies, crackers, and candy don't satisfy your hunger very long. Nuts would do a better job since they also contain significant amounts of protein.

Vitamins and minerals.   Vitamins and minerals in small amounts are essential for good nutrition. Nature has provided amply in the foods we eat, and if we eat the right foods, the vitamins and minerals will be included. The table, below, shows recommended adult daily requirements. Some people (including female adolescents and pregnant and lactating women) require somewhat more.

Recommended Dietary Allowances

	MINERALS			VITAMINS				
	Calcium (mg)	Phosphorus (mg)	Iron (mg)	Vitamin A (IU)	Thiamine (mg)	Riboflavin (mg)	Niacin (mg)	Ascorbic acid (mg)
Male	800	800	10	5,000	1.4	1.6	18	45
Female	800	800	18	4,000	1.0	1.2	13	45

Source: *Recommended Dietary Allowances,* National Academy of Sciences, Washington, DC

A balanced diet.   Vital over the long term, a balanced diet is also important over short periods. Insufficient protein intake, if extended over several days, will cause fatigue, even if you consume enough carbohydrates. In addition, a disproportionate amount of fats in relation to carbohydrates usually results in an upset stomach. This is nature's way of acknowledging poor eating habits. Achieving proper balance, however, is easy if you remember this simple proportion: Measured in calories, food consumption should total about $1/5$ protein, $1/5$ fats, and $3/5$ carbohydrates.

If you want to fine tune your diet, the Appendix table on page 274 should help. The table was extracted from the Department of Agriculture's *Handbook of the Nutritional Contents of Foods.* Though with only a limited listing of wild edibles, it is the most comprehensive and reliable reference available. The table can help you balance your diet, because wild vegetables, fruits, and nuts are shown together with supermarket foods such as beef, milk, and eggs. Food values for wild plants not included are often approximately the same as those of similar cultivated plants. For example, fiddleheads would approximate asparagus in food value.

In addition to the energy content of foods, we've also included values for vitamins and minerals. Foods vary greatly in their nutritional content, and we've included this information to dramatize the need for a balanced diet.

Preparation methods.   Nutritional values of fruits and vegetables depend greatly on preparation. Fresh green leaves or shoots that must be cooked in two changes of water to make them palatable lose much nutritional value compared to those that can be eaten fresh. Also, the longer fresh vegetables are cooked, the greater the loss of vitamins and minerals to the water. Proteins and carbohydrates are less affected by cooking. So for the sake of nutrition, the preferred order of preparation options is raw, quick-cook or steam, bake, boil.

Other plant guides

Since it is impossible to distinguish among all 20,000 North American species in this or any other book, you may also want to refer to identification guides devoted to your own region or state. There are many wildflower guides available, yet even these treat only the most common species.

Here's a sampling of good regional plant guides:

- *The New Britton and Brown Illustrated Flora of the Northeastern U.S. and Adjacent Canada* by H. A. Gleason, third printing, 1963.
- *Manual of Vascular Plants of Northeastern U.S. and Adjacent Canada* by H. Gleason and A. Cronquist, 1963.
- *Manual of Vascular Flora of the Carolinas* by A. Radford, H. Ahles, and C. Bell, 1964.
- *Flora of the Pacific Northwest* by C. Hitchcock and A. Cronquist, 1976.
- *A California Flora and Supplement* by P. Munz, 1968, 1973.
- *Manual of the Vascular Plants of Texas* by D. Correll and M. Johnston, 1970.
- *Rocky Mountain Flora* by W. Weber, 1976.

Good less-technical guides include these:

- *Newcomb's Wildflower Guide* by L. Newcomb, 1977.
- *The Audubon Society Field Guide to North American Wildflowers (Eastern Region* by W. Niering, 1979; *Western Region* by R. Spellenberg, 1979).

For North American trees, we recommend *The Complete Trees of North America* by T. Elias, 1980.

Key to edible-use symbols

The symbols below appear in the "Seasonal Key to Plants" that follows and later in page margins of texts on each plant. After you've read the explanations below, you'll probably find the symbols distinctive enough to make repeated reference to this page unnecessary. You can exploit the symbols in either of two ways based on (1) your general interest in a plant's range of edible uses and (2) your desire to locate plants with specific edible uses.

Trail nibble: plant part eaten as picked along the trail

Salad: used raw in tossed salad (seldom steamed)

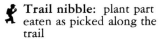 **Cooked "green" vegetable:** boiled or steamed greens, shoots, buds, flowers, or young fruits used as a vegetable

 Underground vegetable: roots, tubers, corms, bulbs, rhizomes prepared as vegetables, usually by boiling or roasting

Fritter: plant part dipped in batter and deep fried

Raw fruit: fruits eaten uncooked, though perhaps with toppings

Cooked fruit: true fruits or nonfruit parts (such as rhubarb) used in pies, baked goods, and other dessert recipes

Jams, jellies, sauces: made from fruits

Syrup and sugar: such as made from maple sap

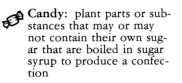 **Candy:** plant parts or substances that may or may not contain their own sugar that are boiled in sugar syrup to produce a confection

 Grains: for cereal and for cooking whole, such as rice

 Nuts, nutlets, large seeds: used whole and for oil extract

Flour or meal: grains, nuts, other seeds, or starchy roots from which flour or meal can be ground

 Hot beverage: from tea or coffee-like preparations

Cold beverage: fruit juices or originally hot tea or coffee-like beverage that has cooled

 Pickle: from pickling recipes

 Seasoning: flavoring from ground, grated, or cooked-whole parts

 Thickener: used like cornstarch to thicken soups

Caution: minor reaction may result from eating wrong part, or too much of right part, or eating at wrong stage

Poisonous: severe reaction results from eating wrong part, or eating at wrong stage

29

Seasonal key to plants

Spring

Page/Plant	Region	Habitat	Edible Uses
FERNS			
58 Ostrich fern *Matteucia struthiopteris*		swamps, bottom-lands, stream banks, ponds	
HERBS: MONOCOTS			
Flowers many in dense heads			
58 Wild onion *Allium cernuum*		dry woodlands, ridges, rocky slopes, prairies	
60 Wild garlic *Allium canadense*		open woodlands, fields, prairies	
60 Wild leek *Allium tricoccum*		moist woodlands	
62 Corn lily *Clintonia borealis*		rich woodlands, thickets	
Flowers single, leaves threadlike			
62 Asparagus *Asparagus officinalis*	Introduced and grows wild. Widespread.	roadsides, disturbed sites	

30

Page/Plant	Region	Habitat	Edible Uses
Flowers in elongate clusters			
64 Eastern camass *Camassia scilloides*		wet meadows, fields, moist open woods	
Vines			
64 Common greenbrier *Smilax rotundifolia*		roadsides, disturbed woodlands	
66 Bullbrier *Smilax bona-nox*		roadsides, fields, open woodlands	
66 Carrion flower *Smilax herbacea*		roadsides, fields, margins of woodlands	
Large semiaquatic			
68 Cattail *Typha latifolia*		ditches, margins of ponds and lakes	
68 Narrow-leaved cattail *Typha angustifolia*		ditches, margins of ponds and lakes	
Small grasslike			
70 Hard-stem bulrush *Scirpus acutus*		edges of ponds, lakes, streams and marshes	
70 Great bulrush *Scirpus validus*		edges of ponds, streams, marshes	

Page / Plant	Region	Habitat	Edible Uses

HERBS: DICOTS

Flowers small, inconspicuous

Page / Plant	Region	Habitat	Edible Uses
72 Pigweed *Amaranthus retroflexus*	Introduced and grows wild. Widespread.	waste areas, roadsides, abandoned land	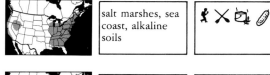
72 Green pigweed *Amaranthus hybridus*	Introduced and grows wild. Widespread.	fields, roadsides, disturbed sites	
74 Lamb's quarters *Chenopodium album*	Introduced and grows wild. Widespread.	vacant lots, roadsides, cultivated land	
74 Poverty weed *Menolepis nuttalliana*		dry salty or alkaline soils	

Flowers tiny, stems & leaves fleshy

Page / Plant	Region	Habitat	Edible Uses
76 Glasswort *Salicornia europaea*		salt marshes, sea coast, alkaline soils	
76 Russian thistle *Salsola kali*		sandy beaches, dry alkaline soils	

Stinging hairs on stem

Page / Plant	Region	Habitat	Edible Uses
78 Stinging nettle *Urtica dioica*		roadsides, trailsides, stream banks	

Page/Plant	Region	Habitat	Edible Uses

Flowers tiny, leaves basal

Page/Plant	Region	Habitat	Edible Uses
78 Plantain *Plantago major*	Introduced and grows wild. Widespread.	yards, roadsides, disturbed sites	

Flowers white

Page/Plant	Region	Habitat	Edible Uses
80 Shepherd's purse *Capsella bursa-pastoris*	Introduced and grows wild. Widespread.	yards, vacant lots, roadsides	
80 Toothwort *Dentaria laciniata*		moist woodlands, ravines, floodplains	
82 Peppergrass *Lepidium virginicum*	Introduced and grows wild. Widespread.	fields, vacant lots, roadsides	
82 Field cress *Lepidium campestre*		fields, vacant lots, roadsides, waste areas	
82 Field pennycress *Thlaspi arvense*	Introduced and grows wild. Widespread.	fields, vacant lots, disturbed soils	
84 Garlic mustard *Alliaria officinalis*		shady woodlands, trailsides	
84 Common chickweed *Stellaria media*	Introduced and grows wild; widespread in East and Midwest	yards, moist soils, woodlands, waste areas	

Page / Plant	Region	Habitat	Edible Uses
84 James chickweed *Stellaria jamesiana*		mountain meadows, seepage areas, woodlands	
86 Cleavers *Galium aparine*		rich woodlands, fields, edges of streams and lakes	
86 Northern bedstraw *Galium boreale*		stream banks, fields, open woodlands	
88 Bugleweed *Lycopus uniflorus*		wet or boggy soils, wet woodlands	
88 Edible valerian *Valeriana edulis*		ditches, moist meadows, prairies, swamps	
90 Wild strawberry *Fragaria virginiana*		open woodlands, fields, margins of woodlands	
90 Spring beauty *Claytonia virginica*		rich woodlands, wet fields, wooded floodplains	
92 Alpine spring beauty *Claytonia megarhiza*		tundra, rocky slopes	
92 Western spring beauty *Claytonia lanceolata*		high mountain slopes, moist woodlands	

Page/Plant	Region	Habitat	Edible Uses
94 Miner's lettuce *Montia perfoliata*		lower mountain slopes, moist sites, springs	
94 Canada violet *Viola canadensis*		bluffs, deciduous woodlands, rich soils	
96 Pale violet *Viola striata*		wooded flood-plains, stream banks, meadows	
96 Pokeweed *Phytolacca americana*	Introduced in West	disturbed soils, roadsides, woodland margins	
98 Japanese knotweed *Polygonum cuspidatum*		disturbed sites, vacant lots, roadsides	

Flowers yellow

Page/Plant	Region	Habitat	Edible Uses
98 Wintercress *Barbarea vulgaris*		fields, wet meadows, ditches, roadsides	
100 Black mustard *Brassica nigra*	Introduced and grows wild. Widespread.	fields, yards, disturbed sites	
100 Marsh marigold *Caltha palustris*		edges of streams, ponds, freshwater swamps	

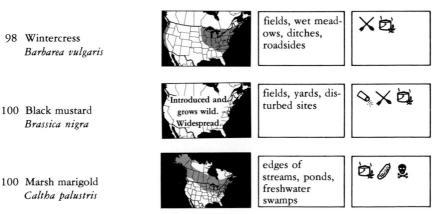

Page/Plant	Region	Habitat	Edible Uses
102 Evening primrose *Oenothera biennis*		prairies, fields, roadsides	
102 Sow thistle *Sonchus arvensis*		roadsides, fields, rights-of-way	
104 Prickly lettuce *Lactuca serriola*	Introduced and grows wild. Widespread.	fields, vacant lots, disturbed sites	
104 Dandelion *Taraxacum officinale*	Introduced and grows wild. Widespread.	lawns, yards, disturbed sites	
106 Goat's beard *Tragopogon pratensis*		roadsides, fields, disturbed sites	

Flowers pink, reddish, or purple

Page/Plant	Region	Habitat	Edible Uses
106 Common milkweed *Asclepias syriaca*		fields, meadows, margins of woodlands, roadsides	
108 Fireweed *Epilobium angustifolium*		ravines, clearings, woodlands	
108 Alfilaria *Erodium cicutarium*	Introduced and grows wild. Widespread.	fields, pastures, roadsides, disturbed sites	
110 Live-forever *Sedum purpureum*		roadsides, disturbed sites, open woodlands	

Page/Plant	Region	Habitat	Edible Uses
110 Lady's thumb *Polygonum persicaria*	Introduced and grows wild in moist soils	low wet sites, roadsides, disturbed sites	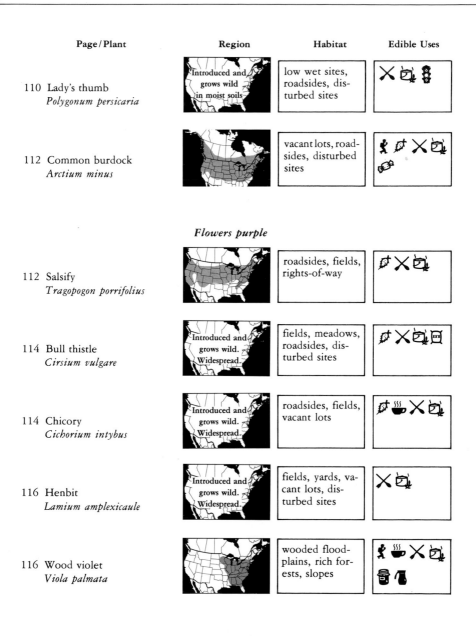
112 Common burdock *Arctium minus*		vacant lots, roadsides, disturbed sites	

Flowers purple

112 Salsify *Tragopogon porrifolius*		roadsides, fields, rights-of-way	
114 Bull thistle *Cirsium vulgare*	Introduced and grows wild. Widespread.	fields, meadows, roadsides, disturbed sites	
114 Chicory *Cichorium intybus*	Introduced and grows wild. Widespread.	roadsides, fields, vacant lots	
116 Henbit *Lamium amplexicaule*	Introduced and grows wild. Widespread.	fields, yards, vacant lots, disturbed sites	
116 Wood violet *Viola palmata*		wooded floodplains, rich forests, slopes	

Flowers tiny, often greenish

118 Orange-flowered jewelweed *Impatiens biflora*		along streams, ponds, springs, wet areas	

Page/Plant	Region	Habitat	Edible Uses
118 Yellow-flowered jewel-weed *Impatiens pallida*		wet meadows, moist woodlands	

Flowers orange to yellow

Page/Plant	Region	Habitat	Edible Uses
120 Sheep sorrel *Rumex acetosella*		old fields, gardens, disturbed sites	
120 Sour dock *Rumex crispus*	Introduced and grows wild. Widespread.	fields, roadsides, vacant lots, disturbed sites	

TREES: CONIFERS

Page/Plant	Region	Habitat	Edible Uses
122 Eastern hemlock *Tsuga canadensis*		cool moist ravines, protected valleys	

TREES: DECIDUOUS

Page/Plant	Region	Habitat	Edible Uses
122 Yellow birch *Betula alleghaniensis*		rich woodlands, wet soils	
122 Sweet birch *Betula lenta*		open woodlands, rich soils	
124 Sassafras *Sassafras albidum*		bottomlands, open woodlands	
124 Sugar maple *Acer saccharum*		eastern deciduous forests	

Summer

Page/Plant	Region	Habitat	Edible Uses

HERBS: MONOCOTS

Large grasses

| 128 Reed grass *Phragmites communis* | | edges of streams, lakes, ponds, marshes, ditches | |
| 128 Wild rice *Zizania aquatica* | | marshes, shallow ponds, lakes, streams, bays | |

Small grasslike

| 130 Chufa *Cyperus esculentus* | | ditches, banks of ponds and streams, low wet soils | |

Semiaquatic, flowers blue

| 130 Pickerelweed *Pontederia cordata* | | edges of lakes, ponds, streams, bays | |
| 132 Lance-leaved pickerel-weed *Pontederia lanceolata* | | shallow water of lakes, ponds, streams | |

Leaves large, swordlike

| 132 Sweet flag *Acorus calamus* | | ditches, ponds, swamps, lakes and streams | |

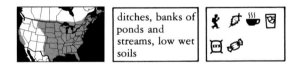

Page/Plant	Region	Habitat	Edible Uses

Flowers white, showy

| 134 Spanish bayonet *Yucca baccata* | | dry slopes, sandy soils | |
| 134 Soapweed *Yucca glauca* | | prairies, roadsides, pastures | |

Flowers orange, showy

| 136 Common day lily *Hemerocallis fulva* | | vacant lots, abandoned home sites, roadsides | |

Flowers blue

| 136 Western camass *Camassia quamash* | | wet mountain meadows | |

Flowers greenish-yellow

| 138 Indian cucumber *Medeola virginiana* | | moist woodlands, bogs, swamps | |

HERBS: DICOTS

Stems large, fleshy

| 138 Indian fig *Opuntia humifusa* | | rocky bluffs, sand dunes, dry grasslands | |
| 140 Prickly pear *Opuntia phaeacantha* | | canyons, valleys, hills, rocky and sandy soils | |

Page/Plant	Region	Habitat	Edible Uses

Flowers white

| 140 May apple *Podophyllum peltatum* | | rich woodlands, shaded road-sides, meadows | |
| 142 Bunchberry *Cornus canadensis* | | bogs, moist woodlands, mountains | |

Stems 4-sided, flowers white

| 142 Peppermint *Mentha piperita* | Introduced and grows wild. Widespread. | ditches, along stream banks, wet meadows | |
| 144 Spearmint *Mentha spicata* | Introduced and grows wild. Widespread. | wet areas, ditches, stream banks | |

Flowers violet to purple

| 144 American brooklime *Veronica americana* | | edges of streams, swamps, springs, ponds | |

Flowers pink

| 146 Marsh mallow *Althaea officinalis* | | edges of salt marshes | |

Flowers white

| 146 Watercress *Nasturtium officinale* | | springs, cool clear streams | |

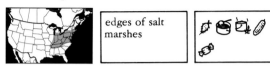
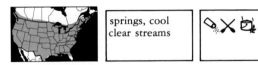

Page/Plant	Region	Habitat	Edible Uses

Flowers yellow

148 Ground cherry
Physalis pubescens

Region: old fields, open woodlands, moist sites

Flowers brownish-purple

148 Groundnut
Apios americana

Habitat: thickets, bottomlands, moist woodlands

Flowers blue

150 Common breadroot
Psoralea esculenta

Habitat: prairies, plains, dry rocky woodlands

Low creeping plants

150 Wintergreen
Gaultheria procumbens

Habitat: rich woodlands, clearings, poor acid soils

152 Creeping snowberry
Gaultheria hispidula

Habitat: subalpine and alpine, northern coniferous forests

Leaves sheathing stems

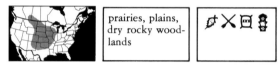

152 Mountain sorrel
Oxyria digyna

Habitat: high mountains, subalpine and alpine fields

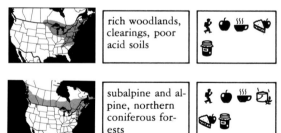

154 American bistort
Polygonum bistortoides

Habitat: along streams, wet meadows, subalpine meadows

Page/Plant	Region	Habitat	Edible Uses
154 Alpine bistort *Polygonum viviparum*		arctic regions, alpine and subalpine slopes	

Flowers yellow

Page/Plant	Region	Habitat	Edible Uses
156 Purslane *Portulaca oleracea*	Introduced and grows wild. Widespread.	fields, vacant lots, waste sites, gardens	
156 Sunflower *Helianthus annus*	Native in West	prairies, plains, roadsides, disturbed sites	
158 Quickweed *Galinsoga parviflora*	Introduced and grows wild. Widespread.	roadsides, yards, gardens, waste areas	

SHRUBS: DICOTS

Leaves evergreen

Page/Plant	Region	Habitat	Edible Uses
158 Bearberry *Arctostaphylos uva-ursi*		higher mountains, subarctic, circumboreal	
160 Salal *Gaultheria shallon*		woodlands, clearings	
160 Creeping wintergreen *Gaultheria humifusa*		subalpine and alpine	
160 Labrador tea *Ledum groenlandicum*		bogs, fens, heaths, northern woods	

Page/Plant	Region	Habitat	Edible Uses
162 Mountain cranberry *Vaccinium vitis-idaea*		subarctic, alpine, bogs, cold seepage areas	
162 Cranberry *Vaccinium macrocarpon*		bogs, swamps, shores of cold acid lakes	

Leaves deciduous

164 Bog bilberry *Vaccinium uliginosum*		arctic, bogs, rocky outcrops	
164 Highbush blueberry *Vaccinium corymbosum*		bogs, low wet woodlands, swamps	
164 Late sweet blueberry *Vaccinium angustifolium*		mountain slopes, barrens, dry rocky soils	
166 Black huckleberry *Gaylussacia baccata*		woodlands, clearings	
166 Beach plum *Prunus maritima*		coastal areas, sandy soils	
168 Golden currant *Ribes aureum*		along streams, ravines, washes, slopes	

Page/Plant	Region	Habitat	Edible Uses
170 Wax currant *Ribes cereum*		canyons, dry ravines, prairies, hillsides	
170 Subalpine prickly currant *Ribes montigenum*		along streams, ravines, washes, forests	
170 Fragrant golden currant *Ribes odoratum*		prairies, open woodlands, bluffs, ravines	
172 American hazelnut *Corylus americana*		thickets, woodlands	
172 Beaked hazelnut *Corylus cornuta*		woodlands, hills, slopes	
174 Sweet fern *Comptonia peregrina*		pastures, old fields, clearings	

Leaves fragrant when rubbed

Page/Plant	Region	Habitat	Edible Uses
174 Southern bayberry *Myrica cerifera*		coastal plains, swamps, edges of ponds, barrens	
176 Sweet gale *Myrica gale*		swamps, along ponds and streams	

Page/Plant	Region	Habitat	Edible Uses
Flowers white			
176 New Jersey tea *Ceanothus americanus*		open woodlands, prairies	
Leaves with silvery scales			
178 Silver buffaloberry *Shepherdia argentea*		canyons, plains, meadows, river banks	
Leaves usually compound			
180 Red raspberry *Rubus idaeus* var. *strigosus*		clearings, margins of woodlands, old fields	
180 Wineberry *Rubus phoenicolasius*		along rivers, streams, roads	
180 Thimbleberry *Rubus parviflorus*		woodlands, canyons, trailsides, stream banks	
182 Common blackberry *Rubus allegheniensis*		old fields, fencerows, edges of woodlands	
182 Black raspberry *Rubus occidentalis*		old fields, fencerows, edges of woodlands	
184 California blackberry *Rubus ursinus*		along trails, roads, canyons, fields	

Page/Plant	Region	Habitat	Edible Uses

Leaves pinnately compound

Page/Plant	Region	Habitat	Edible Uses
184 Smooth sumac *Rhus glabra*		fields, open woodlands, stream banks, trailsides	
186 Squawbush *Rhus trilobata*		foothills, canyons, slopes, washes	
186 Staghorn sumac *Rhus typhina*		fencerows, roadsides, edges of woodlands	
188 Screwbean mesquite *Prosopis pubescens*		washes, riverbottoms, stream banks	
188 Glandular mesquite *Prosopis glandulosa*		desert valleys, grazing lands, range	
190 American elder *Sambucus canadensis*		along streams and rivers, edges of woodlands	
190 Blue elder *Sambucus cerulea*		stream banks, washes, edges of fields	

TREES: CONIFERS

Page/Plant	Region	Habitat	Edible Uses
192 Singleleaf pinyon pine *Pinus monophylla*		foothills, canyons, mountain slopes	

Page/Plant	Region	Habitat	Edible Uses
192 Sugar pine *Pinus lambertiana*		mountain slopes	

Leaves tiny, scaly

Page/Plant	Region	Habitat	Edible Uses
192 Digger pine *Pinus sabiniana*		foothills, lower mountain slopes	
194 Rocky Mountain juniper *Juniperus scopulorum*		ridges, bluffs, dry rocky hillsides	
194 California juniper *Juniperus californica*		dry slopes, canyons, desert slopes	
196 Utah juniper *Juniperus osteosperma*		mesas, mountain slopes, high plains	

TREES: FLOWERING

Evergreen

Page/Plant	Region	Habitat	Edible Uses
196 Sea grape *Coccoloba uvifera*		beaches, sea shores	
198 California laurel *Umbellularia californica*		hillsides, flatlands, lower mountain slopes	

Deciduous

Page/Plant	Region	Habitat	Edible Uses
198 Pawpaw *Asimina triloba*		river valleys, bottomlands	

Page/Plant	Region	Habitat	Edible Uses

Leaves unlobed or 1- to 3-lobed

Page/Plant	Region	Habitat	Edible Uses
200 White mulberry *Morus alba*	Introduced and grows wild. Widespread.	fencerows, road-sides, old fields	
200 Red mulberry *Morus rubra*		river valleys, floodplains, low hills	

Flowers white, showy, early

Page/Plant	Region	Habitat	Edible Uses
202 American plum *Prunus americana*		deciduous wood-lands, stream banks	
202 Flatwood plum *Prunus umbellata*		coastal plain; piedmont; rivers, swamps, ham-mocks	
204 Black cherry *Prunus serotina*		mixed hardwood forests, wood-lands	
204 Common chokecherry *Prunus virginiana*		moist soils of roadsides, fence-rows, woodland margins	
206 Downy serviceberry *Amelanchier arborea*		woodlands, rocky slopes, river banks	
206 Saskatoon serviceberry *Amelanchier alnifolia*		mountain slopes, hillsides, prai-ries, stream banks	

Autumn

Page / Plant	Region	Habitat	Edible Uses

HERBS

Land plant, flowers yellow

| 210 Jerusalem artichoke *Helianthus tuberosus* | | roadsides, low wet ground, waste areas | |

Aquatic plants

| 210 Lotus lily *Nelumbo lutea* | | lakes, ponds, slow-moving streams | |

| 212 Yellow pond lily *Nuphar advena* | | lakes, ponds, slow streams, tidal waters | |

Semiaquatic, flowers white

| 212 Arrowhead *Sagittaria latifolia* | | edges of lakes, ponds, streams, ditches | |

VINES

| 214 Riverside grape *Vitis riparia* | | edges of wood-lands, streams, rivers | |

| 214 Frost grape *Vitis vulpina* | | along streams and rivers, in floodplains and thickets | |

Page/Plant	Region	Habitat	Edible Uses

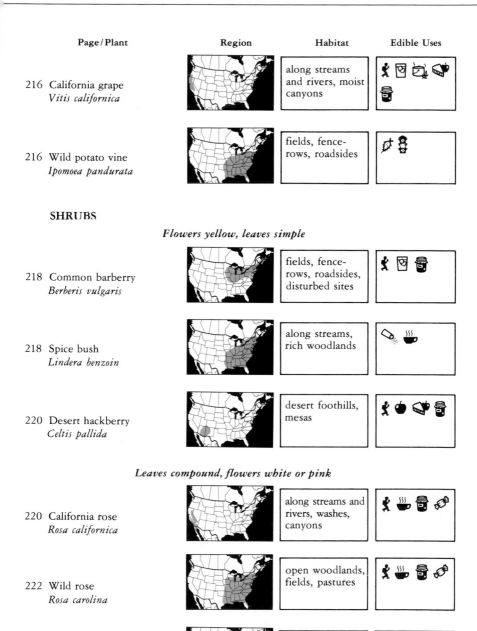

216 California grape
Vitis californica
— along streams and rivers, moist canyons

216 Wild potato vine
Ipomoea pandurata
— fields, fence-rows, roadsides

SHRUBS

Flowers yellow, leaves simple

218 Common barberry
Berberis vulgaris
— fields, fence-rows, roadsides, disturbed sites

218 Spice bush
Lindera benzoin
— along streams, rich woodlands

220 Desert hackberry
Celtis pallida
— desert foothills, mesas

Leaves compound, flowers white or pink

220 California rose
Rosa californica
— along streams and rivers, washes, canyons

222 Wild rose
Rosa carolina
— open woodlands, fields, pastures

222 Sweetbrier rose
Rosa eglanteria
— Introduced and grows wild. Widespread.
— roadsides, old fields, fencerows

Page/Plant	Region	Habitat	Edible Uses
222 Wrinkled rose *Rosa rugosa*		roadsides, sandy dunes, near sea-shores	

Leaves simple, flowers white

Page/Plant	Region	Habitat	Edible Uses
224 Highbush cranberry *Viburnum trilobum*		along streams, wet thickets, moist woodlands	
224 Hobblebush *Viburnum alnifolium*		stream banks, ravines, moist woodlands	
226 Nannyberry *Viburnum lentago*		swamps, stream banks, hillsides	
226 Squashberry *Viburnum edule*		along streams, wet thickets, moist woodlands	

TREES: CONIFER

Page/Plant	Region	Habitat	Edible Uses
228 Pinyon pine *Pinus edulis*		mesas, plateaus, foothills, lower mountain slopes	

TREES: DECIDUOUS

Leaves simple, fruits nuts

Page/Plant	Region	Habitat	Edible Uses
228 White oak *Quercus alba*		eastern deciduous forests	
230 Chestnut oak *Quercus prinus*		slopes and ridges of deciduous forests	

Page / Plant	Region	Habitat	Edible Uses
230 Gambel's oak *Quercus gambelii*		dry foothills, canyons	
230 Blue oak *Quercus douglasii*		interior valleys, rolling hills, mountain slopes	
232 Northern red oak *Quercus rubra*		valleys, ravines, lower mountain slopes	
232 American beech *Fagus grandifolia*		river valleys, deciduous forests, mountain slopes	
234 Allegheny chinkapin *Castanea pumila*		dry woodlands, slopes, sandy coastal areas	

Leaves simple, fruits berrylike or fleshy

Page / Plant	Region	Habitat	Edible Uses
236 Washington hawthorn *Crataegus phaenopyrum*		old fields, stream banks, open woodlands	
236 Downy hawthorn *Crataegus mollis*		along rivers, streams, lowland fields	
238 Fleshy hawthorn *Crataegus succulenta*		hillsides, old fields, coastal areas	
238 Cockspur hawthorn *Crataegus crus-galli*		river valleys, old fields, hillsides	

Page/Plant	Region	Habitat	Edible Uses
238 Common persimmon *Diospyros virginiana*		bottomlands, edges of woodlands, old fields, fencerows	

Leaves compound, fruits berrylike

240 American mountain ash *Sorbus americana*		rocky slopes and ridges, seepage areas	

Leaves compound, fruits nuts

240 Pecan *Carya illinoensis*	Cultivated range / Native range	bottomlands	
242 Big shellbark hickory *Carya laciniosa*		floodplains, bottomlands, river valleys	
242 Shagbark hickory *Carya ovata*		dry upland slopes, well-drained lowlands	
244 Mockernut hickory *Carya tomentosa*		ridges, slopes, river valleys	
244 Black walnut *Juglans nigra*		bottomlands, floodplains, low mixed woodlands	
246 California walnut *Juglans californica*		along streams and rivers, in bottomlands	
246 Butternut *Juglans cinerea*		bottomlands, floodplains, mixed deciduous forests	

Winter

Page / Plant	Region	Habitat	Edible Uses
SHRUBS			
	Leaves compound		
250 Staghorn sumac *Rhus typhina*		fencerows, road-sides, edges of woodlands	
	Leaves simple		
250 Highbush cranberry *Viburnum trilobum*		along streams, wet thickets, moist woodlands	
252 Squashberry *Viburnum edule*		along streams, wet thickets, edges of wood-lands	
TREES: DECIDUOUS			
	Leaf scars alternate		
252 Sweet birch *Betula lenta*		open woodlands, moist slopes	
254 Yellow birch *Betula alleghaniensis*		rich woodlands, lower mountain slopes	
254 American mountain ash *Sorbus americana*		rocky slopes, seepage areas	
	Leaf scars opposite		
256 Sugar maple *Acer saccharum*		eastern decidu-ous forests	

Spring

Spring is the prime season for vitamin-rich shoots and leafy greens. At this time, certain flowers are edible too, and free-flowing sap in trees can be tapped for syrups and tea bases. There's an abundance of plants offering roots, bulbs, and underground stems rich in carbohydrates and other nutrients. Besides, a few other plants already sport nourishing berries and seeds.

The secret for catching the most spring edibles at opportune times is planning. For this, simply consult this book's illustrated table of contents. From it you can make a list of edibles you might encounter on your next spring outing. Or you might even decide to schedule an outing to coincide with the probable readiness of specific plants. Of course, you might prefer a more casual approach and just refer to the book whenever you encounter plants that interest you. Whatever your method, spring's edible bounty awaits you.

Additional spring edibles

Plants listed below have parts that are edible in spring and at least one additional season. Descriptions and photos of these plants appear in a seasonal section other than "Spring," as indicated.

Prickly pear (*Opuntia phaeacantha*),
   p. 140
Red mulberry (*Morus rubra*), p. 200
Reed grass (*Phragmites communis*),
   p. 128
Riverside grape (*Vitis riparia*), p. 214
Soapweed (*Yucca glauca*), p. 134
Spanish bayonet (*Yucca baccata*),
   p. 134
Spice bush (*Lindera benzoin*), p. 218
Sweet fern (*Comptonia peregrina*),
   p. 174

Watercress (*Nasturtium officinale*),
   p. 146
Western camass (*Camassia quamash*),
   p. 136
White mulberry (*Morus alba*), p. 200
Wild potato vine (*Ipomoea pandurata*),
   p. 216
Wintergreen (*Gaultheria procumbens*),
   p. 150
Yellow pond lily (*Nuphar advena*),
   p. 212

Ostrich fern   *Matteucia struthiopteris*
                                    (synonyms: *M. pensylvanica, Pteretis nodulosa*)

Habitat: bottomlands, swamps, streamsides, ponds; rich forest soil. **Identifica-tion:** *perennial herb with 2 leaf types. Larger plumelike, sterile green leaves (fronds) 0.6–1.6 m (1–5 ft) long,* with stiff leafstalks to 40 cm (16 in) long, *leaf blade broadest above middle,* short-tapering at tip, long-tapering at base, with 20 or more pairs of side branches (pinnae), the pairs alternating. *Smaller fertile leaves dark brown when mature,* 40–65 cm (16–26 in) long, stiff, with side branches 3–5 cm (1–2 in) long, bearing powdery reproductive spores. Immature leaves or fiddleheads usually emerge in clusters amid few remaining, upright, brown fertile leaves of previous year, sparsely covered near top with papery, brown scales that fall away as the leaves uncoil; leafstalk (rachis) is conspicuously grooved. **Harvest:** Collect coiled fiddlehead leaves to 20 cm (8 in) tall in April in southern part of range and early May farther north, about same time as flowering of SERVICEBERRY trees. **Preparation:** Scrape inedible brown scales off by hand or wash in cold water. To cook, steam 10 min, season and butter hot; can also be boiled. In field, eat raw as a trail snack or salad item. **Related edible species:** bracken fern *(Pteridium aquilinum)* and cinnamon fern *(Osumunda cinnamomea).* **Poisonous look-alikes:** None.

Wild onion, Nodding onion   *Allium cernuum*
Also edible summer, autumn

Habitat: dry woodlands, rocky slopes, ledges, ridges, prairies. **Identification:** *perennial herb* to 60 cm (24 in) high; underground *bulb usually reddish-pur-ple, slender,* broadest near base, tapering above. Stem (scape) erect except *arch-ing at tip. Leaves* several, from base of plant, linear, mostly 2–4 mm (0.1 in) wide, shorter than stem, *with onion odor when broken,* soft, flexible. Flowers in rounded to flat-topped cluster, nodding when young, erect with age, each long-stalked, stalks 10–24 mm (0.4–0.9 in) long, petallike parts white to pink, 4–6 mm (0.2 in) long. *Fruiting capsules* in summer nearly rounded to broadest near tip, 3–5 mm (0.1–0.2 in) long, *3-parted, each part with 2 pointed crests;* seeds triangular, black. **Harvest:** young tops before flowers appear. Bulbs in spring and fall. **Preparation:** For creamed onions, melt 1 tbsp butter in saucepan, add 2 tbsp flour, ¾ tsp salt, dash of pepper, and cook with constant stirring for 1 min. Add 1 cup boiled onion bulbs and leaves. Stir in milk and simmer until thickened. For wild pickles, pack top bulb clusters in pickle jar, add 1 tbsp mixed pickling spices, and fill with mixture of 2 parts cider vinegar to 1 part water. Seal, store cool for a month or more before using. **Related edible species:** WILD GARLIC and WILD LEEK (next), and several other *Allium* species. **Poisonous look-alikes:** Field garlic *(A. vineale)* is not poisonous but is too strong for most tastes. Avoid all onionlike plants that lack onion odor; some, such as DEATH CAMASS, are highly poisonous.

Ostrich fern: young fronds, or fiddleheads, left; and mature summer leaves (Dykeman).

Wild onion: entire plants and flowers (NYBG).

Wild garlic: flowers (Speas). Entire plant (Kavasch).

Wild leek: rootstocks and entire plants (Dykeman).

Wild garlic

Allium canadense

Also edible summer, autumn

Habitat: common, open woodlands, fields, prairies. **Identification:** *perennial herb* to 58 cm (23 in) high; *underground bulb brown, egg-shaped to nearly globe-shaped, 2–3 cm* (0.8–1.2 in) *across.* Stem (scape) erect. *Leaves* several, from or near base, linear, to 35 cm (13.8 in) long, 2–5 mm (0.1–0.2 in) wide, rarely wider, flat, flexible, *with strong onion odor when broken,* shiny green. *Flower* (spring) *clusters consist of several tiny white to purple bulbils* (miniature bulbs) *and zero to few pink to white flowers on long, flexible stalks.* *Fruiting capsules* rounded or nearly so, 2–3 mm (0.1 in) long, 3-parted, *smooth on top;* seeds triangular, tiny, black. **Harvest:** Use whole plant in early spring before flower stalk appears, or use bulbs in spring and fall. Bundle bulbs with 15–20 cm (6–8 in) stems and dry at room temperature for later use. Pick green top bulb clusters on flower stalk in late spring before ripe. **Preparation:** For salad or vegetable, remove tough outer layers of young whole plant. Chop into green salad or boil whole for ½ hr in salted water, then drain, season with butter, and serve. For soup, use drained-off water to make cream of onion soup. Combine 1 qt onion water, 2 tbsp butter, 1 cup half-and-half. Add smooth mixture of 2 tbsp flour in milk, heat to simmer, and serve. Use this plant in any soup recipes calling for onions or with many cooked vegetables and meats. For other uses, see WILD ONION (preceding). **Related edible species:** WILD ONION, WILD LEEK (next), and several other *Allium* species. **Poisonous look-alikes:** See WILD ONION.

Wild leek, Ramp

Allium tricoccum

Also edible summer, autumn

Habitat: rich, neutral, moist woods, frequently under maples. **Identification:** *colonial herb. Leaves directly from bulb, 2 or 3 in number, 10–30 cm (4–12 in) long, 2–6 cm (0.8–2.4 in) wide, light green, smooth, fleshy, onion scented, appearing in early spring, shrivel by flowering in midsummer.* Flowers small, white, in hemispherical cluster on leafless stalk 15–40 cm (6–16 in) tall. Fruit capsule small, 3-lobed, each lobe with 1 hard seed. **Harvest:** young tops before they unfurl into broad leaves; bulbs from early spring through autumn. **Preparation:** add fine-chopped young leaves to salads or boil whole for 20 min in salted water, drain, season, and serve. Excellent in soup. Bulbs excellent pickled, chopped in salads, cooked alone, or with meat or other vegetables. Add chopped fine bulbs to mashed potatoes. For fried leeks parboil 3 min, drain, add more water, boil until tender. Saute in butter, serve covered with bread crumbs. *Caution:* Leeks are often very strong flavored and may cause gastric distress. Eat sparingly. **Related edible species:** WILD ONION, WILD GARLIC (preceding), and several other *Allium* species. **Poisonous look-alikes:** See WILD ONION.

Corn lily, Clinton's lily   *Clintonia borealis*

Habitat: rich woodlands, deep thickets, higher elevations, cool moist sites.
Identification: *perennial herb* to 40 cm (16 in) high, from a slender underground stem (rhizome); *each plant with 2–5 large basal leaves.* *Leaves* usually broadest near or above the middle, *10–38 cm* (4–15 in) *long,* 4–14 cm (1.6–5.5 in) wide, pointed at tip, entire along margin, dark shiny green. *Flowers 3–8 at top of erect stalk,* nodding, each with 6 greenish-yellow, narrow petallike structures 1.3–1.8 cm (0.5–0.7 in) long. *Fruits are globe-shaped, bright blue berries 8–10 mm* (0.3–0.4 in) *in diameter.* **Harvest:** Gather leaves before fully unfurled. Fully formed leaves are tough and unpleasant tasting. **Preparation:** Chop young leaves into salad with other greens of the season. Boil leaves about 10 min and serve with butter and seasonings. **Related edible species:** White clintonia *(C. umbellata)* has white flowers and black fruit. **Poisonous look-alikes:** *Be positive* of corn lily's young-growth identification features because some similar-looking species are poisonous.

Asparagus   *Asparagus officinalis*

Habitat: roadsides, disturbed sites, especially sandy and well-drained soils.
Identification: *perennial herb* 1–2 m (3.3–6.6 ft) high from thick, white, underground stem (rhizome); *stems* upright, often branched, *green*, becoming very slender at top. *Leaves* alternate, *reduced to small scales, lance-shaped,* to 2.5 cm (1 in) long. *Flowers produced along upper stems, usually singly or in pairs, hanging on slender stalk, narrowly bell-shaped, 3–6 mm* (0.1–0.2 in) *long, yellow to greenish-yellow, 6-lobed. Fruits* are *globe-shaped berries 4–8 mm* (0.2–0.3 in) *in diameter, bright red,* fleshy, containing 3–6 black seeds. **Harvest:** identical to cultivated asparagus. Locate by presence of dried Christmas-tree-shaped stalks of previous year. Slice off young stalks just below ground level when green shoots protrude only a few inches. More shoots will grow, allowing reharvesting. *Caution: Avoid older stalks and other parts, which are mildly toxic.* **Preparation:** Wash stalks and peel off any tough covering near base. Tie stalks in bundle and steam or boil until tender, usually 10–15 min. Serve with butter and seasonings or cream sauce. Excellent prepared as cream soup. See any vegetable cookbook for other recipes. **Related edible species:** none. **Poisonous look-alikes:** none.

Corn lily: flowering and fruiting plants (NYBG).

Asparagus: young shoots (Dykeman). Mature branch with fruit (Elias).

Eastern camass: flower and field (NYBG).

Common greenbrier: fruiting branch (Elias). Flowers (NYBG).

Eastern camass, Camass lily   *Camassia scilloides*
Also edible summer, autumn, winter

Habitat: fields, wet meadows, moist open woodlands. **Identification:** *perenni-al herb* from a globe-shaped bulb 1–3 cm (0.4–1.2 in) in diameter. *Leaves at-tached at base, long-narrow, 20–60 cm* (7.9–23.6 in) *long, 5–17 mm* (0.2–0.7 in) *wide,* pointed at tip. *Flowering stalk upright to 60 cm (24 in) tall;* stalked flowers in narrow cluster; *each flower with 6 white, blue, or violet petals* or petallike structures 7–12 mm (0.3–0.5 in) long. *Fruit* small, nearly globe-shaped, *3-parted capsule* 6–12 mm (0.2–0.5 in) in diameter. **Harvest:** Dig or pull bulbs any season; safest when blue flowers distinguish it from DEATH CAMASS. Dig and transplant in ground free of DEATH CAMASS. Study descriptions of DEATH CAMASS carefully. **Preparation:** Raw bulbs are palatable. May be boiled 25–30 min or baked in foil for 45 min at 175°C (350°F) but best preparation is the pit method used by Indians and described in the Introduction, in which eastern camass is baked for 1–3 days. The baked bulbs are very dark and sugary. Slice pit-baked or boiled bulbs. Then dry in sun or warm oven before storing in paper bag in dry place. Bulbs can be used as a potato substitute. **Related edible spe-cies:** WESTERN CAMASS. **Poisonous look-alikes:** DEATH CAMASS, narrow-leaved plants with green, white, or bronze flowers, single or several in narrow spike.

Common greenbrier, Catbrier   *Smilax rotundifolia*
Also edible summer

Habitat: common plant of roadsides, secondary woodlands, woodland clearings, streamsides, thickets. **Identification:** *climbing perennial vine, stems* tough, becoming woody, *often strongly 4-sided,* green, tendrils many, *armed with stout, sharp thorns. Leaves* alternate, deciduous to almost evergreen (southern part of range), 4–10 cm (1.6–4 in) long, nearly as wide, *broadest near base to nearly circular,* pointed at tip, entire along margin, *leathery,* dark shiny green. Vines bearing either male or female flowers in several-flowered, flat-topped clus-ters, green or yellow. *Fruits bluish-black berries,* globe-shaped 5–9 mm (0.2–0.4 in) in diameter, often containing 2 or 3 seeds. **Harvest:** Gather new shoots and growing tips, plus uncurling leaves and tendrils, while they are still crisp and tender during spring and summer. **Preparation:** excellent raw as trail nibble. For salads use tenderest parts raw or boil slightly older tips 2–3 min, drain and cool. Add your favorite salad dressing. Steam or boil bundled shoots like asparagus or boil tendrils, leaves, and shoots together like spinach. Cook until tender and serve with sauces and seasonings as you would other vegetables. **Related edible species:** several other *Smilax* species, including BULLBRIER and CARRION FLOWER (next). **Poisonous look-alikes:** none.

Bullbrier, Greenbrier
Smilax bona-nox

Also edible summer

Habitat: open woodlands, fields, abandoned farmlands, roadsides, disturbed sites. **Identification:** perennial *climbing vine, stems 4-sided,* becoming woody, frequently branching, green, tendrils present, with scattered stiff thorns or thornless. *Leaves* alternate, deciduous, 4–8 cm (1.6–3.2 in) long, triangular in shape, broadest near base, pointed at tip, entire or with few sharp teeth along *thickened margin,* almost leathery texture. Vines with either male or female flowers in several-flowered, rounded or flat-topped stalked clusters. *Fruits black berries,* globe-shaped or nearly so, *6–9 mm* (0.2–0.4 in) *in diameter,* usually 1-seeded. **Harvest and preparation:** shoots, tips, tendrils, leaves same as COMMON GREENBRIER. Also, dig and clean tuberous roots. Cut them into short pieces and pound them in metal container until fibers are separated and gelatinous sediment is released. Wash sediment from fibers and allow to settle. Strain out fibers and other floating matter. Carefully pour off water and allow sediment to dry and turn red. Boil 1 tbsp powdered sediment per cup of water for 10 min. Cool to make jelly or dilute and sweeten for drink. Also use powder as thickener for stews or substitute for part of flour in pancake batter. **Related edible species:** COMMON GREENBRIER (preceding) and CARRION FLOWER (next). Other tuberous-rooted *Smilax* species, such as China-root (*S. tamnoides*) in the East and *S. californica* in the West, are usable for gelatin. **Poisonous look-alikes:** none.

Carrion flower
Smilax herbacea

Also edible summer

Habitat: open woodlands, margins of woodlands, roadsides, fields. **Identification:** perennial climbing *vine; green stems, never woody,* freely branching, tendrils present, *lacking prickles or thorns.* *Leaves* alternate, deciduous, broadest near base to almost rounded, pointed to rounded at tip, heart-shaped to rounded at base, entire along margin, becoming leathery. Vines bearing either male or female *flowers on long stalks from junctions of uppermost leaves;* flowers in densely-clustered rounded heads. Fruits in dense, rounded clusters, each *fruit a berry,* globe-shaped, *8–12 mm* (0.3–0.5 in) *in diameter, dark blue to bluish-black,* containing several seeds. **Harvest and preparation:** same as for COMMON GREENBRIER and BULLBRIER (preceding). **Related edible species:** COMMON GREENBRIER and BULLBRIER. **Poisonous look-alikes:** none.

Bullbrier: flowering and fruiting branches (NYBG).

Carrion flower: flowering branch (NYBG). Fruiting branch (Kavasch).

Cattail: flowering stalk and roots (Dykeman).

Narrow-leaved cattail: entire plants and flowers (Elias).

Cattail

Typha latifolia

Also edible summer, autumn, winter

Habitat: shallow water of lakes, ponds, bays, ditches, marshes. **Identification:** large upright perennial herb to 3 m (9.8 ft) tall, with large stout, horizontal underground stems (rhizomes). *Leaves* sheathing at the base of stem, *1–2.5 m* (3.2–8.2 ft) *long, 8–24 mm* (0.3–0.9 in) *wide, narrow, swordlike,* pointed at tip, *grayish green.* Flowers at tip of erect stalks, tiny male flowers densely clustered in narrow, cylinder-shaped mass directly above female flowers densely clustered in a cylinder-shape 5–20 cm (2–8 in) long. *Fruits* in *cigar-shaped clusters 2–3.5 cm* (0.8–1.4 in) *thick* which break apart in soft downy-haired seeds in autumn. **Harvest and preparation:** In early spring, dig up roots to locate small, pointed dormant sprouts at ends of roots. Sprouts are edible raw or cooked. Later, similar sprouts appear on roots at bases of leaves. From then until plants are 60–90 cm (2–3 ft) tall, grasp leafy stalks below water surface and pull straight up, usually breaking stalks off at root. Peel away tough leafy layers to tender core, about 12 mm (0.5 in) diameter and to 30 cm (12 in) long. This "Cossack asparagus" is excellent raw, eaten like celery, or sliced into a salad. Or, cover cores with boiling water and simmer about 10 min. Serve with butter, salt and pepper or with oil-and-vinegar. Later pick green bloom spikes while still in papery sheaths and before pollen ripens above them. Remove sheaths and boil spikes in slightly salted water until tender. Eat like corn on cob, or scrape buds from cores for "corn" casserole. As pollen ripens, shake and rub it off stalks into container. Sift through fine screen to remove nonpollen materials. Substitute for part of flour in muffin, fritter, or pancake batter. For white flour, dig roots from fall through early spring. Wash and peel roots, crush cores thoroughly in container of water, and strain out fibers. Wash resulting starch several times, letting it settle and carefully pouring off water after each washing. Dry thoroughly for storage or use wet. **Related edible species:** NARROW-LEAVED CATTAIL (next). **Poisonous look-alikes:** stalks and roots of wild iris species (including YELLOW FLAG, BLUE FLAG). Harvest cattails where old stalks are abundant.

Narrow-leaved cattail

Typha angustifolia

Also edible summer, autumn, winter

Habitat: ponds, lakes, swamps, bays, ditches. **Identification:** *large* upright *perennial herb* to 2 m (6.6 ft) tall, with thick, horizontal, underground stems (rhizomes). *Leaves* sheathing at base of stem, 0.6–1.5 m (2–5 ft) long, *3–8 mm* (0.1–0.3 in) *wide, very narrow,* strap-shaped, flattened, pointed at tip. *Flowers* at tip of erect stalks, *tiny male flowers* densely clustered in narrow, cylinder-shaped column 2.5–7.5 cm (1–3 in), *spaced at intervals above the larger, brown, cylinder-shaped clusters of female flowers* 3–12 cm (1.2–4.7 in) long. *Fruits are narrow, cigar-shaped clusters 5–15 cm* (2–6 in) *long* which break apart into soft, downy-haired seeds in autumn. **Harvest and preparation:** same as for CATTAIL (preceding). **Related edible species:** CATTAIL. **Poisonous look-alikes:** See CATTAIL for details.

Hard-stem bulrush   *Scirpus acutus*
Also edible summer, autumn, winter

Habitat: shores of ponds, lakes, streams, rivers, marshes. **Identification:** *perennial herb* 1–3 m (3.2–9.8 ft) high, from thick, tough, brownish underground stems (rhizomes); *stems upright*, rounded, *stiff, yellowish-green, unbranched,* leaf blades absent or sometimes present, to 10 cm (4 in) long. *Flowering heads (spikes) densely clustered and originating from one place near the tip of the stem,* with 1 to several stalks each bearing several heads, each head cylinder-shaped, 8–18 mm (0.3–0.7 in) long, composed of several overlapping scales. Fruits are hard, somewhat flattened seeds 2–3 mm (0.1 in) long. **Harvest:** See GREAT BULRUSH (next). **Preparation:** Peel and cut firm older roots into sections. Crush them and boil in water until you have white gruel. Separate out any fibers and dry gruel into flour. For biscuit dough, add oil and water to reach right consistency. Add salt and baking powder, knead and roll to about ½-in thickness. Bake at 230°C (450°F) or twisted on stick by campfire. Also prepare flour by drying cleaned roots thoroughly, crush, and remove fibers. Pound and grind remaining material into flour. Use pollen as flour additive. Also grind seeds to use alone or with pollen and root flour for baking. Also see GREAT BULRUSH. **Related edible species:** All North American *Scirpus* species may be edible. **Poisonous look-alikes:** none because the fruiting pattern is distinctive.

Great bulrush, Tule   *Scirpus validus*
Also edible summer, autumn, winter

Habitat: shallow water of lakeshores, ponds, and streams; fresh and brackish water marshes. **Identification:** *perennial herb* to 3 m (9.8 ft) high from tough, reddish scaly underground stems (rhizomes); *stems upright, rounded, soft, pale green, unbranched;* leaf blades absent. *Flowering heads (spikes) produced near stem tips,* with several stalked, branched clusters, each head egg-shaped, 0.4–1 cm (0.1–0.4 in) long, somewhat flattened, composed of a series of overlapping scales. Fruits hard, flattened seeds 2–3 mm (0.1 in) long. **Harvest:** Bulrushes, like CATTAILS, provide food year-round. Cut off young shoots in early spring or when they've formed in autumn. Later remove cores from bases of older stalks. Shake and beat pollen from stalks into bucket in summer and return to collect seeds the same way from late summer into winter. Dig up roots year-round to use firm, sweet ones as vegetable or as sugar source and older ones for flour. **Preparation:** Peel new shoots and youngest rootstocks and separate cores from older stalks. Eat them raw, sliced in salads, or boiled. Roast young shoots and roots, or slice and fry like potatoes. Bruise young roots and boil for several hours, boiling off water to produce sweet syrup. For other preparations, see HARD-STEM BULRUSH (preceding). **Related edible species:** HARD-STEM BULRUSH. **Poisonous look-alikes:** none.

Hard-stem bulrush: flowers (Speas).

Great bulrush: fruiting (Kavasch).

Pigweed, Redroot
Amaranthus retroflexus

Also edible summer, autumn

Habitat: common and widespread; especially recently abandoned land, waste areas, roadsides. **Identification:** *coarse annual herb* to 2 m (6.6 ft) high; stem upright, stout, usually branched. *Leaves* alternate, *long-stalked,* broadest near base, *5–10 cm* (2–4 in) *long, 2.5–6 cm* (1–2.4 in) *wide,* blunt to short-pointed at tip, wavy along margin. *Flowers* late summer and fall, *densely crowded on narrow spikes* 6–18 cm (2.4–7.1 in) long, on upper part of stem. *Fruits* flattened, 1–2 mm (0.1 in) across, dry, each *partially enclosed by rigid pointed bracts 5–8 mm* (0.2–0.3 in) *long;* seeds rounded, shiny black, tiny. **Harvest:** For greens, pick young leaves when plants are only a few inches tall and before stem becomes woody. Use leaves fresh or dry. Pick seed clusters as plants mature but before seeds begin to drop. Dry, thresh by shaking or trampling, winnow by shifting in breeze. Dry on tray at 190°C (375°F) for 40–50 min, stirring occasionally. Store in paper bag in dry place. **Preparation:** Fresh greens excellent as potherb. Boil for 10–20 min until tender and serve with seasonings and butter. For livelier flavor, boil with other greens such as mustard or dandelion, or add vinegar, bacon, hard-boiled eggs, or grated cheese. For salad, use fresh young leaves as major component of tossed salad. Use dried leaves in soups. Seeds edible whole or ground into meal using food mill or stones. For muffins, combine 1 cup pigweed meal, ½ cup whole-wheat flour, 2 tsp baking powder, ½ tsp salt, 3 tbsp honey, brown sugar, or molasses. Add 2 egg yolks, 1¼ cups milk, and ¼ cup butter. Blend until mix is moist. Beat 2 egg whites until stiff and fold into mix. Bake in greased muffin tin about 20 min at 190°C (375°F). Makes approximately 18. Thin batter with milk for pancakes. **Related edible species:** GREEN PIGWEED (next) and several other *Amaranthus* species. **Poisonous look-alikes:** Since pigweed is a concentrator of nitrates, plants from nitrate-fertilized areas should be eaten only in moderation.

Green pigweed
Amaranthus hybridus

Also edible summer, autumn

Habitat: common and widespread in eastern and midwestern North America; fields, roadsides, disturbed sites. **Identification:** *coarse annual herb* to 2 m (6.6 ft) high; stems upright, with several upright branches. *Leaves* alternate, long stalked, broadest below or near middle, *8–15 cm* (3.2–6 in) *long, 2–5 cm* (0.8–2 in) *wide,* short-pointed at tip, wavy along margin. *Flowers* tiny, *densely crowded in slender, green to red spikes.* Fruits tiny, flattened, 1.5–2 mm (0.1 in) across, dry, *partially enclosed by short, flexible bracts* to 2 mm (0.1 in) long; seeds tiny, rounded, shiny black. **Harvest and preparation:** Same as for PIGWEED (preceding). **Related edible species:** PIGWEED and related species. **Poisonous look-alikes:** See PIGWEED.

Pigweed: basal stalk and flowering head (USDA).

Green pigweed: fruiting stalks (Hardin).

Lamb's quarters: basal leaves of young plant and mature stem (Dykeman).

Poverty weed: entire plant (Weber).

Lamb's quarters
Chenopodium album

Also edible autumn

Habitat: common and widespread; yards, vacant lots, roadsides, waste areas, disturbed sites; introduced from Europe. **Identification:** small to medium-size annual *herb* to 0.6 m (2 ft) high; stems erect, usually branched, *with a pale green or whitish cast.* **Leaves** alternate, lower ones *almost triangular,* 3–10 cm (1.2– 4 in) long, *blunt at tip, coarsely toothed along margin, mealy white beneath,* stalked, upper ones smaller. *Flowers* in late spring to autumn, *tiny, inconspicuous, produced in dense short spikes in junctions of upper leaves and at tip.* Fruits tiny, globe-shaped but depressed at tip, enclosed in persistent calyx lobes, in short dense spikes. **Harvest:** Pick young leafy stems to 25 cm (10 in) tall or tender growing tips of older plants. Gather abundant seeds in autumn by rubbing fruiting spikes into paper bag and winnow away chaff. **Preparation:** a superlative green vegetable, lacking strong flavor and high in vitamins A and C. Use leafy stems alone in salad or mix with stronger greens. For potherb, use large quantity of greens because cooking greatly diminishes bulk. Boil young leafy stems in small quantity of water about 5 min until tender. Add butter, salt and pepper or sauce of ¼ cup diced onion, 4 slices crisp bacon chopped fine, ¼ cup vinegar, salt and pepper, simmered gently. Use same sauce on raw greens as salad dressing. Soften seeds by boiling, crush, grind in food mill or blender. This produces nutritious black flour, good mixed with wheat flour for pancakes and muffins. **Related edible species:** Berlandier's lamb's quarters *(C. berlandieri),* Fremont's lamb's quarters *(C. fremontii).* **Poisonous look-alikes:** Species of *Chenopodium* that have bad odor and taste can be somewhat toxic.

Poverty weed
Monolepis nuttalliana

Also edible autumn

Habitat: dry areas of high salinity or alkaline soils. **Identification:** *annual herb* to 55 cm (22 in) tall, spreading; branches numerous, stout, somewhat fleshy, upright or nearly so. *Leaves* alternate, *triangular to lance-shaped,* 1–4 cm (0.4–1.6 in) long, pointed at the tip, entire or irregularly toothed along the margin, sharply lobed at the base. *Flowers small, numerous, inconspicuous, produced in junction of upper, smaller leaves, each bisexual, greenish, petals absent.* Fruits are small, flattened, brown; winged seeds 1 mm (less than 0.1 in) across. **Harvest:** Pick young leafy stems. Roots are edible but usually not tasty. If you have the patience, strip seeds from stems when fully ripe late in growing season. **Preparation:** Like its relative, LAMB'S QUARTERS (preceding), which it superficially resembles, poverty weed is a good green vegetable. Boil young stems in small quantity of water until tender, but avoid overcooking. Serve with butter and seasonings or the following sauce hot: Simmer together for a few minutes ¼ cup dried onion, 4 slices crisp bacon (chopped fine), ¼ cup vinegar, salt and pepper. Southwestern Indians ground seeds with corn and mesquite beans to make pinole. **Related edible species:** Species of the *Chenopodium* genus (including LAMB'S QUARTERS) are of the same family as poverty weed. **Poisonous look-alikes:** none.

Glasswort   *Salicornia europaea*
Also edible summer, autumn

Habitat: sea coast, salt marshes, alkaline soils. **Identification:** *annual herb* to 40 cm (16 in) high; *stems* erect to spreading, *stiff, succulent* (may be unbranched to many branched), green turning orange or red in autumn; leaves opposite, minute, scalelike, *appearing leafless. Flowers* (late summer) tiny, numerous, produced *in erect* to slightly spreading *spikes 2–6 cm* (0.8–2.4 in) *long,* joints longer than broad. Fruits are seeds, tiny, egg-shaped, 1.2–3 mm (0.1 in) in diameter. **Harvest:** Pick tender tips from branches midspring to autumn. **Preparation:** Tips are crispy and salty; good for trail nibble. Or chop and serve raw as salad with spicy vinegar dressing or add to other salad greens. For pickles pack jars with very tender, clean, raw tips or older tips that have been boiled in a little water for 5 min. Make pickling liquid from 4 cups cider or wine vinegar, 3 tbsp pickling spices, 1 grated onion, ½ cup honey or sugar, plus garlic, bay leaves, or other spices. Combine ingredients and boil 5–6 min. Cover glasswort with boiling liquid and seal jars. Store at least 1 month. For vegetable, place tips in boiling water and cook until tender 5–10 min. Serve buttered. **Related edible species:** Other species of *Salicornia* look very similar and are edible; one is perennial (*S. virginica*). **Poisonous look-alikes:** none.

Russian thistle, Saltwort   *Salsola kali*
Also edible summer

Habitat: sandy beaches on East Coast; dry, alkaline soils in West. **Identification:** *annual herb* to 1 m (3.2 ft) high; stems branching, upright to spreading, smooth, hairy, or with mealy appearance. *Leaves alternate,* simple, *fleshy, rounded, 2–5 cm* (0.8–2 in) *long, lance- to needle-shaped, spine-tipped,* entire along margins, lacking distinct leafstalk. Flowers numerous in narrow, elongated spikes in junctions of stems of upper leaves and at branch tips; each flower tiny, bisexual, sepals 5, winged on margins; petals absent. *Fruits are flattened, winged, and nearly circular, 3–6 mm* (0.1–0.2 in) *across,* yellowish to slate-colored. **Harvest:** Pull up shoots of new spring growth when less than 15 cm (6 in) tall; also succulent new plants after rains in late spring and in summer. Beware of spines at leaf tips. *Caution:* Plants occasionally contain toxic levels of nitrates and oxalates. **Preparation:** Cut off roots. Wash tops and boil for about 15 min. Serve like spinach with butter and seasonings, cream sauce, or vinegar. Mix with other greens of season. **Related edible species:** other *Salsola* species mainly in the Southwest. **Poisonous look-alikes:** none.

Glasswort: stems showing two color phases (NYBG).

Russian thistle: flowering branches (NYBG).

Stinging nettle: young plants and flowering plant (Elias).

Plantain: young plant (Dykeman). Mature plant (Elias).

Stinging nettle, Nettle   *Urtica dioica*

Habitat: widespread, especially in moist fertile soils in disturbed areas, margins of woods, trails, stream banks, roadsides, vacant lots. **Identification:** perennial, upright, to 1 m (3.2 ft); erect *stem with bristly, stinging hairs. Leaves opposite, long-stalked,* blade 5–14 cm (2–5.5 in) long, broadest near base, coarsely toothed, veins depressed, *with stiff, stinging hairs on both surfaces.* Each plant either male or female. Flowers produced in junctions of leafstalks, each flower tiny, male or female, borne in many-flowered, loosely branched, elongated, cream-colored clusters. Fruits tiny, inconspicuous, hard, nutletlike, about 2 mm (0.1 in) long. **Harvest:** In spring, wear gloves to avoid stinging hairs, or use scissors to cut young shoots and tender top leaves directly into pot or bag. Later leaves are tough and gritty. **Preparation:** Boiling destroys irritant. As potherb, barely cover with water and simmer until tender. Drain, add seasonings, butter, lemon juice, or wine vinegar. Use cooking water as beverage with lemon and sugar or as soup with salt, pepper, and vinegar. To make a simple stinging nettle puree, rub 2 cups cooked stinging nettles with juice through sieve, or puree in blender. Reheat, add 2 tbsp butter, salt to taste, simmer 10 min more. Stir in ¼ cup light cream; season with black pepper. A versatile plant, stinging nettle cooking juice may also be used as rennet (milk coagulant) for junket pudding and as beer ingredient. Plant is high in vitamins A and C, protein, and minerals. **Related edible species:** wood nettle *(Laporta canadensis),* slender nettle *(U. gracilis).* **Poisonous look-alikes:** none.

Plantain *(Also edible summer, autumn)*   *Plantago major*

Habitat: yards, roadsides, disturbed sites; common weed introduced from Europe. **Identification:** *perennial herb* with fibrous root system. *Leaves basal,* numerous, broadest near or below middle, *5–20 cm* (2–8 in) *long, 2.5–12 cm* (1–4.7 in) *wide,* rounded to pointed at tip, toothed, entire or wavy along margin, *rough on both surfaces,* smooth or hairy. *Flowers tiny, numerous along upper part of erect spike* to 20 cm (8 in) high, each flower with 4 translucent petals. Fruits are tiny capsules produced along spike; each capsule contains 10–18 seeds. **Harvest:** Pick young leaves before flower stalk appears or pick new leaves through summer; otherwise leaves develop stringy veins that are tough to chew. Strip ripe seeds from flower stalks from late spring through fall. **Preparation:** Use tenderest leaves in salads with other greens of season. For cooked vegetable, soak leaves in salt water for 5 min. Boil with little water in covered pot until tender but not overcooked. For beverage, steep handful of leaves in pint of boiling water for ½ hr or longer. Dry seeds thoroughly and grind into flour. For pancakes, combine 2 cups plantain flour with 3 tsp baking powder, ½ tsp salt, 3 tbsp sugar, 2 eggs, 3 tbsp cooking oil, 1 cup milk. Mix thoroughly. Add more milk or flour for proper consistency; add fruit, if desired. Cook on hot griddle. **Related edible species:** Species of the *Plantago* genus are found throughout North America; most are edible. Boil leaves of bitter species in sweetened water. Seaside plantain *(P. juncoides)* is one of the best and is found only along East Coast. **Poisonous look-alikes:** none.

Shepherd's purse: entire plant and flowering stalks (Elias).

Toothwort: flowering plant (NYBG).

Shepherd's purse
Capsella bursa-pastoris

Habitat: yards, vacant lots, roadsides, other disturbed areas; widespread weed, introduced from Europe. **Identification:** small to medium-size *annual or biennial herb* to 60 cm (2 ft) high, unbranched or sparingly branched, *with a flattened, basal rosette of leaves,* the *basal leaves* 4–10 cm (1.6–4 in) long, uniformly wide to broadest near tip, *shallowly to deeply lobed along sides.* Upright stems with few, smaller, narrower leaves. Flowers produced in narrow elongate cluster, each tiny, stalked, with 4 white petals 2–4 mm (0.1 in) long. *Fruits slightly flattened, heart-shaped, notched at tip,* 4–10 mm (0.2–0.4 in) *long.* **Harvest:** Gather leaves before flowering stage. If too peppery, bleach by covering with sawdust, leaves, or flower pots for week or more. Strip off seed pods as they ripen. **Preparation:** Use raw leaves as salad greens, if not too peppery, or with other milder greens. For a potherb, boil leaves in water for about 20 min with one change of water if needed. Season with salt and vinegar. Use dried pods and seeds as seasoning in soups and stews. Western Indians once ground seeds into meal, but process is tedious. **Related edible species:** red shepherd's purse *(C. rubella)* and slender shepherd's purse *(C. gracilis).* **Poisonous look-alikes:** none.

Toothwort
Dentaria laciniata

Habitat: moist deciduous woodlands, ravines, floodplains. **Identification:** perennial herb from a jointed, white underground stem (rhizome); stem upright, to 40 cm (15.7 in) high. Basal leaves absent at flowering, *stem leaves in a whorl of 3 on upper half, deeply 3-parted, leaf segments lance-shaped, coarsely toothed to nearly entire,* the terminal segment often deeply parted. *Flowers* produced in a terminal, elongate, hairy cluster, each flower stalked, *with 4 white petals* 1.2–2 cm (0.5–0.8 in) long. Fruits narrow, elongate, 2–4 cm (0.8–1.6 in) long, splitting open lengthwise at maturity to release the tiny seeds. **Harvest:** Dig rootstocks in small numbers from areas where plentiful. Other plants will grow from pieces of perennial root remaining in the soil. **Preparation:** Use as spicy trail nibble. Wash roots, chop and grind them in vinegar, add a dash of salt; use like horseradish. Add chopped roots to wild tossed green salads to liven flavor. **Related edible species:** At least six other species, similar in appearance, are distributed in moist woodlands of the East and West. All may be used like the species described. **Poisonous look-alikes:** none.

Peppergrass   *Lepidium virginicum*

Habitat: fields, vacant lots, roadsides, other disturbed areas, waste sites. **Identification:** annual or biennial *herb,* upright to 50 cm (19.7 in) high, occasionally taller. *Basal rosette of leaves 4–10 cm* (1.6–3.9 in) *long,* 0.8–2 cm (0.3–0.8 in) wide, broadest near tip, *doubly toothed, lobed, or deeply dissected* along margin; stem leaves smaller, toothed or entire, becoming linear near top. *Flowers* produced in several, narrow, elongate clusters; each flower stalked, *with 4 small white petals. Fruits flattened, widest near middle to almost circular, 2–4 mm* (0.1 in) *long,* nearly as wide, *slightly notched at tip,* containing tiny reddish-brown seeds. **Harvest:** young shoots and leaves in spring. **Preparation:** another member of the mustard family. Use peppergrass greens sparingly in salad with less bitter species. As a potherb boil in 1 or 2 changes of water. Try recipes given for other MUSTARDS. Leaves high in vitamins A and C. Peppery seeds can be used to season meats, soups, and salads. **Related edible species:** Fremont's peppergrass *(L. fremontii)* and FIELD CRESS (next). **Poisonous look-alikes:** none.

Field cress, Cow cress   *Lepidium campestre*

Habitat: fields, vacant lots, roadsides, disturbed sites; introduced from Europe. **Identification:** annual or biennial *herb,* upright to 60 cm (2 ft) high, *stems densely hairy.* Basal leaves 4–8 cm (1.6–3.2 in) long, 1–1.6 cm (0.4–0.6 in) wide, narrow but broadest near tip, coarsely toothed, lobed or dissected along margin; *stem leaves* smaller, almost circular in shape, *lobed at base. Flowers* produced in several, narrow, elongate clusters; each flower stalked, *with 4 small, white petals. Fruits flattened,* widest near tip to *almost round in outline, 2–3 mm* (0.1 in) *long,* slightly notched at tip, narrowly winged, containing tiny dark brown seeds. **Harvest and preparation:** same as for PEPPERGRASS (preceding). **Related edible species:** PEPPERGRASS and related species. **Poisonous look-alikes:** none.

Field pennycress   *Thlaspi arvense*

Habitat: fields, vacant lots, waste areas, other disturbed sites; more common in northern portion of its range. **Identification:** *annual herb* 40–80 cm (16–32 in) high; stems branched, upright, smooth. Basal leaves narrow, widest near tip, withering and absent at flowering. *Stem leaves 2–10 cm* (0.8–4 in) *long,* 0.4–3 cm (0.2–1.2 in) wide, *lance-shaped* to narrow but broadest near tip, wavy or coarsely toothed or entire along margin, *lobed at base, lobes pointed. Flowers* numerous in narrow, elongate clusters (racemes), each flower stalked, *with 4 white petals. Fruits flattened, nearly circular in outline, 0.8–1.8 cm (0.3–0.7 in) in diameter, deeply notched at tip, broadly winged,* containing several tiny black seeds. **Harvest:** young shoots and leaves in spring. **Preparation:** Since plant has characteristic bitterness of MUSTARD family, boil shoots and leaves in 1 or 2 changes of water for 15–25 min. Serve with butter, salt and pepper. Use tender greens if not too bitter with other species in tossed salads. **Related edible species:** pennycress *(T. perfoliatum)* and many other members of mustard family Cruciferae. **Poisonous look-alikes:** none.

Peppergrass: fruiting plant
(Elias).

Field cress: top photo, wilting flowers
after being picked and entire plant
(Dykeman).

Field pennycress: flowers, top, and fruits
on lower portion of flowering cluster
(Dykeman).

Garlic mustard: young plants and flowering plant (Dykeman).

Common chickweed: flowering plants (NYBG).

James chickweed: flowering branch and flower (NYBG).

Garlic mustard *(Also edible summer)*   *Alliaria officinalis*
Habitat: partially shaded roadsides, paths in open woods, shady disturbed areas.
Identification: *biennial herb, 2nd year growth to 90 cm (3 ft). Leaves triangular to heart-shaped, coarsely toothed, long-stalked, with garlic odor when crushed. Flowers white,* 6–8 mm (0.2–0.3 in) across, in *clusters at tips of stems and at leaf bases,* April–June. Fruits are very *slender pods (siliques) to 5 cm (2 in) long,* containing numerous tiny seeds. **Harvest:** young leaves, blossoms, and seed pods in spring and early summer. **Preparation:** chop tender growth raw in salad; for cooked vegetable steam or boil in little water, season with salt and butter. Use for garlic flavor with meats and vegetables. **Related edible species:** no other *Alliaria* species present; many other members of MUSTARD family *(Cruciferae)* are edible. **Poisonous look-alikes:** none.

Common chickweed *(Also edible summer, autumn, winter)*   *Stellaria media*
Habitat: yards, disturbed sites, moist and wet areas, cultivated land, woodlands; common weed introduced from Europe. **Identification:** annual herb sometimes to 30 cm (12 in) high; stems weak, trailing along ground before becoming upright, with rows of hairs. *Leaves opposite,* simple, *1–3.5 cm* (0.4–1.4 in) *long, about ⅔ as wide,* usually broadest near base or middle, pointed at tip, entire along margin, rounded at base, lower leaves with a conspicuous leafstalk. *Flowers single* or in few-flowered clusters at tips, *long-stalked, each flower with 5 deeply lobed, white petals that are shorter than sepals.* Fruits are small reddish-brown capsules 5–8 mm (0.2–0.3 in) long, egg-shaped, containing many small seeds. **Harvest:** Pick tender leaves and stems from young plants any time they are not blooming; available year-round in some regions. Quicker method, pull up the whole plant and cut off tender growth with scissors. **Preparation:** Mild flavored chickweed is excellent by itself or with other, stronger greens. Use generously raw in salads. Boil only 2–5 min; add it to other less delicate greens near end of their cooking period. Serve with butter, seasonings, and a little chopped onion. Also see JAMES CHICKWEED (next). **Related edible species:** JAMES CHICKWEED. **Poisonous look-alikes:** none.

James chickweed *(Also edible summer, autumn)*   *Stellaria jamesiana*
Habitat: mountain meadows, seepage areas, woodlands, usually between 1,220–2,590 m (4,000–8,500 ft) elevation. **Identification:** *small perennial herb* to 35 cm (14 in) tall from slender roots with thickened tuberlike structures; stems erect or nearly so, branched frequently, hairy. *Leaves opposite,* simple, *4–15 cm* (1.6–6 in) *long, about one-fourth as wide, lance-shaped,* long pointed at tip, entire along margin. *Flowers produced in loose, spreading clusters at tips* and at junctions of upper leaves in spring and early summer. *Each flower with 5 deeply notched white petals.* Fruits are small tan capsules, 3–5 mm (0.2 in) long, containing many tiny, dark brown seeds. **Harvest:** same as COMMON CHICKWEED (preceding). **Preparation:** Add chickweed to soups and stews. For pancakes, drain and blot 1–2 cups leaves. Blend into prepared pancake batter (2 cups mix to 1½ cups water). Adjust consistency. Fry and serve with butter and tart jelly. **Related edible species:** COMMON CHICKWEED, star chickweed *(S. pubera),* and mouse-ear chickweed *(Cerastium vulgatum).* **Poisonous look-alikes:** none.

Cleavers, Goosegrass, Bedstraw
Galium aparine
Also edible summer

Habitat: wide spread on moist sites, rich woodlands, along streams, lakes, vacant lots and fields. **Identification:** *annual herb;* stems weak, slender, often leaning on other plants or rambling along ground, 4-sided, with numerous tiny, stiff, hooked hairs causing plants to cling to clothing; *leaves in whorls of 8,* each very narrow but *widest above middle,* 4–8 cm (1.6–3.2 in) long, 2–6 mm (0.1–0.2 in) wide, with recurved hairs along margin. Flowers tiny, white, produced in usually 3-flowered, stalked clusters in junction of upper leaves in late spring or early summer. *Fruits consist of twin, fused, globe-shaped, dry structures 2–4 mm (0.1 in) long, covered with numerous hairs hooked at tip.* **Harvest and preparation:** Pick young greens in spring when tender. Steam leafy stems in strainer or colander over boiling water for 5–10 min or boil in small amount of water until tender. Serve with butter and seasonings. Combines well with nettle greens. For salad take 3 cups boiled, cooled cleavers and add 1 cup cooked asparagus cut in 1 in lengths, ½ cup slivered nuts, ¾ cup French dressing. Gather fruits in June and July as they turn brown. For excellent noncaffeine coffee substitute, roast fruits in warm oven 150°C (300°F) until dark and crisp, about 1 hr. Grind in blender or crush on any hard surface. Simmer ¾ cup prepared fruits in 1 qt water until medium to dark brown. Strain and serve. **Edible related species:** NORTHERN BEDSTRAW (next). *Note:* The many species of cleavers or bedstraw in North America are difficult to tell apart; however, none of them is known to be poisonous. **Poisonous look-alikes:** none.

Northern bedstraw
Galium boreale

Habitat: stream banks, fields, open woodlands. **Identification:** *perennial herb;* stems usually upright, to 1 m (3.2 ft), slender, 4-sided, smooth. *Leaves in whorls of 4, each narrowly lance-shaped, 2.5–5 cm* (1–2 in) *long,* 2–7 mm (0.1–0.3 in) wide, with 3 main veins, finely hairy along margins. Flowers tiny, white, produced in compact many-flowered, branched, elongated clusters (inflorescences) at or near growing tips. *Fruits consist of 2 fused, globe-shaped structures (rarely 1) that are 2–3 mm (0.1 in) in diameter, smooth or with long straight hairs or shorter ones hooked at tip.* **Harvest and preparation:** same as for CLEAVERS (preceding). **Edible related species:** See CLEAVERS. **Poisonous look-alikes:** none.

Cleavers: flowering stalks (C. S. Webber, Jepson Herbarium).

Northern bedstraw: flowering stalks (NYBG).

Bugleweed: flowering stalk and flowers (NYBG).

Edible valerian: flowering stalks (NYBG).

Bugleweed

Lycopus uniflorus

Also edible autumn, winter

Habitat: low wet or boggy ground in North, wet woodlands and mountain bogs in South. **Identification:** *perennial herb* to 1 m (3.2 ft) tall; stems upright, unbranched or sparingly branched, finely hairy. *Leaves opposite,* simple, 3–10 cm (1.2–4 in) long, 0.6–3.4 cm (0.2–1.3 in) wide, *lance-shaped* to almost uniformly wide, pointed at tip, *with few teeth along margin,* tapering at base, light green and papery; leafstalks absent. *Flowers produced in compact, many-flowered clusters in junctions of upper leaf stems;* each flower tiny, *petals white,* fused, with 2 upper and 3 lower lobes. Fruits are tiny, flattened, irregular nutlets 1–2 mm (less than 0.1 in) long, with small bumps (tubercles) on top. **Harvest:** Tubers grow best close to the base of old stems in loose sandy soil. Dig tubers from fall through early spring when they are highest in stored nutrients. **Preparation:** Add peeled, sliced tubers to tossed salad or chop fine as mild relish. Boil tubers in salted water until tender, about 10–15 min. Serve with butter and seasonings. For pickles, peel tubers, boil in water about 5 min, drain and cover with wine vinegar. Store for several weeks before using. **Related edible species:** sessile-leaved water horehound *(L. amplectens)* is found in sandy East Coast areas. Other species of *Lycopus* lack tubers. **Poisonous look-alikes:** none.

Edible valerian

Valeriana edulis

Also edible autumn, winter

Habitat: open moist sites, meadows, prairies, ditches, swamps. **Identification:** *perennial herb* to 1.2 m (3.8 ft) from large, elongated root. *Leaves opposite,* featherlike (pinnate) divided; *basal leaves spoon-shaped,* widest near tip, 12–30 cm (4.7–12 in) long, *entire or sometimes featherlike (pinnate) divided* with narrow lateral segments, thick, hairy along margins; stem leaves pinnately divided into few narrow segments, smaller. *Flowers tiny, produced in* tightly branched, elongated, *many-flowered clusters* at tips in late spring; each flower white to pink, 3–5 mm (0.1–0.2 in) long. Fruits dry, flattened, 1-seeded, egg-shaped, 3–4 mm (0.2 in) long. **Harvest and preparation:** Dig roots in autumn and early spring, when firm. Steam 24 hr or longer to remove disagreeable odor. Then use in soups as you would potato or squash. Dry and grind steamed roots into flour for use in bread, as did the Indians. Bake Indian pit style 2 days. **Related edible species:** Other valerians have been used in folk medicine. **Poisonous look-alikes:** toxicity of look-alikes not well documented.

Wild strawberry: mature fruits and flower (Elias).

Spring beauty: flowering stalk (NYBG).

Wild strawberry
Fragaria virginiana
Also edible summer

Habitat: open woodlands, margins of woodlands, fields. **Identification:** small perennial herb, lacking distinct stem, sometimes producing runners. *Leaves basal, compound and 3-parted* (trifoliolate), leaflets widest near or above middle, 2–10 cm (0.8–4 in) long, sharply toothed along margin, hairy beneath. *Flowers* several in short spreading cluster, each *with 5 white petals* 8–14 mm (0.3–0.5 in) long. *Fruits are tiny, hard (achenes), embedded in large, fleshy tissue (receptacle)* that is 0.5–2 cm (0.2–0.8 in) in diameter, *red, sweet.* **Harvest:** one of the best wild fruits. Locate your site early and check regularly from early June for ripe berries. Collect leaves anytime but best in late summer. **Preparation:** Use wild strawberries in any strawberry recipes. For quick beverage, crush handful of berries and mix with 1 cup water and a little sugar. For fruit leather, add ½ tbsp sugar or honey to each cup of fruit. Bring just to boil, cool, and process through food mill. Pour no more than 5 mm (0.2 in) thick onto Teflon cookie sheet. Heat in oven at lowest setting for 6–7 hr. When leathery, roll and seal in plastic wrap. Stores well at any temperature. See basic pie and jam recipes in book's introductory material. For tea high in vitamin C, steep 2 handfulls fresh or ½ cup dried leaves in 1 qt boiling water for 5 min. To dry leaves, spread on clean surface in warm, dry area (sun or shade). When thoroughly dried (use warm oven, if necessary), crumble leaves and store in paper bag in dry place. **Related edible species:** Several are widely distributed, basically alike, and easy to identify. **Poisonous look-alikes:** none.

Spring beauty
Claytonia virginica

Habitat: rich woodlands, wooded floodplains, wet fields. **Identification:** *perennial herb* to 40 cm (16 in) tall, *from globe-shaped, bulblike tuber 1–5 cm (0.4–2 in) in diameter;* stems several, upright, weak, sometimes leaning. *Leaves* simple, *5–14 cm (2–5.5 in) long, 0.2–2 cm (0.1–0.8 in) wide, linear* to narrow but widest above the middle, blade gradually merging with leafstalk. *Flowering stem with 5–20 weakly stalked flowers, each flower white to pink with dark pink veins, petals 5,* 1.2–2 cm (0.5–0.8 in) across. Fruits are egg-shaped to nearly globe-shaped capsules 5–10 mm (0.2–0.4 in) long, containing numerous, tiny, dark red seeds. **Harvest:** Because this is a beautiful spring flower, use only where very abundant or when desperately needed. In spring, pick young leaves and dig tubers when identifiable by blossoms. Keep only largest tubers; replant others. **Preparation:** Use leaves as trail nibble or chop a few in green salads. Boil leaves for a few minutes in salted water for edible but not exceptional vegetable. Eat washed tubers raw or add to salads. Boil tubers with jackets in salted water about 10–15 min. Peel and serve whole or mashed, fried, or in salad like potatoes. Tubers also good baked; peel before eating. **Related edible species and poisonous look-alikes:** See ALPINE SPRING BEAUTY (next).

Alpine spring beauty   *Claytonia megarhiza*

Habitat: rocky crevices, rock slides in alpine zone, tundra. **Identification:** *low perennial herb* from thick, fleshy, purple to dark-red taproot. *Basal leaves spreading, forming large rosette,* leaves 2–15 cm (0.8–6 in) long, *broadest near tip to almost circular in outline,* pointed to rounded at tip, entire along margin, gradually tapering and winged at base; stem leaves alternate, linear to narrow and broadest near tip. *Flowers* stalked, produced in elongate cluster; each flower 1.2–2.5 cm (0.5–1 in) across, *with 5 white to pink petals with red veins,* 6–10 mm (0.2–0.4 in) long. Fruits are tiny, 3-parted, egg-shaped capsules. **Harvest:** Because of habitat and scarcity, use as survival food only. Pick rosettes of leaves or pull up whole plant for fleshy root. **Preparation:** similar to SPRING BEAUTY (preceding). Peel roots before boiling to avoid strong flavor and use like tubers of SPRING BEAUTY. **Related edible species:** SPRING BEAUTY, WESTERN SPRING BEAUTY (next); also Carolina spring beauty *(C. caroliniana),* widely distributed in northern U. S. **Poisonous look-alikes:** To avoid confusion with poisonous lilies, learn to identify leaves or collect when in bloom.

Western spring beauty   *Claytonia lanceolata*

Habitat: mid to high mountain slopes, moist woodlands to alpine zone. **Identification:** *perennial herb* to 20 cm (8 in) high, *from nearly globe-shaped,* bulblike underground *stem base* (corm) 1–2 cm (0.4–0.8 in) in diameter; stems 1 to several, upright. Basal leaves 1 or 2, 4–8 cm (1.6–3.2 in) long, broadly lance-shaped; *stem leaves 2, opposite, 3–6 cm* (1.2–2.4 in) *long,* narrow to broadly lance-shaped, 0.8–2 cm (0.3–0.8 in) wide. *Flowering stems* upright, *with 3–15 stalked flowers, each bowl-shaped, with 5 pink petals* 0.8–1.2 cm (0.3–0.5 in) long. Fruits are egg-shaped capsules 3–5 mm (0.1–0.2 in) long, containing a few shiny, black seeds. **Harvest and preparation:** Because of habitat and scarcity, use as survival food only. Similar to SPRING BEAUTY. Leaves are edible but not exceptional; boil 10–15 min. Crispy but small tubers are good raw or cooked for about 25 min at about 1,640 m (5,400 ft) altitude. **Related edible species and poisonous look-alikes:** See ALPINE SPRING BEAUTY (preceding).

Alpine spring beauty: flowering plant (NYBG).

Western spring beauty: flowering plant (NYBG).

Miner's lettuce: flowering plants (NYBG).

Canada violet: flower and flowering plant (NYBG).

Miner's lettuce
Montia perfoliata
Also edible summer
(synonym: *Claytonia perfoliata*)

Habitat: valleys, lower mountain slopes, springs, moist sites. Introduced from Europe; miner's lettuce has expanded its range in the East. **Identification:** *annual herb* to 30 cm (12 in) high, *from fibrous root system.* Leaves mostly basal, simple, 6–20 cm (2.4–8 in) long including the long leafstalk, blade variable, usually broadest below or above middle, entire along margin, smooth; *stem leaves 2, opposite and fused into a circular disc just below flowering stalk.* Flower stalk elongate, bearing numerous, whorled, short-stalked flowers, each tiny, with 5 white, clawed petals 3–6 mm (0.1–0.2 in) long. Fruits are tiny, 3-parted capsules containing 1–3 shiny, black seeds. **Harvest:** blossoms, leaves, stems, and roots any time during growing season. **Preparation:** Young upper leaves and stems are excellent as picked or in salads. Include blossoms when available. For salad add chopped hard-boiled eggs and oil and vinegar dressing. For cooked vegetable, boil leaves and stems in very little water until tender; boil young leaves as little as 3–4 min. Excellent source of vitamin C. Wash roots and boil for just a few minutes. Butter and lightly season to bring out water chestnut flavor. **Related edible species:** Siberian miner's lettuce *(M. sibirica)* of southern Alaska. **Poisonous look-alikes:** none.

Canada violet
Viola canadensis
Also edible summer

Habitat: mixed deciduous woodlands, bluffs, rocky to deep, rich soils. **Identification:** perennial herb with thick underground stem (rhizome); stems upright, smooth, to 40 cm (16 in) high. *Leaves basal and along stem, simple 4–12 cm (1.6–4.7 in) long, nearly as wide, broadest near base, long pointed at tip,* toothed along margin, *heart-shaped at base,* leafstalks long, *with small, lance-shaped bract (stipule)* at base of each leaf. *Flowers* produced on upper third of plant, each stalked, *white often with purple on back, 2–3 cm* (0.8–1.2 in) *across, petals 5, lateral ones fringed.* Fruits are egg-shaped to nearly globe-shaped capsules 5–10 mm (0.2–0.4 in) long, containing several tiny brown seeds. **Harvest:** Strip blossoms from plants, avoiding stems. When possible gather bright green leaves which are young and tender, but even older leaves in late summer are edible. **Preparation:** Leaves and blossoms are superior sources of vitamin C; the leaves are high also in vitamin A. Use blossoms as snack straight from plant or for jelly, jam, syrup, and candy. For jelly, see book's introduction. Use leaves and flowers raw with other ingredients in tossed salad. Cook chopped leaves with minimum water in covered pot for about 15 min. Season and serve alone or with mustard greens. For tea, dry leaves in warm shade and store in paper bag in cool dry places. Steep 1 oz dried leaves per cup of boiling water. **Related edible species:** PALE VIOLET (next), and WOOD VIOLET, and SOUTHERN WOOD VIOLET. It is likely that all of the species of violets are edible, with some more palatable than others. Some, especially yellow-flowered violets, may be cathartic. Thus, moderate initial consumption is advised. **Poisonous look-alikes:** Violet leaves may resemble leaves of other wildflowers, some of which are toxic. So it's safest to collect violet leaves only when flowers are in bloom.

Pale violet

Viola striata

Also edible summer

Habitat: wooded floodplains, meadows, stream banks. **Identification:** *perennial herb* with short thick underground stem (rhizome); stems several, upright or reclining, smooth, to 50 cm (20 in) high. Basal leaves soon withering; *stem leaves simple, 3–8 cm* (1.2–3.2 in) *long,* as wide or nearly so, *broadest near base and almost circular in outline,* pointed to blunt at tip, toothed along margin, shallowly heart-shaped at base, leafstalks long; *with large, leaflike bract (stipule) at base of each leaf. Flowers* usually produced at tips of stems, each on a slender stalk, *creamy white with purplish-brown veins near base, 2–2.5 cm (0.8–1 in) across, petals 5, lateral ones densely fringed, forming spur 3–6 mm* (0.1–0.2 in) *long on backside.* Fruits are egg-shaped to globe-shaped capsules 4–8 mm (0.2–0.3 in) long. **Harvest and preparation:** same as for CANADA VIOLET (preceding). **Related edible species:** CANADA VIOLET. **Poisonous look-alikes:** See CANADA VIOLET for details.

Pokeweed

Phytolacca americana

Habitat: woodland margins, disturbed sites, waste ground, roadsides, fencerows. **Identification:** *large, perennial herb* to 3 m (9.8 ft) tall with thick fleshy roots; stems branched, upright, smooth, *with disagreeable odor when broken.* Leaves alternate, 9–30 cm (3.5–12 in) long, 3–12 cm (1.2–4.7 in) wide, broadest near base, pointed at tip, entire along margin; leafstalks to 5 cm (2 in) long. *Flowers greenish to white, produced in narrow elongate clusters* (racemes); each flower 2–4 mm (0.1 in) long, petals absent. *Fruits are 5–12-parted berries, wider than long, 6–10 mm* (0.2–0.4 in) *in diameter, green turning purplish-black at maturity.* **Harvest:** young shoots up to 15 cm (6 in) long in late spring before leaves unfold. Identify from presence of previous year's stalks. Cut stems from perennial root as you would asparagus. *Caution: The root is poisonous; avoid all parts of the plant except young shoots.* If shoots show any purple coloration, avoid them as well as mature stems. For winter use, dig root in fall and plant in large container of soil. After hard freeze move to warm area and water regularly. Harvest shoots as above. **Preparation:** Boil shoots 10 min with 1 or 2 water changes; drain, add fresh boiling water and season, cover, and simmer until tender. Serve like broccoli or asparagus with butter, cheese, or other sauces. For casserole, alternate layers of cooked pokeweed shoots, white sauce, and sliced, boiled eggs. Top with seasoned bread crumbs. Bake 30 min at low temperature 165°C (330°F). Boiled, peeled shoots may also be pickled. **Related edible species:** none. **Poisonous look-alikes:** None, but see *caution* above.

Pale violet: flowering plant (Mohlenbrock).

Pokeweed: fruiting stalks (Crow). Flowers (Elias). Young shoots attached to cut root top (Dykeman).

Japanese knotweed: young shoots (Dykeman). Flowering branch (Feldman).

Wintercress: entire plant, leaf, and flowering head (Dykeman).

Japanese knotweed   *Polygonum cuspidatum*

Habitat: disturbed and waste sites, vacant lots, roadsides; introduced weed from Asia. **Identification:** *large perennial herb to 3 m* (9.8 ft) *high,* often forming dense colonies; *stems* upright, *with hollow core,* smooth, mottled, frequently branching. *Leaves* alternate, simple, *10–16 cm* (4–6.3 in) *long, 6–12 cm* (2.4–4.7 in) *wide, broadest near base,* long tipped, *wavy along margin,* squared to rounded at base, almost leathery; *leafstalk* stout and *enclosed at base by membranous sheath that also surrounds stem.* Flowers produced in elongate, branched clusters in junctions of upper leaves, each flower tiny, 1–2 mm (less than 0.1 in) long, white. Fruits are dark brown, shiny, winged nutlets. **Harvest:** Locate papery dry stalks of previous year. Gather young shoots up to 30 cm (1 ft) long for potherb, up to 90 cm (3 ft) for other use. **Preparation:** Boil tips of young shoots in salt water or steam 4–5 min. Serve like ASPARAGUS, hot on toast with butter or white sauce, or cold in salad. Also, force cooked shoots through mill for puree. Add salt, butter, sweetener, to taste, and reheat. Or prepare casserole of cooked young shoots, bread crumbs, grated cheese, cream, and seasonings; bake at 200°C (390°F) until top is browned. Peel older stalks 30–90 cm (1–3 ft) and use like rhubarb. For sauce combine 4 cups peeled and cut shoots, 1 cup sugar, and nutmeg. Simmer until soft. Serve hot or cold. See basic jam recipe in book's Introduction. Prepare pie from peeled shoots using rhubarb pie recipes. **Related edible species:** giant knotweed *(P. sachalinense),* Alaskan knotweed *(P. alaskanum),* AMERICAN BISTORT, ALPINE BISTORT, LADY'S THUMB and others. Some may cause a light-sensitive skin reaction. **Poisonous look-alikes:** none.

Wintercress   *Barbarea vulgaris*
Also edible autumn, winter

Habitat: fields, wet meadows, ditches, roadsides; common and widespread, introduced from Europe. **Identification:** *biennial or perennial herb* to 0.7 m (28 in) high; stems erect, sparingly branched above. Lower *stem leaves* broadest near or above middle, 7–15 cm (2.8–6 in) long, *deeply lobed along sides,* stalked; leaves of upper stem much smaller, stalkless and lobed at base, coarsely toothed. *Flowers from April to June, numerous in cylinder-shaped clusters, each flower* narrow, stalked, *with 4 narrow, yellow petals. Fruit pods very narrow, 1.5–3 cm (0.6–1.2 in) long, tipped with short beak to 3 mm (0.1 in) long,* splitting open lengthwise to release tiny seeds. **Harvest:** Pick leaves after frosty weather and into spring until flower stalks appear. Leaf rosettes grow on warm winter days; become bitter in spring. Leaves blanch and lose bitterness if you tie them in bundle with plant rooted and cover with a bucket. Pick buds and flowers until blooming is over, April or May. **Preparation:** Use early and blanched leaves in salads with other late-winter foods such as COMMON DAY LILY tubers and WATERCRESS. Boil later, bitter leaves in 2 changes of water until tender and treat as for BLACK MUSTARD (next). Buds and flowers are excellent with cheese sauce. Cover clusters with boiling water for 1 min. Drain, cover with fresh boiling water, heat, and boil 3 min more. Drain, season, and cool for 5 min. **Related edible species:** early wintercress *(B. verna).* **Poisonous look-alikes:** none.

Black mustard   (Also edible summer)   Brassica nigra

Habitat: common and widespread, fields, yards, disturbed sites; introduced from Europe. **Identification:** *medium-size to large annual herb* to 1.2 m (4 ft) high; stems erect, hairy on lower parts. Leaves alternate, stalked, usually broadest above or near the middle, 8–18 cm (3.2–7 in) long, *lower leaves lobed, upper leaves narrower, wavy toothed. Flowers few in narrow, elongate, loose clusters,* each *flower* stalked, about 1 cm (0.4 in) across, *with 4 yellow petals. Fruits* narrow linear *capsules 1–2 cm* (0.4–0.7 in) *long, roughly 4-sided,* upright, *beaked, beak 1–2 cm* (0.4–0.8 in) *long,* splitting open lengthwise to release tiny seeds. **Harvest:** leaves very early in spring or blanch later leaves as with WINTERCRESS (preceding). Pick buds and flowers until nearly all flowers have opened. Avoid bitter leaves. For seeds, harvest during summer when oldest pods open. Pile them on fine cloth or plastic tarp and sun-dry for several days. Beat with flail to release seeds, remove stalks, winnow seed from chaff. **Preparation:** Use early and blanched leaves in salads. Boil older greens with 1 change of water for about 30 min. Season with butter and vinegar or mix with crumbled bacon and chopped wild onions. Top with hard-boiled egg slices and French dressing or vinegar. Excellent source of vitamins A, B, and C. For buds and flowers, treat as WINTERCRESS. Sprinkle seeds lightly on salad. To make mustard, grind seeds in food mill; use dried. Or for mustard spread, combine equal parts mustard powder and oven-browned flour with half-and-half mix of vinegar and water. Add other spices to taste. **Related edible species:** field mustard *(B. rapa),* Chinese mustard *(B. juncea),* and others. **Poisonous look-alikes:** none.

Marsh marigold, Cowslip   Caltha palustris

Habitat: freshwater swamps, wet meadows, along streams, ponds, lakes. **Identification:** *perennial herbs* to 70 cm (28 in) high; stems partially spreading to upright, hollow, smooth. *Basal leaves long-stalked, blade rounded to almost kidney-shaped, 1–2.8 cm* (0.4–1.1 in) *long, 0.4–2.2 cm* (0.2–0.8 in) *wide,* rounded at tip, toothed along margin, heart-shaped at base; stem leaves smaller, lacking stalks. *Flowers large, showy,* 2.5–4 cm (1–1.6 in) across, *with 5 bright yellow petallike sepals.* Fruits are elongate, somewhat rounded, 1–1.7 cm (0.4–0.7 in) long, splitting open along one side when mature to release small seeds. **Harvest:** Cut leaves from plant when young, best before flowers open. Pick tightly closed buds for pickling. **Preparation:** *Raw leaves and buds are poisonous until properly treated!* Wash leaves and cover with boiling water. Reheat to boiling, then drain. Repeat 2 or 3 times, then cook in very little water until tender. Drain and serve with butter and seasonings or with cream or cheese sauce. For pickles, treat buds with boiling water as described for leaves. Do not boil. Drain and pack in jars. Cover with hot pickling liquid and seal. Store for at least a month before eating. Do not consume used pickling juice. To make pickling liquid, slowly add mix of ¼ cup salt, ½ cup sugar, 1 tbsp ground mustard, and 1 tbsp celery seed to 2 cups vinegar and 1 cup water. Boil 10 min with stirring. **Related edible species:** none. **Poisonous look-alikes:** Flowers resemble COMMON BUTTERCUPS yet leaves are very different.

Black mustard: entire plants (NYBG).

Marsh marigold: plants in typical streamside habitat and entire plant (Dykeman).

Evening primrose: basal leaves (Dykeman). Flowering stalks (Pawloski).

Sow thistle: fruiting head, left, and flower (Mathisen).

Evening primrose
Oenothera biennis

Also edible autumn, winter

Habitat: disturbed sites, along roads, prairies, fields. **Identification:** biennial herb of 1.6 m (5.3 ft) high, from elongated taproot; stems upright, hairy. Leaves of first year in low rosette; second year leaves on flower stalk, alternate, lance-shaped to broadest near middle, 8–18 cm (3.2–7 in) long, 2–6 cm (0.8–2.4 in) wide, pointed at tip, entire to toothed along margin, tapering at base, hairy. *Flowers second year, many in terminal, elongated cluster, each flower with narrow, tubular calyx 1.5–3 cm* (0.6–1.2 in) *long, 4 large spreading, bright yellow petals 1.5–3 cm* (0.6–1.2 in) *long. (Flowers open after dusk and often close by midmorning.) Fruits are cylinder-shaped, angled capsules 1–4 cm* (0.4–1.6 in) *long,* containing many small, reddish seeds. **Harvest:** Dig taproots of first year growth between autumn and early spring. Pick leaves from rosettes in early spring or even earlier from areas clear of snow. **Preparation:** Peel taproots and boil in 2 changes of water for 20–30 min. Serve with butter and seasonings or slice and fry. Cook sliced roots with meat or in stews, partially boiling roots first if flavor is too strong. Simmer boiled roots in sugar syrup for 20–30 min until candied. Peel leaves and use sparingly in salads. Or boil leaves 15–20 min in 2 changes of water and serve with butter or vinegar. **Related edible species:** other species of this large genus. **Poisonous look-alikes:** none, but don't confuse leaves with those of other early-blooming species.

Sow thistle
Sonchus arvensis

Habitat: disturbed sites such as roadsides, fields, railroad right-of-ways, gravel banks; introduced weed from Europe. **Identification:** Not to be mistaken for the more common and generally more palatable thistles of the *Cirsium* genus, sow thistle is a *perennial herb* to 1 m (3.2 ft) high with deep vertical and spreading horizontal coarse roots; stems upright, smooth, with milky sap. *Leaves* alternate, simple, broadest near or above middle, 10–35 cm (4–14 in) long, 4–14 cm (1.6–5.5 in) wide, *deeply lobed along margin, upper leaves less so, spiny-toothed, lobed leaf bases clasping stems,* usually smooth. *Flowering heads* produced in loosely branched, elongated, erect cluster, each head *3–5 cm* (1.2–2 in) *across,* with lance-shaped bracts on the outside and many small *yellow flowers* within. Fruits are small, dark-brown nutlets 2.5–3 mm (0.1 in) long. **Harvest:** Locate by noting concentrations of mature plants the previous year. Pick when only a few inches tall; leaves become increasingly bitter with age. *Caution: Sow thistle occasionally contains toxic levels of nitrates.* **Preparation:** If not too bitter, cut and mix leaves with other, blander salad greens. Boil in very little water for 3–4 min, change water, and then boil until tender. Serve with butter and seasonings or vinegar. If too bitter, mix with blander greens such as LAMB'S QUARTERS. **Related edible species:** Several species of the *Sonchus* genus are variously distributed and edible when very young. Some have leaf spines that must be removed. **Poisonous look-alikes:** none.

Prickly lettuce   *Lactuca serriola* (synonym: *L. scariola*)
Habitat: disturbed sites such as fields, roadsides, vacant lots; introduced weed from Europe. **Identification:** *annual or biennial herb* to 2 m (6.6 ft) high, *with milky juice in stems and leaves,* stems upright, slender, usually armed with spreading prickles. Stem *leaves* alternate, *lance-shaped,* 5–25 cm (2–10 in) long, 1.5–12 cm (0.6–4.7 in) wide, *with several deep lobes or lobeless, toothed and spiny along margin* and spiny along main vein on lower leaf surface, with pointed lobes at base and often clasping stem. *Flowering heads* sparingly produced in branched clusters, each head *1–1.5 cm* (0.4–0.6 in) *long,* 3–6 mm (0.1–0.2 in) *across, containing 6–12 yellow flowers.* Fruits are tiny gray to brown nutlets 3–4 mm (0.1 in) long. **Harvest:** Like other wild lettuce species, prickly lettuce is good only when very young. Pick leaves when plants are less than 20 cm (8 in) tall. **Preparation:** Use alone or with other greens in tossed salad. Boil leaves in very little water for 2–3 min. Serve with butter and seasonings. For wilted lettuce pour boiling water over lettuce leaves and let sit for 5 min. Drain. Make dressing of 3 slices of crisp bacon crumbled into ¼ cup hot vinegar with 1 tsp sugar and ½ tsp salt. Pour over hot lettuce. *Caution: Large quantity of raw young leaves may cause digestive upset.* **Related edible species:** many species of the *Lactuca* genus widely distributed; most noticeable of these is wild lettuce *(L. canadensis),* which lack prickles on leaves and lower stem. **Poisonous look-alikes:** none.

Dandelion   *Taraxacum officinale*
Also edible autumn, winter

Habitat: lawns, yards, disturbed sites; common weed introduced from Europe. **Identification:** *perennial herb, with large,* sometimes branched *taproot.* *Leaves all basal,* 8–40 cm (3.2–16 in) long, 0.8–14 cm (0.3–5.5 in) wide, widest near tip, rounded to pointed at tip, *variously and irregularly lobed along margin,* tapering to narrow base, hairy beneath, *with milky juice.* Flowers produced throughout spring in large heads at tip of hollow stalks. *Flowering heads 2–5 cm* (0.8–2 in) *across, composed of numerous, small, narrow, orange-yellow flowers, remaining closed on cloudy days. Fruits* on elongated, upright hollow stalks, *forming delicate ball* composed of many tiny seeds each tipped with white featherlike tuft (pappus) easily dispersed by wind. **Harvest:** Best lawn areas are those with taller grass. Dig roots with crown at top of root and leaves attached from time leaves (rich in vitamin A) appear until they are too bitter to use. Dig older roots in fall and winter. Cut out developing bud clusters and pick fully opened flowers in spring. **Preparation:** For flowers, leaves, and older roots, see CHICORY. Peel young roots, slice thin, and boil in 2 changes of water for about 20 min, adding pinch of baking soda to first water. Serve with butter and seasonings or saute cooked slices in butter until brown. Season with paprika. Boil buds just a few minutes, butter and serve. Dip blossoms in fritter batter; fry in oil and serve with syrup or garlic salt. **Related edible species:** several other species of *Taraxacum,* all similar to common dandelion in appearance/preparation. Also, CHICORY in early growth. **Poisonous look-alikes:** none.

Prickly lettuce: flowering branch and entire plant (Kavasch). Leaves (Dykeman).

Dandelion: flowering plant (Elias).

Goat's beard   *Tragopogon pratensis*

Habitat: roadsides, fields, other disturbed sites; introduced from Europe. **Identification:** *perennial* or biennial *herb* to 76 cm (30 in) high with taproot and milky juice; stems upright. *Leaves* alternate, linear, *grasslike, 15–30 cm* (6–12 in) *long, 1–2 cm* (0.4–0.8 in) *wide,* pointed at tip, entire along margin, base partially circling stem, smooth. *Flowering heads* produced singly at tip of stems, *resembling dandelion, with 8 lance-shaped outer bracts, many yellow flowers.* Fruiting heads globe-shaped, light, fluffy, consisting of numerous small nutlets, each tipped with light, featherlike bristles. **Harvest:** See SALSIFY (preceding). Roots of goat's beard may be smaller, tougher, less palatable. **Preparation:** Same as SALSIFY. Cool boiled roots and saute in oil until browned or prepare like potatoes. Roasted and ground roots make coffee substitute. Use very young leaves in salad if not bitter or boil for 5–10 min and serve with butter and seasonings. **Related edible species:** SALSIFY, yellow goat's beard *(T. dubius)*. **Poisonous look-alikes:** none in the flowering stage.

Common milkweed   *Asclepias syriaca*
Also edible summer

Habitat: fields, meadows, roadsides, woodland margins. **Identification:** *perennial herb* to 1.8 m (6 ft) tall; stems upright, usually unbranched, hairy. *Leaves opposite,* broadest near base or middle, *10–28 cm* (4–11 in) *long, 4–12 cm* (1.6–4.7 in) *wide,* pointed at tip, entire to wavy along margin, *thick, leathery, hairy above, with milky sap. Flowers in dense, rounded heads 6–10 cm* (2.4–4 in) *across, each flower rose, dull purple to greenish-white,* 8–12 cm (3.2–4.7 in) long, with 5 reflexed petals. *Fruits are elongated pods,* broadest near base and gradually tapering to curved point, 8–14 cm (3.2–5.5 in) long, covered with small, soft, green projections. Seeds small, each with conspicuous, soft, featherlike hairs at one end. **Harvest:** Cut new shoots when less than 20 cm (8 in) tall. Pick newly opened leaves until buds are formed; then pick clusters of buds and flowers. Later pick firm pods 2–3 cm (0.8–1.2 in) long. **Preparation:** To remove bitterness from all parts, cover with boiling water and bring back to boil. Discard water and repeat 2–3 times with boiling water. Do not use cold water in process. Cook treated shoots like ASPARAGUS. After treatment boil young leaves, bud clusters, and pods until tender, usually 10–15 min. Serve with butter and seasonings or with sauce. Use treated pods in soup like okra *(Hibiscus esculentus)*. **Related edible species:** Showy milkweed *(A. speciosa)* is good. **Poisonous look-alikes:** all narrow-leaved milkweed species, especially BUTTERFLY WEED; some are more toxic than others. Young DOGBANE, also with milky sap, has branches (common milkweed does not) and its young shoots lack hairs.

Goat's beard: fruiting head, flower bud, rootstock (Dykeman).

Common milkweed: flowering head and entire plant (Elias).

Fireweed: flowering stalk (Elias). Flowers (NYBG).

Alfilaria: entire plant with flowers and fruits (Ross).

Introduced and grows wild. Widespread.

Fireweed
Epilobium angustifolium
Also edible summer

Habitat: woodlands, ravines, clearings; commonly grows after fires. **Identification:** *perennial herb* 1–2 m (3.2–6.5 ft) high; stems erect, usually single, smooth. Leaves alternate, narrow and broadest near base, 5–20 cm (2–8 in) long, to 3 cm (1.2 in) wide, nearly stalkless, long-pointed at tip, entire or nearly so along margin. *Flowers* many on elongate spikes; each flower stalked, spreading, *with 4 pink to purple, rarely white, clawed petals* 1–2 cm (0.4–0.8 in) long. *Fruit a narrow capsule 3–8 cm* (1.2–3.2 in) *long,* with reddish or purplish cast, 4-parted. **Harvest:** Cut young shoots in spring; new leaves, flower bud clusters, and mature stems later. Older leaves are good for tea but too bitter for potherb. **Preparation:** Not a very tasty food plant but widespread, abundant, easy to identify, and has several edible parts. Cook young shoots like ASPARAGUS and season with butter, hollandaise, or cheese sauce. Use young leaves and later flower-bud clusters in salad with other greens. For potherb, stir 4 cups small leaves and 3 tbsp water into 2 tbsp melted butter in skillet over high heat. Cover and cook 2–3 min, season and serve. Boil flower bud clusters 10–15 min and serve with butter, salt and pepper. Peel stems too old for cooking and chew on raw pith or use pith in soups. Dry mature leaves and blend with other suitable leaves for a tea. **Related edible species:** dwarf fireweed *(E. latifolium)* and other related but smaller species. **Poisonous look-alikes:** none.

Alfilaria, Filaree, Storksbill
Erodium cicutarium

Habitat: fields, pastures, roadsides, other disturbed sites; common weed introduced from Europe. **Identification:** *annual or biennial herb* with 1 to several spreading stems, hairy. *Leaves* emerge at base and along stem, alternate, *2–10 cm* (0.8–4 in) *long, featherlike (pinnate) compound, leaflets (pinnae) cleft and coarsely toothed. Flowers* 2–10 in small, branched, rounded-headed cluster at tips of shoots; each flower about 2.5 cm (1 in) across, *with 5 rose-purple petals.* Fruits are narrow, elongate capsules 2–4 cm (0.8–1.6 in) long, opening from base toward tip. **Harvest:** Gather young, overwintered leaves in early spring when other wild foods are scarce. Be certain leafstalks are hairy. **Preparation:** Chop leaves for salad with other greens. Boil leaves in lightly salted water until tender, about 10–20 min. Serve with butter, lemon juice, and herbs. **Related edible species:** none recommended. **Poisonous look-alikes:** Leaves resemble those of the parsley family including POISON HEMLOCK. Picking only hairy-stemmed leaves very early in spring should help you avoid errors. Be sure of identification!

Live-forever, Orphine
Sedum purpureum
Also edible autumn, winter

Habitat: roadsides, open slopes, woodlands, and disturbed sites; introduced European weed. **Identification:** *perennial herb* to 80 cm (32 in) tall, from fleshy tubers. *Stems upright, succulent; leaves* alternate or whorls of 3, simple, *fleshy, 3–6 cm* (1.2–2.4 in) *long*, 1–3 cm (0.4–1.2 in) wide, pointed or blunt at tip, entire or toothed along margin, green to bluish-green. *Flowers* produced in a compact, branched cluster at tips of branches, each flower bisexual, 6–10 mm (0.2–0.4 in) across, *with 5 reddish-purple to deep pink petals.* Fruits small capsules 4–6 mm (0.2 in) long, splitting open along 1 side only. **Harvest:** young leaves in spring and tubers from fall through spring, as long as they are firm and crisp. **Preparation:** Add raw, very young leaves to salads. Boil leaves gathered through early summer for 5–10 min and serve as cooked green. Pour hot pickling liquid over tubers and leave for several days before eating. For pickling liquid boil 2 tbsp mixed pickle spices in cloth bag in solution of 1 qt vinegar and 1 cup sugar. Boil tubers like those of COMMON DAY LILY for about 20 min. Serve with butter and seasonings. **Related edible species:** Other *Sedum* species provide edible leaves; some are more pungent than others. Roseroot *(S. rosea)* is the most frequently used. **Poisonous look-alikes:** none.

Lady's thumb
Polygonum persicaria
Also edible summer

Habitat: disturbed sites, especially low wet ground, along roadsides, lakes, streams, ponds; widespread weed introduced from Europe. **Identification:** *annual herb* to 1 m (3.2 ft) high; stems soon branching, spreading to upright, smooth. *Leaves* alternate, *narrowly lance-shaped,* 4–12 cm (1.6–4.7 in) long, 0.6–3 cm (0.2–1.2 in) wide, *often with irregular or triangular purplish spot above,* pointed at tip, wavy along margin, tapering at base, *enclosed at base by membranous sheath that also surrounds stem.* Mature stems reddish. *Flowers* numerous, dense *in cylinder-shaped spikes* 2–4 cm (0.8–1.6 in) long, each flower *pink to rose.* Fruits are tiny, broadly egg-shaped nutlets 2–2.5 mm (0.1 in) long. **Harvest:** Gather young leaves, mainly in spring but later if not too peppery. **Preparation:** Add chopped raw leaves to tossed salad. Boil leaves in small amount of water for 5–10 min. Serve with vinegar. **Related edible species:** ALPINE BISTORT, JAPANESE KNOTWEED. Known as the smartweeds, other *Polygonum* species may be as good as lady's thumb, and none are known to be poisonous. *Caution: Some species may cause light-sensitive reactions.* **Poisonous look-alikes:** none.

Live-forever: flowering head (Kavasch). Entire plant (Speas).

Lady's thumb: entire plant and stem (Dykeman).

Introduced and grows wild in moist soils

Common burdock   *Arctium minus*
Also edible summer, autumn

Habitat: roadsides, vacant lots, disturbed sites; introduced from Europe and Asia. **Identification:** *biennial herb* to 1.8 m (6 ft) high; stems upright, often branched, usually smooth. *Leaves* alternate, *basal leaves large, 30–50 cm* (12–20 in) *long, 20–30 cm* (8–12 in) *wide,* widest near base, *deeply lobed at base,* with conspicuous hollow stalk; upper-stem leaves smaller and not lobed at base. *Flowering heads produced during second year along upper stems* or in branched elongated clusters; heads 1.7–2.8 cm (0.7–1.1 in) across, outer bracts spine-tipped; *flowers pink to purple.* Seeds small, hard nutlets 4–6 mm (0.2 in) long. **Harvest:** Dig roots of first-year plants during summer, later if necessary. Pick first-year basal leafstalks and young flower stalks of second year. **Preparation:** Peel roots, slice ½-in thick and boil 20 min with pinch of baking soda. Change water and boil until tender. Serve with butter and seasonings, or mash pieces and make fried patties. Peel flower stalk, removing all green rind. Eat like celery, slice into salad, or boil until tender. Good in casseroles and many other recipes. Simmer pieces of cooked flower stalk in maple syrup to make candy. Eat peeled leafstalks raw or boiled, but since they are hollow, there's not much left after peeling. **Related edible species:** Just as good, great burdock *(A. lappa)* is larger, with larger burrs on solid leafstalks. **Poisonous look-alikes:** Leaves resemble rhubarb leaves but flowers are greatly different.

Salsify, Oyster plant   *Tragopogon porrifolius*

Habitat: roadsides, fields, railroad right-of-ways, other disturbed sites; introduced weed from Europe. **Identification:** *biennial or perennial herb* to 1 m (3.2 ft) with long taproot and milky juice; *stems* upright, *swollen just below flowering heads.* Leaves alternate, lance-shaped, 18–32 cm (7–12.6 in) long, to 2 cm (0.8 in) wide, long-pointed at tip, entire along margin, base circling stem. *Flowering heads* solitary, *usually 3–4 cm* (1.2–1.6 in) *long, with 6–11 lance-shaped outer bracts and numerous purple flowers.* Fruiting heads globe-shaped, fluffy, consisting of many small nutlets, each tipped with featherlike bristles. **Harvest:** This is the cultivated species of salsify or oyster plant that also grows wild. Roots and leaves must be harvested before plant produces flowerstalk. This is a problem since grasslike leaves grow among leaves of many other plants. Learn to recognize leaves so you can harvest them and dig roots while still palatable. **Preparation:** Scrub and scrape roots as you would carrots, putting them in cold water to prevent discoloring. Cut into ½-in slices. If they are tough, add pinch of baking soda to cooking water and boil for 10 min, then change water and cook until tender. Drain and serve with butter and seasonings or with white sauce. For other uses see GOAT'S BEARD (next). **Related edible species:** GOAT'S BEARD. **Poisonous look-alikes:** none in flowering stage.

Common burdock: flowering stalk (Speas). Basal leaves (Dykeman).

Salsify: flowers, side view (NYBG). Flower (Ross).

Bull thistle: young plant (Dykeman). Flowering head (Elias).

Chicory: basal leaves and young plants (Dykeman). Flowers (NYBG).

Bull thistle   *Cirsium vulgare*

Habitat: fields, meadows, roadsides, disturbed sites; introduced from Europe and Asia. **Identification:** *biennial herb* to 1.8 m (6 ft) high, from taproot; *stems* upright, hairy, *winged, wings lobed and armed with spines.* **Leaves** alternate, broadest near or above middle, *deeply and variously dissected along margin,* 8–30 cm (3.2–12 in) long, 4–12 cm (1.6–4.7 in) wide, *stiff, spiny,* stiffly hairy above, with soft white to green hairs below, leaf bases extending onto stem. *Flowering heads* second year, several, outer bracts spiny, 2–4 cm (0.8–1.6 in) long; flowers *purple.* Seeds are hard, 3–4 mm (0.2 in) long and tipped with bristles. **Harvest:** Dig roots of first-year growth (thistles without stems). With gloves and knife, harvest leaves and young second-year stems at top of root early in growing season. **Preparation:** Peel young stems and remove spines from leaves before using raw in salad or boiling until tender for green vegetable. Remove all spiny covering from core of leaf bases. Boil cores with washed, peeled roots for about 15 min, changing water if necessary to remove bitterness. Serve salted with butter or vinegar. Slice boiled roots and fry until browned. Boil roots several hours until mushy, dry and grind into flour. Because of spines, you may prefer to use thistles only as survival food. **Related edible species:** Many species of thistles are available; some are more palatable than others. **Poisonous look-alikes:** HORSE NETTLE is a low herb with prickly stems but no spines on leaves.

Chicory   *Cichorium intybus*
Also edible autumn, winter

Habitat: roadsides, fields, vacant lots, other disturbed sites; introduced weed from Europe. **Identification:** *perennial herb* to 1.5 m (5 ft) high, *with large deep taproot;* stems erect or nearly so, often branching. **Leaves** alternate, lance-shaped to broadest above middle, *10–32 cm* (4–12.6 in) *long,* 2–8 cm (0.8–3.1 in) wide, upper leaves reduced, *toothed and often lobed along margin,* sap milky. *Flowering heads produced along upper part of stems in junctions of upper smaller leaves; each head* 1–1.6 cm (0.4–0.6 in) long, *3–4 cm* (1.2–1.6 in) *across in flower, containing many bright blue, rarely pink or white, 5-lobed flowers.* Fruits are tiny, brown or black nutlets 2–4 mm (0.1 in) long. **Harvest:** Pick leaves, including crown at top of root, as early as possible. Dig root, fall through spring. Chicory leaves are similar to those of DANDELION; collect and use leafy parts of the two together. **Preparation:** Slice bleached underground portion of leaf crown for use raw in salad, along with oil and vinegar or with other spring edibles. Boil crown bases about 5 min and serve with butter and seasonings. Same for leaves but water changes may be needed to remove bitterness, especially later in spring. For coffee substitute, scrub roots and roast slowly in oven until brown throughout. Grind and brew like coffee. **Related edible species:** none, but similar to DANDELION in early stages. **Poisonous look-alikes:** none.

Henbit   *Lamium amplexicaule*

Habitat: fields, yards, vacant lots, disturbed sites; introduced from Eurasia, common and widespread. **Identification:** small *annual herb* to 40 cm (16 in) tall; *stems* usually branching with upper parts upright, *4-sided. Leaves opposite,* mainly on lower half of stem, 0.7–3.4 cm (0.3–1.3 in) long, *nearly rounded, coarsely round-toothed along margin,* heart-shaped at base, hairy above, lower leaves long-stalked. *Flowers purple,* produced near tip, each *narrow, funnel-shaped,* 12–18 mm (0.5–0.7 in) long, *2-lipped,* lower lip 2-lobed, upper lip 3-lobed, hairy on outer surface. Fruits are 4 small nutlets, partially enclosed by persistent calyx. **Harvest:** young leaves and shoots in spring. **Preparation:** Combine with other greens in salads; use young leafy shoots as potherb. For spiced henbit, chop 4 cups shoots, cover with water, and boil 10 min. Separately melt 3 tbsp butter or margarine, add 1 tsp curry powder, 2 whole cloves, and ¼ tsp ground cinnamon. Stir and cook 1 min. Stir in 2 tbsp flour and cook 1 more min. Add ½ cup water from boiling henbit and stir until smooth. Add cooked henbit and ¾ cup sour cream. Simmer 15 min gently. **Related edible species:** Henbit (*L. purpureum*), with the same distribution, is very similar except leaves are stalked. **Poisonous look-alikes:** none.

Wood violet   *Viola palmata*
Also edible summer

Habitat: wooded floodplains, rich deciduous forests, especially on slopes and ledges. **Identification:** *perennial herb* from thick, elongated underground stem (rhizome); above ground stem absent. *Leaves* simple, *6–12 cm* (2.4–4.7 in) *long,* often wider, broadest near base, *blade deeply 5- to 11-lobed,* lobes variously toothed, smooth or hairy, leafstalks long, to 20 cm (8 in); with linear to narrowly lance-shaped bracts (stipules) at base of each leaf. *Flowers produced singly at tip of stalk as long as leaves, deep reddish-violet to violet,* 1.7–4 cm (0.7–1.6 in) across, petals 5, lateral ones bearded, with short spur in back. Fruits are egg-shaped capsules 6–12 mm (0.2–0.5 in) long. **Harvest:** Gather flowers, leaving stems behind. Give preference to bright-green, young, tender leaves; but older darker-green summer leaves are edible too. **Preparation:** Use fresh flowers as trail snack or for jelly, jam, syrup, candy. For jelly, cover 2 cups flowers with boiling water in jar and leave overnight. Then strain and discard flowers. Add juice of 1 lemon and 1 pkg pectin. Bring to boil and add 4 cups sugar. Boil again for 1 min. Pour into sterilized jars and seal. For syrup, pour 2 cups boiling water over 6 cups flowers and leave overnight. Strain and discard flowers. Combine liquid with 2 cups sugar. Boil until syrup thickens. Store in covered jars in refrigerator. For other uses, see CANADA VIOLET. **Related edible species:** CANADA VIOLET, PALE VIOLET, western mountain violet, (*V. purpurea*), and southern wood violet (*V. hirsutula*). It is likely that all of the violet species are edible, with some more palatable than others. Some may have a cathartic effect. **Poisonous look-alikes:** Violet leaves resemble leaves of other wildflowers, some of which are toxic. So it's safest to collect leaves only when flowers are in bloom.

Henbit: flowering stock (Elias).

Wood violet: flowering plant (Elias).

Orange-flowered jewelweed: flowering plant (Dykeman). Young plant (Elias).

Yellow-flowered jewelweed: flowering stalks (Elias).

Orange-flowered jewelweed, Spotted touch-me-not   *Impatiens biflora*
                                                      (synonym: *I. capensis*)

Habitat: widespread in wet areas, along streams, ponds, springs, swamps, low moist woodlands, floodplains, bottomlands. **Identification:** annual herb; *stems* upright, to 1.5 m (5 ft) high, branched, *very juicy,* smooth. Leaves alternate, 4– 12 cm (1.6–4.7 in) long, 3–7 cm (1.2–2.8 in) wide, broadest at or below middle, blunt- or round-toothed along margin, long-stalked. Flowers showy, in few-flow-ered, spreading clusters; each *flower* stalked, *with conspicuous saclike spur in rear, orange to orange-yellow spotted with reddish, yellow, or white spots on face.* **Fruit** elongate, cylinder-shaped capsule 1.5–2.5 cm (0.6–1 in) long, at maturity *exploding suddenly when touched to scatter seeds.* **Harvest and prep-aration:** For potherb, pick *young shoots* to 15 cm (6 in) high; wilts quickly, so use immediately. Cover with water; boil 10–15 min, draining and adding fresh boiling water twice. Season and butter. *Caution:* Frequent use as a potherb is not recommended because of abundance of calcium oxalate crystals. Seeds: As pods ripen, shake plant over fine net; separate seeds from rest of fruit. Tastes like BUTTERNUTS; eat as gathered or use as topping for desserts. Medicinal use: Applied to skin, juice prevents and relieves symptoms of POISON IVY, NETTLES, and fungal dermatitis. Apply raw juice or concentrated boiled juice of crushed stems. Ex-tract spoils quickly, but frozen extract retains medicinal properties. Antifungal agent is 2-methoxy-1, 4-naphthoquinone. **Related edible species:** YELLOW-FLOW-ERED JEWELWEED (next). **Poisonous look-alikes:** none.

Yellow-flowered jewelweed, Pale touch-me-not   *Impatiens pallida*

Habitat: moist woodlands, wet meadows; not as abundant and usually occurring in slightly drier sites than ORANGE-FLOWERED JEWELWEED. **Identification:** annual herb; *stems* upright, to 2 m (6.6 ft) high, freely branched, *very juicy,* smooth. Leaves alternate, long stalked, blades 4–14 cm (1.6–5.5 in) long, 3–8 cm (1.2– 3.2 in) wide, broadest at or below middle, blunt or round toothed along margin. *Flowers showy, in few-flowered clusters* in junctions of upper leaves; *each flower stalked, with conspicuous saclike spur in rear, pale yellow with reddish spots on face. Fruit elongate, cylinder-shaped capsule 2–2.6 cm (0.8–1 in) long, at maturity exploding suddenly when touched to scatter seeds.* **Harvest and preparation:** same as for ORANGE-FLOWERED JEWELWEED (preceding). **Related edible species:** ORANGE-FLOWERED JEWELWEED. **Poisonous look-alikes:** none.

Sheep sorrel: flowering stalk (Elias). Basal leaves and leaf (Dykeman).

Sour dock: flowering stalks (Elias).

Sheep sorrel
Rumex acetosella

Also edible summer, autumn

Habitat: disturbed sites, gardens, old fields, mainly on acid soils. **Identification:** annual or perennial *herb* to 50 cm (20 in); stems upright, 4-sided, unbranched or branched. Basal leaves present, shaped like a narrow arrowhead. *Stem leaves 2.4–5 cm* (1–2 in) *long,* 0.5–2 cm (0.2–0.8 in) wide, *narrow arrowhead-shaped,* pointed at tip, *with slender pointed lobes at base,* with papery sheath around stem where leaves are attached. *Flowers tiny,* green, yellow, red to purple, *clustered on narrow elongate spikes.* Fruits are tiny nutlets 1.2–1.8 mm (less than 0.1 in) long, 3-angled, shiny yellow-brown, enclosed by persistent calyx. **Harvest:** Pick or cut leaves from healthy, deep green clumps from spring until autumn, but flowering clumps may be tough. **Preparation:** Sour taste makes sheep sorrel leaves an excellent thirst-quenching trail nibble. Use leaves liberally with bland greens in tossed salad. For beverage boil 1 cup loosely packed leaves in 1 qt water for 2–3 min; then cover and steep for at least 15 min. Strain, add sugar or honey to taste, and serve hot or cold. Boil leaves in 2 changes of water for pleasantly sour potherb or mix with other cooked greens. Use leaves with chicken broth to make soup or sauce to use with fish, rice, or vegetables. *Caution: Large quantity may cause stomach upset.* **Related edible species:** Many species of dock, including SOUR DOCK (next), are edible; sheep sorrel has the most distinctive sour flavor. **Poisonous look-alikes:** none.

Sour dock, Curled dock, Yellow dock
Rumex crispus

Also edible summer, autumn, winter

Habitat: common in disturbed sites, fields, roadsides, vacant lots. **Identification:** *large herb,* usually biennial, to 1.5 m (5 ft) tall; stems upright, smooth, ribbed. *Leaves* 14–24 cm (5.5–9.4 in) long, 2–6.5 cm (0.8–2.5 in) wide, uniformly wide to widest near base, pointed at tip, *strongly wavy and curled along margin,* rounded to heart-shaped at base, dark green, *with papery, straw-colored sheath around stem where leaves are attached.* Flowers small, usually greenish, stalked, densely clustered on 1 to several narrow, elongated stalks. *Fruits 3-parted,* 4–6 mm (0.2 in) across, dark red to reddish-brown, each *enclosing 3 nutlets* 1.5–3 mm (0.1 in) in diameter. **Harvest:** leaves in early spring, or even through late winter when they may be tinged with red and yellow. Strip seeds from stalks in late summer and autumn. **Preparation:** Young leaves cooked for about 10 min in small amount of water taste like young beet greens. Older leaves may need longer cooking with 1–2 water changes to make them tender and remove bitterness. Cook with other wild greens of season. Serve with butter, bacon, hard-boiled egg, seasonings. *Caution: Large quantity may cause stomach upset.* With much effort seeds can be hulled, winnowed, ground, and sifted to produce palatable flour. Use half and half with regular flour. **Related edible species:** While most species of dock are likely edible, sour dock is one of the most flavorful. **Poisonous look-alikes:** none.

Eastern hemlock *Tsuga canadensis*

Habitat: cool moist ravines, protected valleys, lowlands. **Identification:** medium or large *evergreen tree* to 25 m (82 ft), rarely taller, with deeply furrowed, reddish-brown or cinnamon red bark. *Leaves small,* 0.7–1.6 cm (0.3–0.6 in) long, 1–2 mm (less than 0.1 in) wide, *linear, arranged in 1 plane horizontal to ground, flattened,* dark yellowish-green *with 2 whitish bands underneath.* Male flowering cones tiny, yellowish, at tips of branches; female cones small, green, leathery. *Fruiting cones 1.2–1.9 cm* (0.5–0.7 in) *long,* hanging, widest near middle, rounded or pointed at tip, *light brown;* cone scales nearly rounded; seeds tiny, egg-shaped, winged. **Harvest:** needles any time but preferably young ones in spring. Inner bark best in winter and early spring. **Preparation:** For tea, boil needles in covered pot and steep about 10 min. Tea is high in vitamin C. To avoid damage to tree, use inner bark only in emergency. It may be eaten raw or boiled, or dried and ground to mix with flour. **Related edible species:** Carolina hemlock *(T. caroliniana),* western hemlock *(T. heterophylla),* mountain hemlock *(T. mertensiana).* **Poisonous look-alikes:** AMERICAN YEW is a commonly cultivated shrub that has longer needles and bright red, fleshy pulp surrounding seeds.

Yellow birch *Betula alleghaniensis*
Also edible autumn, winter (synonym: *B. lutea*)

Habitat: rich woodlands, lower slopes, and occasionally cool marshlands, usually below 1,000 m (3,300 ft) elevation. **Identification:** medium-size tree with rounded crown and peeling ragged-edged, reddish-brown *bark* turning *dull yellow or yellowish-brown. Broken twigs have mild wintergreen fragrance.* Leaves alternate, deciduous, simple, 7–11 cm (2.8–4.3 in) long, 3–5 cm (1.2–2 in) wide, usually broadest near base, with double row of sharp-pointed teeth along margin. Male and female flowers in separate catkins on same tree in spring. *Fruits broad, upright cones 2.5–3.5 cm (1–1.4 in) long,* with numerous 3-lobed scales and tiny winged seeds. **Harvest:** For sap, tap like SUGAR MAPLE, 3–4 weeks after maple sap flow begins. Flow copious but sugar content lower than from maple. For use of twigs and inner bark, see instructions under more flavorful SWEET BIRCH (next). **Preparation:** Boil sap in shallow open container outdoors, adding more as volume decreases, until evaporation leaves viscous, molasses-flavored syrup with temperature about 104°C (220°F). Ratio of sap to ultimate syrup is far greater than for SUGAR MAPLE. Store in sterilized, filled, sealed jars. **Related edible species:** SWEET BIRCH. **Poisonous look-alikes:** none.

Sweet birch, Black birch *(Also edible summer, autumn, winter)* *Betula lenta*

Habitat: forest or open woods, especially moist, north-facing, protected slopes, in deep, rich, well-drained soils. **Identification:** medium-size tree with rounded crown and *smooth, dark red to almost black bark. Broken twigs have wintergreen fragrance.* Leaves alternate, deciduous, simple, 6–15 cm (2.4–6 in) long, 4–8 cm (1.6–3.2 in) wide, broadest near base, *with double row of fine, sharp-pointed teeth along margin.* Male and female flowers in separate, small catkins on same tree in spring. Fruits in erect, brownish cones 2.5–3 cm (1–1.2 in) long, containing many tiny, winged seeds. Fruits maturing in late summer and early

Eastern hemlock: branch with young leaves and branch with mature cones (Elias).

Yellow birch: trunk (Dykeman). Branch with fruits (Elias).

Sweet birch: spring branch with male flowers (Dykeman). Fruit in summer (Elias). Trunk (Dykeman).

Sassafras: summer branch with fruits (Elias). Spring branch with flowers (NYBG).

Sugar maple: fruiting branch (Soderstrom).

fall. **Harvest:** twigs, red inner bark, larger roots: year-round but best in spring. For sap in spring, 3–4 weeks later than SUGAR MAPLE. See instructions under YELLOW BIRCH (preceding). **Preparation:** inner bark raw as emergency food, boiled like noodles, or dried and ground into flour. Dry inner bark at room temperature; store in sealed jars. For tea, steep (do not boil) twigs or fresh or dried inner bark in water or, preferably, birch sap. Boiling destroys volatile wintergreen oil. For birch beer, pour solution of 4 gal birch sap and 1 gal honey (or 5 gal sap and 3 lb sugar), which has been boiled 10 min, over 4 qt fine twigs in crock. Cool, strain to remove twigs, add 1 cake yeast. Cover; ferment about 1 week, until cloudiness starts to settle. Bottle and cap tightly. For birch syrup, see YELLOW BIRCH. **Related edible species:** YELLOW BIRCH. **Poisonous look-alikes:** none.

Sassafras *(Also edible summer, autumn, winter)*   *Sassafras albidum*

Habitat: bottomlands, moist soil of open woodlands, lower slopes. **Identification:** small to medium-size tree with open, flat-topped crown and smooth to deeply and irregularly furrowed, reddish-brown bark on older trees. Leaves alternate, deciduous, simple, *in 3 shapes (entire or with 2 or 3 lobes), 10–15 cm (4–6 in) long,* 5–10 cm (2–4 in) wide, broadest near base, *bright green, with spicy odor when crushed.* Flowers produced in clusters in spring, each small, yellow, and either male or female (each tree male or female). Fruits egg-shaped 1–1.5 cm (0.4–0.6 in) long, dark blue, stalked, enclosed at base by small red cup. **Harvest and preparation:** year-round. Carefully pull several suckers near base of parent tree to obtain small roots. For larger harvest, brittle roots require digging. Flavor is in root bark. Boil washed roots or root bark in water (or maple sap) until liquid is red. Sweeten to taste; drink hot or cold. Roots may be reused. Dried, pulverized root bark is pungent meat spice. Dried, pulverized leaves flavor and thicken soups and gravies. Use green winter buds and young leaves in salads. *Caution:* Sassafras reportedly has carcinogenic properties. Basic jelly recipe: Make jelly with 3 cups strong sassafras tea, 3 oz powdered pectin, 1/2 tsp citric acid, 4 cups sugar; or use 2 cups tea, 1 pkg pectin, 3 cups honey, powdered root bark to taste. **Related edible species:** SPICE BUSH. **Poisonous look-alikes:** none.

Sugar maple *(Also edible summer, winter)*   *Acer saccharum*

Habitat: eastern deciduous forest, common and widespread, especially at lower elevations. **Identification:** medium-size to tall *tree* to 30 m (98 ft) with rounded crown, slightly fissured to furrowed dark gray bark. *Leaves opposite,* simple, 7.5–20 cm (3–8 in) long and broad, broadest near base, *3- to 5-lobed, lobes with a few coarse teeth along margin,* bright green, smooth above and below. Flowers small, bisexual, produced in slender hanging clusters before leaves emerge. *Fruits are winged (samaras), 3–3.5 cm* (1.2–1.4 in) *long,* wings spreading at 60° angle. **Harvest:** Obtain sap from first spring flow, until buds swell. Good sap flow requires freezing nights and warm days. Drill hole [11 mm (7/16 in) for commercial spile] slightly upward and 5–8 cm (2–3 in) into trunk. Drive spile in far enough to hold bucket, not so hard to split wood. Collect sap and store cold until you have 25–30 gal. Collect winged seeds before fully ripe, usually from June to September. **Preparation:** Boil sap outdoors, indoors only if

you like sticky walls. Use large surfaced, open pan, adding sap as water boils off. After adding all sap, continue boiling until temperature is 4°C (7°F) above that of boiling water on that particular day. You may wish to boil for the last two degrees on a controllable stove. Pour syrup through milk filter, filling sterilized canning jars, and seal. Yields about 3 qt. For maple sugar, boil 1 pt syrup in saucepan with frequent stirring until temperature is at least 110°C (230°F). Remove from heat, cool and stir until surface loses sheen. Pour quickly onto foil or waxed paper. When partially hardened, score into pieces with knife. Use sap fresh as beverage, fermented to form mild vinegar, or reduced by boiling to ¼ original volume as base for teas. Soak seeds and remove wings. Boil until tender, drain, season, and roast for 10–15 min. **Related edible species:** Sap of all native maples may be used for syrup. Sugar maple is sweetest. **Poisonous look-alikes:** none; avoid Norway maple *(A. platanoides),* which has milky sap.

Summer

By summer most of the leafy edibles that were tender in spring have toughened and become unpalatable. Yet many late-starting plants are usable through the summer and include the mints of fields and water's edge as well as purslane from the untended garden. Spring strawberries are succeeded by a host of other delicious fruits including raspberries, mulberries, blueberries, blackberries, serviceberries, and beach plums. So summer is the prime season for pies, jams, jellies, and juices, as well as food-drying projects.

As the days grow shorter in late August and September, fewer and fewer shrubs and trees yield juicy, flavorful fruits. Yet this slow period before the fall fruit and nut season can still keep a forager busy. Now you can find ripe seed clusters from many of the same plants whose greens served as edibles in spring; some of these include lamb's quarters, amaranth, plantain, and dock. Threshed, winnowed, and ground, these seeds provide tasty and nutritious flour supplements.

Of course, summer is also the season to beware of stinging nettles, poison ivy, and pesky briars, the briars coming in many disguises.

Additional summer edibles

Plants listed below have parts that are edible in summer and at least one addition-al season. Descriptions and photos of these plants appear in a seasonal section other than "Summer," as indicated.

Allegheny chinkapin (*Castanea pumila*), p. 234
Arrowhead (*Sagittaria latifolia*), p. 212
Black mustard (*Brassica nigra*), p. 100
Bullbrier (*Smilax bona-nox*), p. 66
Butternut (*Juglans cinerea*), p. 246
California grape (*Vitis californica*), p. 216
California rose (*Rosa californica*), p. 220
Canada violet (*Viola canadensis*), p. 94
Carrion flower (*Smilax herbacea*), p. 66
Cattail (*Typha latifolia*), p. 68
Common burdock (*Arctium minus*), p. 112
Common chickweed (*Stellaria media*), p. 84
Common greenbrier (*Smilax rotundifolia*), p. 64
Common milkweed (*Asclepias syriaca*), p. 106
Eastern camass (*Camassia scilloides*), p. 64
Fireweed (*Epilobium angustifolium*), p. 108
Frost grape (*Vitis vulpina*), p. 214
Garlic mustard (*Alliaria officinalis*), p. 84
Glasswort (*Salicornia europea*), p. 76
Great bulrush (*Scirpus validus*), p. 70
Green pigweed (*Amaranthus hybridus*), p. 72
Hard-stem bulrush (*Scirpus acutus*), p. 70
James chickweed (*Stellaria jamesiana*), p. 84

Lady's thumb (*Polygonum persicaria*), p. 110
Lotus lily (*Nelumbo lutea*), p. 210
Miner's lettuce (*Montia perfoliata*), p. 94
Narrow-leaved cattail (*Typha angustifolia*), p. 68
Pale violet (*Viola striata*), p. 96
Pigweed (*Amaranthus retroflexus*), p. 72
Plantain (*Plantago major*), p. 78
Riverside grape (*Vitis riparia*), p. 214
Russian thistle (*Salsola kali*), p. 76
Sassafras (*Sassafras albidum*), p. 124
Sheep sorrel (*Rumex acetosella*), p. 120
Sour dock (*Rumex crispus*), p. 120
Spice bush (*Lindera benzoin*), p. 218
Squashberry (*Viburnum edule*), p. 226, 252
Sugar maple (*Acer saccharum*), p. 124, 256
Sweet birch (*Betula lenta*), p. 122, 252
Sweetbrier rose (*Rosa eglanteria*), p. 222
Wild garlic (*Allium canadense*), p. 60
Wild leek (*Allium tricoccum*), p. 60
Wild onion (*Allium cernuum*), p. 58
Wild potato vine (*Ipomoea pandurata*), p. 216
Wild rose (*Rosa carolina*), p. 222
Wild strawberry (*Fragaria virginiana*), p. 90
Wintercress (*Barbarea vulgaris*), p. 98
Wood violet (*Viola palmata*), p. 116
Wrinkled rose (*Rosa rugosa*), p. 222
Yellow pond lily (*Nuphar advena*), p. 212

Reed grass: flowering plants (Feldman). Flowers (Mohlenbrock).

Wild rice: flower stalk with male flowers topmost and stalks with female flowers (Elias).

Reed grass, Phragmites *(Also edible autumn, winter, spring)*   *Phragmites communis*

Habitat: margins of streams, lakes, ponds, marshes, springs, ditches. **Identification:** *tall perennial grass,* with long, spreading underground stems (rhizomes), often forming dense clumps; *stems upright, 2–4 m* (6.6–13 ft) *high,* stout; *leaf blades* flat, long, *18–60 cm* (7–24 in) *long,* narrow, 1–6 cm (0.4–2.4 in) wide, smooth, base of leaf sheathing part of stem. *Flowers many in large, dense, elongated, branched, plumelike clusters 15–40 cm* (6–16 in) *long,* purplish at first, turning tan to whitish at maturity, side branches ascending, each spikelet (small simple cluster of flowers sharing the same stalk) 1–1.6 cm (0.4–0.6 in) long, *with numerous long, silky hairs.* Fruits are tiny, hard, reddish grains (seeds) many people overlook. **Harvest:** Gather new shoots (at base of old stalks) and leaves early in growing season. Collect hardened sap from wounded stems. Cut whole stems before blooming. Gather seed heads in late summer and autumn. Failure to produce seed is common. Dig roots and underground stems all year. **Preparation:** Eat early shoots raw, or boil or steam until tender; serve as vegetable. Eat hardened gum fresh or toast near fire. Dry stems in sun, beat or grind, sift out fine powder. Moisten powder and place near fire to swell and toast like marshmallows. For gruel, remove seeds by hand. Crush seeds with hulls and mix with spicy berries. Add boiling water and cook until thin reddish gruel, about 30 min; add sweetener. For use of roots and underground stems, see CATTAIL. **Related edible species:** none. **Poisonous look-alikes:** none, but avoid roots and shoots of iris (YELLOW FLAG, BLUE FLAG) and other inedibles.

Wild rice *(Also edible autumn)*   *Zizania aquatica*

Habitat: marshes, shallow ponds, lakes, streams, or bays of fresh and brackish water. **Identification:** *tall annual grass;* stems upright, usually 1–3 m (3–10 ft), stout; leaf blades long, narrow 0.3–1 m (12–39 in) long, 2–5 cm (0.8–2 in) wide, soft. *Flowers many, in large, open, branched, elongate, plumelike clusters to 60 cm (2 ft) high,* side branches 15–20 cm (6–8 in) long, *lower branches* spreading to ascending and *only with male flowers; upper branches erect, bearing only female flowers,* each about 2 cm (0.8 in) long; seed case tipped with long, stiff, hairlike structures; seed narrow, hard, brown. **Harvest and preparation:** Grains ripen in late summer to early fall. Timing is critical; ripe seeds easily fall from plant. Small, shallow-draft boat or canoe provides best harvesting container. Carefully bend stalks over boat and knock ripe grains into it. Several visits days apart needed for maximum harvest. Spread grains to dry; then parch, stirring occasionally, for 3 hr at 175°C (350°F). Thresh husks from grains by pounding or rubbing. Winnow by pouring from one container to another in natural or fan-generated breeze. Wash grains in cold water to eliminate smoky flavor. Use like cultivated rice. Cooking: Bring 3 cups water and 1 tsp salt to boil. Stir in 1½ cups rice grains and return to boil. Cover and simmer until tender, 30–45 min. Serve buttered or with sweetener. For flour, substitute ground rice for part of wheat flour in baking recipes. **Related edible species:** Texas wildrice (*Z. texana*). **Poisonous look-alikes:** none, but poisonous pink or purple fungus (*Claviceps* species) occasionally replaces some grains. Learn to recognize and avoid it.

Chufa, Yellow nut grass

Cyperus esculentus

Also edible autumn, winter, spring

Habitat: ditches, margins of ponds and streams, low wet soils, waste places. **Identification:** *perennial herb with* slender underground stems (rhizomes) and *nearly rounded tubers* 6–10 mm (0.2–0.4 in) in diameter; *stems triangular in cross section,* upright, 20–90 cm (8–36 in) tall, stout, smooth; stem leaves narrow, 5–10 mm (0.2–0.4 in) wide; *with 3–10 leaves at base of flowering clusters* but much longer than flower clusters. *Flowering clusters broadly cylinder-shaped to almost globe-shaped,* composed of numerous spikelets (small simple cluster of flowers on same stalk); spikelets narrow, elongate, 0.5–3 cm (0.2–1.2 in) long, 4-sided, many-flowered. Fruits are small *nutlets, 1–1.5 mm* (less than 0.1 in) *long, triangular-shaped, yellowish.* **Harvest:** Gather tubers best from loose or sandy soil where whole plant with tubers is easily pulled or dug from depth of less than a few inches. Gather any time ground is not frozen. **Preparation:** Tubers palatable and useful raw, boiled, candied, dried, and ground into flour, and as beverage base. For flour, dry slowly until tubers break apart instead of mash when hammered lightly. Grind fine in blender or food mill. Use flour half and half with wheat flour. For beverage soak 1½–2 cups tubers for 2 days. Drain and mash or blend in 1 qt water with ¼ cup sugar or honey. Strain out solids before drinking. For coffee substitute, roast tubers until dark brown throughout. Grind and brew 1 tbsp per cup. **Related edible species:** Several species of *Cyperus* have tubers or tuberlike structures. **Poisonous look-alikes:** none.

Pickerelweed

Pontederia cordata

Also edible autumn

Habitat: along shores or in shallow water of lakes, ponds, slow moving streams, bays. **Identification:** *perennial herb* to 1 m (3.2 ft) high, with short, thick underground stem. *Leaves basal, blade* 6–20 cm (2.4–8 in) long, 2–12 cm (0.8–4.7 in) wide, broadest near base to very narrow, shape variable but usually *arrowhead-shaped,* smooth; *leafstalk stout, 6–32 cm* (2.4–13 in) *long.* Flowering stalk slightly taller than leaves, bearing 1 or 2 leaflike bracts, *attractive blue flowers densely clustered on spike 5–16 cm* (2–6.3 in) *long, each flower funnel-shaped, 2-lipped.* Fruits are stiff, egg-shaped capsules 4–10 mm (0.2–0.4 in) long, enclosed by persistent ragged remains of flower. **Harvest:** Pick young leafstalks in early summer before leaves are fully unfurled. Strip fruits off spikes as they ripen in early autumn. **Preparation:** Wash, chop, and add young leafstalks to salads. As potherb boil leafstalks about 10 min, drain, and season. Fruits each contain a solid seed, edible as trail snack or dried and ground like grain. **Related edible species:** LANCE-LEAVED PICKERELWEED (next), used the same as this species. **Poisonous look-alikes:** none.

Chufa: fruiting cluster (Mohlenbrock).

Pickerelweed: flowering stalk (NYBG). Plants (Dykeman).

Lance-leaved pickerelweed: plant and flowering stalk (NYBG).

Sweet flag: leaves (Dykeman). Flowering spike (Elias). Rootstock (Dykeman).

Lance-leaved pickerelweed

Pontederia lanceolata

Also edible autumn

Habitat: shallow water along shores of lakes, ponds, streams, marshes. **Identification:** perennial herb to 1 m (3.2 ft) tall with thick, creeping underground stem (rhizome). *Leaves mainly basal,* blade 6–20 cm (2.4–8 in) long, 2–12 cm (0.8–4.7 in) wide, variable in shape but usually narrowly heart-shaped to arrowhead-shaped, smooth; *leafstalk stout, 8–30 cm* (3.2–12 in) *long.* Flowering stalk as tall or slightly taller than leaves, usually with a leaflike bract about midway; flowers densely clustered on narrow spike 6–18 cm (2.4–7 in) long, *each flower blue to purple,* funnel-shaped, 2-lipped, *covered with short glandular hairs. Fruits* stiff, *egg-shaped capsules 4–8 mm* (0.2–0.3 in) *long, usually as broad or broader than long.* **Harvest and preparation:** See PICKERELWEED (preceding). **Related edible species:** PICKERELWEED. **Poisonous look-alikes:** none.

Sweet flag, Calamus

Acorus calamus

Habitat: ditches, swamps, pond edges, lakes, and streams; may grow with BLUE FLAG, water flag, and CATTAILS. **Identification:** perennial herb with large, stout, aromatic underground stem (rhizome). *Leaves* crowded near base, erect, narrow, *linear, swordlike but flexible, usually 1–1.5 m* (3–5 ft) *long,* rarely to 2 m (6.6 ft), 1–3 cm (0.4–1.2 in) wide, *midvein off-center, greenish-yellow, with aromatic, almost spicy, odor when cut.* Underground stem portions red. *Flowers* tiny, bisexual, *numerous on narrow, tapering spike (spadix) produced about ⅓ of way up leaflike stalk;* spikes often overlooked. Fruits inconspicuous, borne on flowering spike. **Harvest and preparation:** Harvest tender young stalks when less than 30 cm (1 ft) tall with short underground stems. Grasp and pull firmly. Vertical stem usually breaks off at rhizome. To obtain underground stem, dig with trowel to sever anchoring roots. Inner portions of tender young stems provide spicy trail snack or salad ingredient. For candy, use especially red underground part of stem. Remove roots, wash, peel, slice into 1 cm (0.4 in) long pieces. Cook in several changes of boiling water until pungency is tolerable. Simmer 20 min in syrup of 1 cup water to 2 cups sugar. Drain, dry, roll in sugar. **Related edible species:** none. **Poisonous look-alikes:** Irises (YELLOW FLAG, BLUE FLAG) cause severe digestive upset. Iris leaves lack spicy odor when cut. Flowers are showy.

Spanish bayonet, Datil *(Also edible spring)*   *Yucca baccata*

Habitat: dry slopes, usually in sandy or rocky soils from 920–2,440 m (3,000–8,000 ft). **Identification:** *long-lived perennial* with short inconspicuous trunk, sometimes in clumps. *Leaves clustered near base, blade lance-shaped, 50–76 cm* (20–30 in) *long, 3–7 cm* (1.2–2.8 in) *wide,* stiff, tip sharp-pointed and ending in stout spine, with coarse, recurved fibers along margin, flattened or concave, grayish-green. Flowering stalk in spring, upright 1–1.5 m (3.2–5 ft) high, densely flowered along upper half, flowers showy, fleshy, sepals 3, reddish-brown on outer surface, petals 3, cream-white, 6–12 cm (2.4–4.7 in) long. *Fruits are fleshy capsules, 14–18 cm* (5.5–7 in) *long,* broadest near the middle, 3-parted, turning reddish brown at maturity and splitting open to release seeds. **Harvest:** young flower stalks before buds expand and fruits as they are available late spring through summer. Use buds and flowers as described for SOAPWEED (next), but not as good. **Preparation:** Cut young flower stalks into sections, boil 25–30 min or roast until core is tender. Peel off tough rind. Serve with butter, lemon juice, and seasonings. Eat fruit raw or cooked. Roast whole fruits until tender, scrape out pulp and separate from seeds. Sweeten if desired. Use raw pulp for pie. Strain pulp and dry by boiling to paste and finishing in oven as thick sheet. Eat dry or dissolve for beverage. Roast seeds at 190°C (375°F) until dry and crisp. Grind coarsely and boil as vegetable until tender. **Related edible species and poisonous look-alikes:** See SOAPWEED.

Soapweed *(Also edible spring)*   *Yucca glauca*

Habitat: prairies, roadsides, pastures—usually in dry, well-drained sandy or rocky soils. **Identification:** perennial with short stem. *Leaves densely clustered near base* and covering stem, *blade linear, 38-60 cm* (15-24 in) *long, 0.8-1.2 cm* (0.3-0.5 in) *wide,* stiff, hard and sharp-pointed at tip, with narrow white band and occasional loose threadlike strands along margin, concave, gray-green. Flowering stalk in spring, upright to 1 m (3.3 ft), with stalked flowers along upper half, flowers bowl-shaped, showy, with 3 greenish-white sepals, 3 white petals 4.5–5.5 cm (1.8–2.2 in) long. *Fruits are cylinder-shaped dry capsules 5–8 cm* (2-3.2 in) *long,* 3–4.5 cm (1.2–1.8 in) in diameter, turning brown, 3-parted and splitting open at maturity to release seeds. **Harvest:** Pick young flower stalks before buds expand. Pick flowers and buds as available. **Preparation:** Cover 1 cup flowers or buds with water and boil until tender, 15–20 min. Drain and chop coarsely. Add with pimento or green pepper to several eggs and little milk. Cook like scrambled eggs. For salad boil 1 cup flowers and buds as above. Drain, chop, and cool. Add celery, chopped apple, raisins, nutmeats, cabbage, and mayonnaise as in Waldorf salad. For flower stalks see SPANISH BAYONET (preceding). Unripe fruits are bitter but can be made palatable by boiling or baking. **Related edible species:** all *Yucca* species including SPANISH BAYONET. Flower and bud uses apply best to dry-fruited species, fruit uses to fleshy-fruited species. Spiny leaved *Agave* looks similar and is also edible. **Poisonous look-alikes:** none.

Spanish bayonet: plants (NYBG).

Soapweed: flowering stalk (NYBG). Plants (NYBG).

Common day lily   *Hemerocallis fulva*
Also edible autumn, spring

Habitat: garden plant that commonly grows wild in abandoned home sites, vacant lots, along roads. **Identification:** large perennial herb from a fibrous root system with short, fingerlike tubers, with numerous *long, narrow basal leaves.* Each leaf 0.5–1.5 m (1.7–5 ft) long, 1.5–3 cm (0.6–1.2 in) wide, gradually tapering to long narrow tip, tapering with edges folded inward at base, light green to greenish-yellow. Flowers in clusters of 3–5 at tip of upright stalks, stalks to 2 m (6.6 ft); flower buds narrow, tubular; each *flower 10–15 cm* (4–6 in) *long,* narrowly tubular at base, *funnel-shaped* above, *with 6 large, showy petallike segments, orange to tawny-orange,* darker inside, flowering from late May to July, each flower open 1 day only. Fruits fleshy, 3-parted capsules. **Harvest:** tubers 1 cm (0.4 in) × 2–3 cm (0.8–1.2 in). Spade roots over; pick only firm tubers all year. Replant roots. Tubers regenerate rapidly. Pick buds when half to nearly full size. Pick flowers when fully opened or wilting. **Preparation:** Raw tubers give sweet nutty flavor to salads, or boil in salted water until tender, season. Excellent potato substitute. Boil buds a few minutes, butter, and season. Great cooked vegetable; raw they irritate the throat. Dip buds or flowers in egg batter and fry in hot oil or add them to soups at end of preparation for gelatinous quality. Dry buds and flowers at air temperature about a week; store in sealed jars for later use in soups or other recipes. *Caution: Eat in moderation to avoid laxative effect.* **Related edible species:** none. **Poisonous look-alikes:** Leaves slightly resemble those of iris (YELLOW FLAG, BLUE FLAG), but common day lily leaves arch over with tip pointed to ground; iris leaves are upright and darker.

Western camass, Camass lily   *Camassia quamash*
Also edible autumn, winter, spring

Habitat: coastal mountain forests, wet meadows of interior mountains. **Identification:** *perennial herb* to 80 cm (32 in) high, from bulb 2–3 cm (0.8–1.2 in) across; *grasslike leaves* several from base, narrowly lance-shaped, 20–50 cm (8–20 in) long, 0.6–1.8 cm (0.2–0.7 in) wide, pointed at tip. Flower stalk 20–80 cm (8–32 in) high, *flowers several, stalked, showy, with 6 blue to bluish-violet petals* or petallike structures, each 2–3.6 cm (0.8–1.4 in) long. Fruits are dry capsules 0.8–2.4 cm (0.3–1 in) long, egg-shaped, splitting open at maturity to release seeds. **Harvest:** Dig or pull bulbs any season, safest when blue flowers distinguish it from DEATH CAMASS. Dig and transplant to safe place where you know there is no DEATH CAMASS. *Be certain of identification!* **Preparation:** Raw bulbs are palatable potato substitute. May be boiled 25–30 min or baked in foil for 45 min at 175°C (350°F). Indians baked bulbs in pit up to 3 days, the resulting product being very dark and sugary. Slice pit-baked or boiled bulbs, dry in sun or warm oven, store in paper bag in dry place. **Related edible species:** EASTERN CAMASS. **Poisonous look-alikes:** DEATH CAMASS (*Zigadenus* species), narrow-leaved plants with green, white, or bronze flowers, single or several in narrow stalk.

Common day lily: flowers (Dykeman).

Western camass: field of camass (Ross). Flowering stalks (NYBG). Flowers (Ross).

Indian cucumber: leaves and root (Dykeman). Flowering plant (NYBG).

Indian fig: plant (Folkerts).

Indian cucumber
Medeola virginiana

Habitat: rich moist woodlands, protected slopes, margin of bogs and swamps. **Identification:** *perennial herb, with* swollen *tuberlike white underground stems (rhizomes)* horizontal to ground; stem erect, to 80 cm (2.8 ft), usually about 30 cm (1 ft), slender, covered with wooly hairs when young, *bearing a whorl of 5–10 leaves about midway and another whorl of 3 leaves near top.* Leaves simple, parallel-veined, to 10 cm (4 in) long, and uniformly wide to broadest near tip; upper leaves smaller and broadest near base. *Stalked flowers 3–9 in cluster at tip of stem, some flowers hanging beneath upper leaves,* in May and June, each flower with 6 pale greenish-yellow petals 6–10 mm (0.2–0.4 in) long. *Fruits* small, rounded, dark purple berries 6–8 mm (0.2–0.3 in) in diameter, *not edible.* **Harvest:** common, easily identified plant a reliable source of limited quantity of tubers for trail food. Digging destroys plant, but any remaining tubers will produce new growth. **Preparation:** Wash and eat tubers raw as trail snack or in salad. Has delicate cucumber flavor. For pickles combine 1½ cups tubers, ½ cup water, ½ cup vinegar, 1 tbsp salt, 2 tsp sugar, 1 clove garlic, ¼ small, chopped red pepper, 1 tsp pickling spice. Bring to boil, place in small hot sterilized jars, covering tubers with liquid, and seal. Store at least 2 months. **Related edible species:** none. Unrelated, inedible starflower *(Trientalis borealis)* looks similar except for net-veined leaves. **Poisonous look-alikes:** none.

Indian fig, Prickly pear *(Also edible spring, autumn)*
Opuntia humifusa

Habitat: rocky bluffs, sand dunes, dry rocky or sandy grasslands. **Identification:** perennial herb with fibrous root system, sprawling along ground, often forming clumps. *Fleshy segments or joints nearly circular* to broadest above middle, sometimes uniformly wide, *5–20 cm* (2–8 in) *long, strongly flattened,* pale to dark green, dotted with small reddish-brown bumps containing numerous tiny, barbed hairs; spines absent or occasionally 1. *Flowers* produced June–July on upper part of segments, *showy, yellow with red center,* 5–9 cm (2–3.5 in) across, usually with 10–12 petals. *Fruit* broadest above middle to nearly club-shaped, *3–6 cm* (1.2–2.4 in) *long, red to purple, becoming fleshy,* containing many flattened, nearly circular seeds. **Harvest:** Wear leather gloves to ward off spines and barbed hairs. Cut young segments during spring and summer. Pick fruits as they ripen in late summer and autumn. **Preparation:** Flame segments to remove spines, roast segments over fire, then peel or peel first, then slice and use like string beans. Edible but somewhat sticky. Also, deep fry like onion rings. Dry pulp for later use. To eat fruits fresh, chill if possible, trim off both ends, cut skin lengthwise, scoop out sweet pulp. Or, dip 1–2 min in boiling water and peel. Be careful, fruits also have fine, spiny bristles. Dry fruit pulp for later use, stew it for dessert, or boil it down and strain out seeds to make syrup or to prepare jelly. Briefly roast seeds and grind into meal for soup thickener or flour. For emergency water, peel and chew leafy segments. **Related edible species:** Fleshy fruits and segments of all flat-stemmed *Opuntia* species are edible. **Poisonous look-alikes:** none.

Prickly pear, Indian fig   *Opuntia phaeacantha*
Also edible autumn, spring

Habitat: hills, canyons, valleys, usually in rocky or sandy soils. **Identification:** shrub to 1 m (3.2 ft), sometimes sprawling or forming clumps to 6 m (19.7 ft) in diameter. *Fleshy cactus segments or joints rounded or nearly so,* sometimes widest above middle, *10–25 cm* (4–10 in) *long, flattened, bluish-green; cacti spines usually on upper half, 1–6 per cluster, 2.5–7.5 cm* (1–3 in) *long, straight or curved.* Flowers produced near top of upper segments, *showy, yellow,* 6–8 cm (2.4–3.2 in) long, to 8 cm (3.2 in) in diameter, with many petallike structures. *Fruits elongate,* usually broadest above middle, *3–6 cm (1.2–2.4 in) long, to 3.8 cm (1.5 in) in diameter, fleshy, red,* depressed at tip, containing numerous, flattened and rounded seeds. The several varieties of this prickly pear differ primarily in segment shape, spine distribution, color, and length. **Harvest and preparation:** INDIAN FIG (preceding). **Related edible species:** all flat-stemmed prickly pear cacti. **Poisonous look-alikes:** none.

May apple, Mandrake   *Podophyllum peltatum*

Habitat: rich deciduous woodlands, meadows, moist shaded road banks. **Identification:** *perennial herb* to 50 cm (20 in) tall, frequently in large dense patches with creeping underground stems and thick, fibrous roots, short stem, first-year plant with 1 leaf, second-year flowering plants with 2. *Leaves large, umbrellalike, 12–36 cm* (4.7–14 in) *in diameter, nearly circular in outline, deeply 5–9-parted,* toothed; *leafstalk attached at center of leaf. Flowers solitary, produced in junction of 2 leaves,* stalked, nodding, each with 6 sepals, 6–9 waxy white petals 2.5–4 cm (1–1.6 in) long. Fruit an egg-shaped berry 2.5–5 cm (1–2 in) long, usually yellow, but red in one form. **Harvest:** Gather fruit when yellow; practically falls from plant into your hand. Leaves will be turning yellow by this time. Unripe fruit and other parts of plant contain poison podophyllin. The root has a long history of medicinal use. **Preparation:** Eat ripe fruit fresh; taste sensation varies from person to person. For preserves, jam, or pie filling, remove both ends, quarter fruit, and force through food mill to remove seeds before cooking. If skins are desired in final product, squeeze pulp from quartered fruit before removing seeds. Chop skins and add to pulp later. See recipes for jam and pie early in book. Also combine juice with lemonade, sumac ade, or other juices for new flavors. **Related edible species:** none. **Poisonous look-alikes:** none; do not attempt to use unripe May apples or any other part of the plant.

Prickly pear: plant (Elias). Fruits (Dykeman).

May apple: flowering plant (Dykeman). Fruit (NYBG).

Bunchberry: flowers and fruiting plants (Elias).

Peppermint: flowering stalks (Speas).

Bunchberry
Cornus canadensis

Habitat: northern moist woods, bogs, woodlands, mountains especially in southern part of range. **Identification:** perennial, forming mats from spreading underground stems (rhizomes); aboveground stems 8–24 cm (3.2–9.4 in) high, *each stem with whorl of 4–6 leaves near top* and 1–2 pair smaller leaves below. Leaves 4–7 cm (1.6–2.8 in) long, 1.5–3.5 cm (0.6–1.4 in) wide, broadest near base or tip, pointed at tip, with 2–3 pair lateral veins. *Flowers* produced in May or June, *tiny, in tight, dense clusters surrounded by 4 conspicuous, white, petallike bracts* (flower clusters plus bracts resemble a single flower). Fruit produced in midsummer to autumn, in dense clusters, each a fleshy stone-fruit, globe-shaped, 6–8 mm (0.2–0.3 in) in diameter. **Harvest:** Berries ripen through July in clusters of a few to 12. Ripe when scarlet; usually plentiful and easily picked in quantity. **Preparation:** Eat nearly tasteless berries raw, but pulp is difficult to separate from seeds. Better cooked and strained for use with more flavorful fruits or for pudding. **Related edible species:** Swedish bunchberry *(C. suecica)* in northern regions has sweeter and more acid fruits. Laplanders make pudding from this species by boiling fruits with whey until thick. **Poisonous look-alikes:** none.

Peppermint
Mentha piperita

Habitat: wet places, especially ditches, along streams, wet meadows. **Identification:** perennial herb, stems erect, 0.6–1.1 m (2–3.6 ft) tall, *4-sided,* purplish, smooth to slightly hairy. *Leaves opposite,* each pair alternating along stem, *each with short leafstalk,* blade 3.2–6.4 cm (1.3–2.5 in) long, 1–1.6 cm (0.4–0.6 in) wide, usually broadest near base, sharply toothed along margins, *with distinct peppermint smell when broken or crushed.* Flowers tiny, light purple, crowded together in dense, many-flowered, interrupted spikes at tips, June–October. Fruits with 4 tiny nutlets enclosed by persistent calyx. **Harvest and preparation:** Pick leaves at any stage. Great variation in flavor among populations from different areas. Collect leaves on dry day and dry on paper in warm area. Store in tight container. Jelly: Add 2 cups boiling water to 2 cups crushed fresh leaves in saucepan. Place inverted lid on saucepan, with small amount of ice and water in lid to condense water vapor and flavorful oils. Bring mint mix to simmer, remove from heat, steep 10 min. Strain; add 4 cups sugar and ¼ cup cider vinegar to 2 cups mint flavored water. Add green food coloring, if desired. Stir until sugar is dissolved. Dissolve 1 pkg powdered pectin in ¾ cup water, heat and boil hard 1 min. Add pectin solution to mint syrup, stir, pour into sterilized glasses, and seal. For other uses, see SPEARMINT (next). **Related edible species:** SPEARMINT, several hybrids of native and introduced species. **Poisonous look-alikes:** none.

Spearmint   *Mentha spicata*

Habitat: grows in wild, especially in wet areas along roads, ditches, streams. **Identification:** perennial, spreading by creeping rootstock; *stems* erect to 1 m (3.2 ft), *4-sided,* smooth or nearly so. *Leaves opposite,* each pair alternating along stem, leafstalks absent or nearly so, blade 2.5–7.5 cm (1–3 in) long, 0.8–2.4 cm (0.3–1 in) wide, broadest at or below middle, toothed along margin, with *strong smell of spearmint when crushed or broken.* Flowers tiny, light purple to near white, produced in dense, elongate, many-flowered clusters 4–12 cm (1.6–4.7 in) long, at growing tips. Fruits tiny nutlets enclosed in persistent calyx. **Harvest and preparation:** Pick leaves at any stage. Great variation in flavor among plants from different areas. Collect leaves on dry day and dry on paper in warm area. Store in tight container. For tea pour 1 cup boiling water over ½ tsp crumbled, dried leaves or ¼–½ cup fresh leaves. Cover; steep 5 min. Do not boil. Strain, add sweetener and lemon to taste. High in vitamin C. Chop fresh leaves in green salad. Crush fresh leaves in iced tea. For candy wash and pat dry 2 doz fresh leaves. Beat 1 egg white until stiff. Dip leaves, one at a time in egg white, then in confectioner's sugar. Dry in oven at low heat, about 100°C (210°F), for 30 min or until crisp. Real mint-leaf candy! For jelly recipe see PEPPERMINT (preceding). **Related edible species:** PEPPERMINT, several other *Mentha* species, and many hybrids between native and cultivated species. **Poisonous look-alikes:** none.

American brooklime   *Veronica americana*
Also edible spring

Habitat: common, along stream banks, swamps, clear ponds, springs, often with watercress. **Identification:** *Perennial herb, usually creeping* or sprawling; stems smooth, fleshy. *Leaves opposite,* lanceshaped to broadest near base, 3–8 cm (1.2–3.2 in) long, 1–4 cm (0.4–1.6 in) wide, pointed at tip, toothed along margin, stalked. *Flowers stalked, produced along terminal, elongated spikes;* each *flower with 4 pale violet to lilac petals, 4–8 mm (0.2–0.3 in) across.* Fruits are small, nearly round capsules, 3–5 mm (0.1–0.2 in) across, almost as long. **Harvest:** young growth tips from unpolluted water during late spring and summer. If water quality is questionable, wash tips in clean water to which iodide purifying tablets sold in camping stores have been added. Rinse with potable water. **Preparation:** Use like WATERCRESS in salads or as potherb with bland greens to offset bitterness of brooklime. **Related edible species:** several other species of speedwells (*Veronica* spp.), some widely distributed. **Poisonous look-alikes:** none.

Introduced and
grows wild.
Widespread.

Spearmint: (Elias photo).

American brooklime: flowering stalk (Dykeman).

Marsh mallow *(Also edible autumn, winter)*   *Althaea officinalis*

Habitat: edges of brackish and salt marshes; introduced from Europe and now grows wild. **Identification:** *perennial herb* from 0.6–1.2 m (2–4 ft) tall, from thick, large taproot; stems upright, often branched, stout, hairy. *Leaves* alternate, simple, broadest near base, 6–12 cm (2.4–4.7 in) long, about ⅔ as wide, *often shallowly 3-lobed,* short-pointed at tip, rounded at base, *irregularly and coarsely toothed along margin,* densely hairy. *Flowers* several *in cluster at base of upper leaves in summer; each with 5 pink, spreading petals* 2–3 cm (0.8–1.2 in) long. *Fruit is dry, flattened disc, divided into 15–20 segments.* **Harvest:** leaves in early summer, flower buds in summer, and roots from late summer through winter. **Preparation:** whole plant contains mucilagelike material; roots are best source. Use young leaves in early summer as okra-like soup thickener or as potherb. Pickle flower buds. Boil thin sliced, peeled roots for 20 min in enough water to cover them. Strain off roots; for candy sweeten the liquid and boil until very thick. Beat and drop spoonfuls on waxed paper to cool. Roll pieces in confectioner's sugar. For vegetable, fry boiled root slices with butter and chopped onion until browned. Use water from boiling any parts of plant as substitute for egg white in meringue or chiffon pies. Also used for hand lotion and cough syrup. Use leaves for poultices for infected wounds. **Related edible species:** other Mallow family species, especially those of genus *Malva.* Eat *Malva* fruits raw or substitute roots for meringue. **Poisonous look-alikes:** none.

Watercress   *Nasturtium officinale*
Also edible autumn, winter, spring   (synonym: *Rorippa nasturtium-aquaticum*)

Habitat: slow moving clear water, especially springs, cool streams; introduced from Eurasia. **Identification:** *perennial herb, growing in shallow water* or mud; stems weak, partially floating in water or lying flat in mud with white roots growing from floating stems. *Leaves alternate,* 4–16 cm (1.6–6.3 in) long, 2–5 cm (0.8–2 in) wide, *dissected into 3–11 lobed and usually rounded dark green leaflets;* upper leaves nearly rounded. *Flowers numerous in narrow, elongate clusters,* each flower stalked, with *4 white petals,* 3–5 mm (0.2 in) long. Fruits narrow, slender, capsulelike, 1–2.5 cm (0.4–1 in) long, beaked, containing several tiny reddish-brown seeds. **Harvest:** Collect young growth nearly all year from unpolluted water sources. Removal does not hurt plant. If water quality is questionable and plant is to be eaten raw, disinfect shoots by washing in water with iodide purifying tablets sold in camping stores. Rinse in potable water. **Preparation:** As potherb, cook and serve just like spinach or add to more bland potherb greens, or stir-fry 4–5 min in skillet with 2 tbsp cooking oil and 1 tbsp fresh grated ginger root. Serve with soy sauce. Watercress is an excellent soup ingredient. Use radish-tasting stems and blossoms as garnish or as main salad ingredient. For nasturtium salad: Make slightly sweetened oil and vinegar dressing. Mix 1 cup young watercress leaves, 1 cup watercress buds and blossoms, 2 cups mixed mild greens, and 1 chopped scallion in large bowl. Add dressing, toss and serve. Vary ratio of watercress to other greens to get desired taste. High in vitamins and minerals. **Related edible species:** none. **Poisonous look-alikes:** none.

Marsh mallow: flowering stalk (Speas).

Watercress: flowering plant (Mohlenbrock).

Ground cherry: flowering plant (NYBG). Flower and fruits (Pawloski).

Ground nut: flowering plant (NYBG). Underground tuber (Kavasch).

Ground cherry   *Physalis pubescens*

Habitat: moist sites, open woodlands, recently cultivated fields, disturbed sites. **Identification:** *annual herb* to 60 cm (24 in) high; *stems* weak, wide branching, *often trailing,* hairy. *Leaves* alternate, simple, broadest near base, 3.5–8 cm (1.4–3.2 in) long, 1.7–6 cm (0.7–2.4 in) wide, pointed at tip, variably rounded at base, nearly entire, *thin, pale green, hairy,* long stalked. *Flowers* stalked, in junction of upper leaf stems, 5–10 cm (2–4 in) across, *yellow with dark center. Fruit a sweet yellow berry* 1.2–1.8 cm (0.5–0.7 in) in diameter, *enclosed by 5-sided inflated persistent calyx resembling paper lantern 2–3 cm* (0.8–1.2 in) long, *angled,* with conspicuous veins. **Harvest:** Fruits fall before fully ripe. So pick mid to late summer and ripen in husks a few weeks until fruits are yellow and sweet. Unripe fruit and green plant parts are strong flavored and somewhat poisonous. **Preparation:** excellent trail snack and dessert. For pie recipe, see book's Introduction. To preserve fruits boil until clear and tender in syrup of 1 cup sugar, 2 cups water, 3 tbsp lemon juice. Seal in sterilized jars. For jam boil for 5 min 1 qt crushed fruits, ¼ cup lemon juice, ½ cup water, and 1 pkg pectin. Add 3 cups sugar, boil again to reach jelly point, 115°C (240°F). Seal in sterilized jars. Use cherries in relishes. **Related edible species:** Several *Physalis* species are distributed throughout North America. Ripe fruits yellow, red, purple, or blue-black according to species; all are identifiable by lanternlike husk. Use only ripe fruit! **Poisonous look-alikes:** Learn to distinguish species of *Physalis* from poisonous nightshades *(Solanum)* (see JIMSON WEED and HORSE NETTLE).

Groundnut *(Also edible autumn, winter, spring)*   *Apios americana*

Habitat: moist woodlands, bottomlands, thickets. **Identification:** *perennial vine* from 1 or more fleshy tubers arranged in a row, the tubers 1–2 cm (0.4–0.8 in) thick; stems smooth, twining around nearby plants; very white and easy to spot when mature, milky juice. *Leaves* alternate, *featherlike compound* (pinnate), 10–20 cm (4–8 in) long, *composed of 5–9 leaflets,* rarely less, leaflets usually 3–6 cm (1.2–2.4 in) long, lance-shaped, pointed at tip, rounded at base, smooth to hairy. *Flowers* July-September, densely clustered on short stalk 5–15 cm (2–6 in) long, each flower *with 5 brownish-purple petals, resembling pea flower;* fragrance resembles that of the violets. Fruits are dry, linear pods 5–12 cm (2–4.7 in) long, 4–7 mm (0.2–0.3 in) broad, containing 2 to several seeds, splitting open lengthwise into 2 spirally twisting valves. **Harvest:** Pick pods in midsummer to autumn as seeds mature; pods seldom abundant though. Dig tubers, starting at base of stem, working along root to obtain whole string. Good all year. **Preparation:** Roast pods at 190°C (375°F) for 20–25 min. Cool; remove seeds and brown in oil over low heat. Boil tubers in heavily salted water until tender. Season. Slice and fry leftovers, or grease and roast to regain tenderness, flavor. Also thinly slice raw tubers and fry like potatoes in butter or pork; season. Or bake at 175°C (350°F) 45–60 min until tender. Flavor turnip-like. **Related edible species:** groundnut *(A. priceana)* with 1 large tuber. **Poisonous look-alikes:** species of vetchlings *(Lathyrus),* rattlebox *(Crotalaria),* milk vetches *(Astragalus),* and point locoweeds *(Oxytropis).*

Common breadroot   *Psoralea esculenta*

Habitat: prairies, plains, dry rocky woodlands. **Identification:** *perennial herb* to 38 cm (15 in) tall, *developing from 1 or more swollen, elongated taproots* 4–10 cm(1.6–4 in) long; stems short, stout, frequently branched, hairy. *Leaves* alternate, *handlike (palmate) compound,* long-stalked, *composed of 5 leaflets,* each 3–6 cm (1.2–2.4 in) long, uniformly wide to widest above middle, covered with long hairs. *Flowers produced in dense elongate clusters 3–8 cm (1.2–3.2 in) long,* each flower with leaflike bract, flowers *blue,* composed of 5 petals shaped like clover flower. Fruits are small pods 5–8 mm (0.2–0.3 in) long, broadest near base, long beaked, splitting open lengthwise along 2 valves. **Harvest:** Dig taproot from its hard prairie soil in early summer as stems and leaves begin to turn brown. Later above-ground parts dry and blow away making roots nearly impossible to locate. **Preparation:** important wild food staple. Peel and eat root raw, roast in campfire or boil until tender. Season like potatoes. For storage, peel and dry slowly. Grind dried root into flour or meal and use for baking. Indians cooked meal with meat and corn. Reconstitute with water to use as vegetable. **Related edible species:** *P. hypogala,* also of the plains region, produces a smaller but similar taproot. **Poisonous look-alikes:** Scurf pea *(P. tenuifolia)* and other *Psoralea* species have been toxic to horses and cattle, and so should not be eaten.

Wintergreen, Checkerberry   *Gaultheria procumbens*
Also edible autumn, winter, spring

Habitat: woodlands, clearings, usually in poor acid soils. **Identification:** small herb with slender stems creeping along soil surface and erect leafy stems to 18 cm (7 in). *Leaves* crowded near top, each widest near or above middle, 2–5 cm (0.8–2 in) long, entire or with tiny rounded teeth along margin, *leathery texture, shiny, with wintergreen smell when crushed. Flowers usually solitary on short drooping stalk, white,* urn-shaped to cylinder-shaped, 5-parted at tip, 6–10 mm (0.2–0.4 in) long. *Fruits bright red berries 6–10 mm (0.2–0.4 in) in diameter,* globe-shaped to elongate. **Harvest:** leaves any time of year; berries from fall through winter. **Preparation:** Use leaves as trail nibble or brew into tea. Cover 1 qt young leaves with boiling water, cover container loosely and steep 1–2 days. Reheat gently, sweeten, and enjoy. Wintergreen oil concentration in tea increases with prolonged steeping. Berries ripen in fall but improve with freezing so look for them in winter and spring and use as trail nibble; add to pancakes and muffins, or, if plentiful, make uncooked jam. Combine in blender 2 cups fresh berries, 1 oz lemon juice, 1 cup strong wintergreen tea. Blend until smooth, pour into mixing bowl, add 4 cups sugar. In saucepan bring to hard boil 1 pkg pectin and ¾ cup water. Boil 1 min and stir into berry mix. Mix thoroughly, ladle into sterile jars, and seal. Store in refrigerator or freezer. Leaves and fruits contain aspirin like methyl salicylate and effectively reduce fevers and minor aches and pains. **Related edible species:** CREEPING SNOWBERRY (next). **Poisonous look-alikes:** none.

Common breadroot: July plant with remnant flower cluster on right (Young).

Wintergreen: fruiting plant, top (Dykeman). Flowering plant (Elias).

Creeping snowberry: fruiting plant (Elias).

Mountain sorrel: fruiting plant (Elias).

Creeping snowberry
Gaultheria hispidula

Also edible autumn, winter, spring

Habitat: northern coniferous forests, mountains in subalpine and alpine zone. **Identification:** *small creeping herb* with very leafy stems; *leaves* alternate, simple, *evergreen,* broadest near base, to *almost round, 0.5–1 cm (0.2–0.4 in) long,* entire, bright green and smooth above, paler with long stiff hairs beneath. Flowers May-June, solitary in junction of leaves, each tiny, white, bell-shaped, 2–3 mm (0.1 in) long, on short drooping stalk. *Fruits are fleshy bright white berries 6–10 mm (0.2–0.4 in) long,* slightly longer than wide, with spicy aromatic smell when crushed, bristly. Ripen by August. **Harvest and preparation:** leaves same as WINTERGREEN (preceding). Also prepare as cooked green vegetable. Fruits ripen mid through late summer. Excellent fresh and in baked goods, jam (see WINTERGREEN), and preserves. For no-cook preserves wash and smash or grind fruit thoroughly. Add equal amount of sugar slowly with constant stirring. Pack in sterile jars and seal. **Related edible species:** WINTERGREEN, CREEPING WINTERGREEN, SALAL, and *G. ovatifolia,* also called salal, of northwest U. S. **Poisonous look-alikes:** none.

Mountain sorrel
Oxyria digyna

Habitat: high mountains, subalpine and alpine fields, usually in rocky places 2,450–3,950 m (8,000–13,000 ft). **Identification:** perennial herb to 40 cm (16 in) high; stems upright, simple or sparingly branched, smooth. *Leaves* alternate, sometimes kidney shaped, simple, *mostly basal, blades usually rounded,* 1.6–3.2 cm (0.6–1.3 in) across, entire, smooth, long-stalked, stalk 6–12 cm (2.4–4.7 in) long. *Flowers* small, *arranged in densely flowered, elongate, compact clusters;* each flower stalked, bisexual, with 4 red to greenish sepals that persist in fruiting. *Fruits* flattened, *broadly winged, rounded, dark red, small, dry, hard, 1-seeded,* not splitting open at maturity. **Harvest:** leaves while still tender, before plant flowers. **Preparation:** Use fresh leaves as trail nibble or in salad. Combination of sour mountain sorrel and pungent species such as WATERCRESS works well with other, more neutral greens. Use a plain oil dressing. Add leaves to other greens for added flavor when cooked. In arctic regions, natives ferment mountain sorrel as sauerkraut. For puree, mash greens with food mill or blender and add to small amount of boiling water. Boil 5–10 min. Add 3 cups puree to 1 qt hot milk (or 1 cup milk and 3 cups chicken stock). Salt and pepper to taste. Bring to boil and simmer 5–10 min with stirring. Slowly add 3 beaten egg yolks. Add flour paste for desired thickness. Blend in 4 tbsp melted butter. For other uses see SHEEP SORREL. **Related edible species:** none, but SHEEP SORREL and SOUR DOCK are used similarly. **Poisonous look-alikes:** Some species of dock (RUMEX) accumulate sour-tasting oxalates.

American bistort: flowering plants (NYBG).

Alpine bistort: flowering stalks (NYBG).

American bistort, Western bistort
Also edible autumn, spring

Polygonum bistortoides

Habitat: along streams, wet meadows, subalpine meadows. **Identification:** *perennial herb* to 70 cm (28 in) high, from *thick, fleshy, horizontal rootstock;* stems erect, slender, smooth. Leaves alternate, entire, mostly basal, 10–25 cm (4–10 in) long, 2–5 cm (0.8–2 in) wide, lower leaves uniformly wide to broadest near tip, upper ones lance-shaped and smaller, stalked, each sheathing stem at base. *Flowering spikes cylinder-shaped at end of stem, 2–6 cm* (0.8–2.4 in) *long,* to 1.5 cm (0.6 in) thick, *pink to white,* individual flowers tiny, lacking petals. Fruits are small, shiny brown nutlets 3–4 mm (0.1–0.2 in) long. **Harvest and preparation:** Use rootstocks and young leaves as for ALPINE BISTORT (next). Rootstock larger in American bistort, but edible bulblets are absent from flower stalks. Both species provide valuable survival fare in mountain regions where other wild foods may be unavailable. **Related edible species and poisonous look-alikes:** See ALPINE BISTORT.

Alpine bistort, Alpine smartweed
Also edible autumn, spring

Polygonum viviparum

Habitat: arctic regions, alpine and subalpine slopes, gravelly and rocky soils. **Identification:** *perennial herb* to 45 cm (18 in) high, *from short, thickened, usually twisted, underground stem;* stem upright, sheathed at base of leaves. *Lower leaves* alternate, simple, *3–10 cm* (1.2–4 in) *long, to 2.5 cm* (1 in) *wide, narrowly lance-shaped,* pointed at tip, tapering at base, long stalked, upper leaves much smaller. Flowering spike 3–8 cm (1.2–3.2 in) long, *upper flowers pink or white,* tiny, lacking petals, lower flowers producing tiny reddish or purple bulbils. Fruits are small, reddish-brown, 3-angled nutlets 2–4 mm (0.1–0.2 in) long. **Harvest and preparation:** Strip tiny bulbils from lower part of flower stalks and eat raw. Dig rootstocks (easiest to find during growing season) and eat raw, boil, or roast. Young roots tender but older ones may require cooking. Boil 40 min or bake at 165°C (330°F) for 40 min. Season like potatoes. Though appearance of unpeeled roots may not be inviting, flavor is good. Use young leaves in salad with other greens or prepare as cooked greens. Boil until tender and season with butter, salt and pepper. **Related edible species:** AMERICAN BISTORT (preceding) and LADY'S THUMB used as cooked or salad green. Also JAPANESE KNOTWEED, giant knotweed *(P. sachalinense),* Alaskan knotweed *(P. alaskanum),* and others. **Poisonous look-alikes:** No species of *Polygonum* are known to be poisonous. But some may cause light-sensitive skin reaction. They vary in usefulness as cooked or salad greens, some being very peppery or acid; some, like tartary buckwheat *(P. tataricum),* produce edible seeds.

Purslane, Pusley
Portulaca oleracea

Habitat: fields, vacant lots, waste sites; common garden weed. **Identification:** annual *herb, lying flat on ground* or nearly so and *forming mats to 1 sq ft, stems smooth, fleshy, shiny, often reddish purple. Leaves* alternate and opposite, 2–5 cm (0.8–2 in) long, 1–2 cm (0.4–0.8 in) wide, *fleshy, broadest near the rounded tip,* entire along margin. *Flowers* single, or few clustered at tips of branches, flower 0.5–1 cm (0.2–0.4 in) wide, *with 5 yellow petals. Fruits are capsules,* 4–8 mm (0.2–0.3 in) long, broadest near base and rounded at tip, *top portion falling away at maturity* to expose dark red to black seeds. **Harvest:** Pinch or cut young leafy tips June–September. Pick larger stems in midsummer for pickles. To gather seeds, spread whole mature plants on sheet to dry for 2 weeks, then sieve and winnow. **Preparation:** One of best wild shoots cooked or in salad. Common and nutritious; acid taste; high in iron. For tossed salad combine raw shoots with other ingredients. Use oil and vinegar dressing. Cook young plants as potherb 10 min and season with butter and salt. For casserole chop cooked shoots, stir in 1 beaten egg and enough bread crumbs to make damp mix. Add salt and pepper, bake in moderate oven. Pickle stems same as cucumbers. Blanch and freeze tips for later use. To dry, boil thick stems in a little water for 20 min. Drain, dry in warm shady area, store in paper bag for later use in soups or stews as thickener. Dry seed 1 week in shade, store in paper bag. Grind and use half and half with flour. **Related edible species:** at least 2 *(P. neglecta* and *P. retusa)* which are very similar. **Poisonous look-alikes:** none.

Sunflower *(Also edible autumn)*
Helianthus annuus

Habitat: prairies, plains, roadsides, disturbed sites. **Identification:** *perennial herb 1–2.5 m (3.2–8.2 ft) high,* from large taproot; stem upright, unbranched to branched, with stiff hairs. *Leaves* mostly alternate, simple, *6.5–30 cm (2.6–12 in) long,* nearly as wide at base, *broadly to narrowly triangular,* tapering to short- or long-pointed tip, toothed near tip, heart-shaped at base, with stiff hairs on both surfaces. Flowers produced in heads to 15 cm (6 in) across, single, stalked, base of head cup-shaped, *ray flowers with yellow petals 2.5–5 cm (1–2 in) long,* central disc flowers lacking showy petals, brown. Fruit flattened, dry, 1-seeded, 4–6 mm (0.2 in) long. **Harvest:** Gather seed heads in late summer to early autumn before seeds are dry enough to be released. Hang in warm, dry place. **Preparation:** Indians parched then ground unshelled seeds into fine meal. Meal was added to water and drunk or mixed with marrow to form dough and eaten. To separate nutmeats from shells, break hulls with chopper, very coarse grinder, or food mill. Pour broken seeds into water, stir vigorously, let settle. Nutmeats will sink and shells will rise to top. Skim shells for making coffee. For use in nut recipes, drain, dry, and roast nutmeats. Grind nutmeats into meal and use for part of flour in muffin and bread recipes. For nut butter grind raw nutmeats into paste; add honey or maple syrup if necessary to improve flavor. To produce oil, thoroughly crush or grind raw seeds. Boil in water. Skim oil off broth. **Related edible species:** All of the nearly 60 species in North and South America are edible. **Poisonous look-alikes:** none.

Purslane: flowering plant (NYBG).

Sunflower: flowering stalks (Elias). Cultivated
form with larger flowering head (Feldman).

Quickweed: flowering plant and flowers (NYBG).

Bearberry: fruiting branches (Elias).

Quickweed, Galinsoga   *Galinsoga parviflora*

Habitat: disturbed sites, roadsides, yards; also garden weed. **Identification:** annual herb to 70 cm (28 in) high, often bushy, stems usually spreading, smooth to slightly hairy. *Leaves opposite,* simple, usually lance-shaped, 2.5–8 cm (1–3.1 in) long, 1.2–4 cm (0.5–1.6 in) wide, pointed at tip, small blunt teeth along margin, tapering to rounded at base, with 3 principal veins, papery, usually stalked. *Flowers tiny, produced in heads, 4–5 outer scale-like bracts (involucre) 2–3 mm (0.1 in) high, green; outer (ray) flowers white, inner (disc) flowers yellow.* Fruits small hard nutlets 1–1.5 mm (0.1 in) long, nearly black, hairy. **Harvest:** young plants during middle of growing season. **Preparation:** Discard roots. Boil tops about 15–25 min and serve with salt, pepper, and butter. Add more flavorful greens and vinegar to compensate for quickweed blandness. **Related edible species:** *G. ciliata* (also called quickweed) plus a few other *Galinsoga* species, all introduced from southwest U.S., Mexico, and points south. **Poisonous look-alikes:** none.

Bearberry, Kinnikinick   *Arctostaphylos uva-ursi*

Habitat: circumboreal, subarctic; sandy or rocky soils, higher elevations in southern part of range. **Identification:** *low spreading shrub, forming mats* with tough flexible twigs. *New twigs hairy and sticky; mature ones* dark reddish-brown or gray, *papery and peeling.* *Leaves* alternate, simple, *evergreen, 1– 3 cm* (0.4–1.2 in) *long,* broadest near rounded tip, entire, shiny above, leathery. Flowers tiny, 5–12 per elongated cluster, each white to pale pink, urn-shaped, 4–6 mm (0.2 in) long. *Fruits bright or dull red berries 4–10 mm (0.2–0.4 in) in diameter, mealy,* not tasty. **Harvest and preparation:** leaves called *kinnikinick,* an Indian tobacco substitute also used by frontiersmen. For smoking, leaves are mildest in summer; dry in sun or near fire, crumble, and light up. Dried leaves make medicinal tea, good for indigestion. Fruits ripen late in growing season. Raw, they are bland and dry, but cooked they become palatable with cream and sugar. Not great snack but useful survival food. **Related edible species:** alpine bearberry *(A. alpina)* and several manzanitas plus many species in other genera in heath family. **Poisonous look-alikes:** none.

Salal, Western wintergreen *(Also edible autumn)*   *Gaultheria shallon*

Habitat: woods, clearings, brushy areas below 800 m (2,630 ft), from West Coast to west slope of Cascades. **Identification:** *upright, many branched shrub* 0.3–2.5 m (1–8.2 ft) tall, frequently forming dense thickets. *Leaves evergreen,* alternate, simple, uniformly wide to broadest near middle, 3–10 cm (1.2–4 in) long, finely toothed, dark, shiny above, paler beneath. Flowering clusters narrow, elongate, composed of 5–15 stalked flowers, each urn-shaped, white or pink, 8–10 mm (0.3–0.4 in) long; prominent leaflike bract and 2 bractlets at base of flower stem. *Fruits dark-purple berries,* 7–8 mm (0.3 in) in diameter, nearly round, thick skinned, star-shaped depression on end, with several seeds. **Harvest:** Fruits ripen in summer and persist several weeks. **Preparation:** edible fresh but sometimes quite spicy and not juicy; better cooked. Also dry in sun or warm attic. Good in jam, jelly, pies, baked goods. See basic jelly and jam recipes, in book's Introduction. For beverage crush and boil berries, extract juice, and add equal amount of water. Sweeten, if necessary. **Related edible species:** WINTERGREEN, CREEPING WINTERGREEN (next), CREEPING SNOWBERRY, and *G. ovatifolia,* also called salal, of northwest U.S. **Poisonous look-alikes:** none.

Creeping wintergreen *(Also edible autumn, winter)*   *Gaultheria humifusa*

Habitat: subalpine and alpine zones and moist slopes of western and Pacific Northwest mountains. **Identification:** low shrub with short spreading branches along ground. *Leaves* alternate, simple, *evergreen,* broad, *broadest near base or middle, 1–2 cm (0.4–0.8 in) long, almost as wide,* entire or with tiny teeth along margin, leathery. Flowers solitary in junction of leaves, each white, urn-shaped, 3–4 mm (0.1–0.2 in) long. *Fruits are dry berries 4–8 mm (0.2–0.3 in) in diameter,* rounded, *red at maturity.* **Harvest and preparation:** same as WINTERGREEN. Dryness makes fruit less palatable than other *Gaultheria* species. **Related edible species:** See SALAL (preceding). **Poisonous look-alikes:** none.

Labrador tea *(Also edible autumn, winter, spring)*   *Ledum groenlandicum*

Habitat: bogs, fens, heaths, northern woods, exposed bluffs. **Identification:** low shrub up to 1 m (3.2 ft) high, with erect, reddish-brown branches, densely hairy when young. *Leaves* alternate, simple, *evergreen,* fragrant, crowded near tip of twigs, 1.5–5 cm (0.6–2 in) long, 4–12 mm (0.2–0.5 in) wide, uniformly wide to slightly wider at middle, rounded at tip, *margin entire and rolled under, leathery,* dull dark green above, *densely hairy beneath, white at first, turning rusty.* Flowers produced in late spring or summer in rounded clusters, each with 5 cream-white petals, stalked. Fruits are dry capsules 4–6 mm (0.2 in) long, slender, long-stalked, splitting open from base. **Harvest:** any time but least good in midwinter. Pick leaves when dense pile beneath is rust colored. Dry in sun, over low fire, or in oven. **Preparation:** Steep 1 tbsp dried leaves in 1 cup boiling hot water for 10 min. Do not boil water with leaves in it, which may release a harmful alkaloid. Serve hot or cold. **Related edible species:** northern Labrador tea *(L. palustre).* **Poisonous look-alikes:** mountain Labrador tea *(L. glandulosum)* is described by some sources as poisonous.

Salal: fruiting and flowering branches (Ross).

Creeping wintergreen: fruiting plants (Mulligan).

Labrador tea: flowering plant (Elias).

Mountain cranberry: flowers (NYBG). Fruiting plant (Elias).

Cranberry: flowering plants (NYBG). Fruit (Elias).

The BLUEBERRY and CRANBERRY GENUS   *Vaccinium*

Blueberries, cranberries, huckleberries, and bilberries are all closely related groups of species of the *Vaccinium* genus. There are perhaps 35 species in North America, but hybridization is common. Fruits of most species are edible and range in taste from tart to sweet. The domesticated blueberries are selections of the highbush blueberry *(V. corymbosum)*. Wild blueberries sold commercially are commonly obtained from late sweet blueberry *(V. angustifolium)* or velvet-leaved blueberry *(V. myrtilloides)*. The supermarket cranberry *(V. macrocarpon)* is the same as the wild. Berries are rich in vitamin C.

Mountain cranberry, Lingenberry, Foxberry   *Vaccinium vitis-idaea*
Also edible autumn, winter

Habitat: widespread subarctic and alpine plant, bogs, cold seepage areas, rocky acid soils. **Identification:** *small, creeping plant,* to 15 cm (6 in) with slender stems; *leaves* alternate, simple, *evergreen,* broadest above middle, *0.6–1.8 cm (0.2–0.7 in) long, 4–10 mm (0.2–0.4 in) wide,* entire, leathery, with scattered black glandular hairs beneath, midrib furrowed. Flowers tiny, pink to reddish, 6–8 mm (0.2–0.3 in) long, narrowly bell-shaped. *Fruits red berries, rounded, 6–10 mm (0.2–0.4 in) in diameter,* often persisting over winter, slightly acid tasting. **Harvest and preparation:** Fruits ripen August and September; many persist on plant through winter. Tart to bitter at first; flavor improves after frost. Good trail snack, better used in any cooked cranberry recipes. **Related edible species:** CRANBERRY (next). **Poisonous look-alikes:** none.

Cranberry *(Also edible autumn, winter)*   *Vaccinium macrocarpon*

Habitat: widespread northern plant; bogs, swamps, shores of cold acid lakes. **Identification:** *low, trailing shrub* with slender brown, flaky-barked stems; *leaves* alternate, simple, *evergreen,* uniformly wide to broadest near middle, *5–16 mm (0.2–0.6 in) long,* rounded at tip, leathery, whitish beneath. Flowers single or in few-flowered clusters on long stalks in junction of upper leaves, each stalk with 2 leaflike bracts, each flower pink, urn-shaped, 4 petals bent back, 6–10 mm (0.2–0.4 in) long. *Fruits* are *berries 1–2 cm (0.4–0.8 in) in diameter,* globe-shaped, green turning *bright red at maturity,* each on long slender stalk. **Harvest:** Fruits ripen September through October and persist into winter in protected areas. Fruits may be harvested with toothed scoop. **Preparation:** Fresh acidic fruits keep well in cool storage. Freeze or dry for long storage. To dry berries, spread on tray or foil in oven for 4 hr at 110°C (230°F). Experiment with substituting dried, powdered berries for part of flour in baking recipes. Most common use of fresh and frozen berries is in sauce served with roast turkey. Bring to boil 2 lb fresh cranberries, 2 cups sugar, 1 cup water (or berries plus 1 cup maple sugar and 1 cup cider). Reduce heat and simmer until all berries pop, and mix looks glassy. For storage, ladle into sterile jars and seal. Check recipe books. **Related edible species:** MOUNTAIN CRANBERRY (preceding); small cranberry *(V. oxycoccos)* is similar but smaller. HIGHBUSH CRANBERRY is not related but has almost identical fruits. **Poisonous look-alikes:** none.

Bog bilberry   *Vaccinium uliginosum*

Habitat: widespread boreal and arctic plant; bogs, rocky outcrops, high mountain slopes. **Identification:** *low shrub to 0.6 m* (2 ft) high; branches stout, usually spreading; *leaves* alternate, simple, *deciduous, broadest near tip or middle to uniformly wide, 0.5–2 cm* (0.2–0.8 in) *long,* rounded at tip, entire, firm to leathery texture, dull green. Flowers *solitary or in clusters of 2–4 on short stalks* in junctions of leaves; each pink to whitish, urn-shaped. *Fruits fleshy berries 5–8 mm (0.2–0.3 in) in diameter, dark blue to black,* sweet, with many tiny seeds. **Harvest and preparation:** same as LATE SWEET BLUEBERRY. **Related edible species:** See LATE SWEET BLUEBERRY. **Poisonous look-alikes:** none.

Highbush blueberry, Swamp blueberry   *Vaccinium corymbosum*

Habitat: widespread in eastern North America; bogs, low wet woodlands, swamps, occasionally drier soils. **Identification:** *shrubs,* variable in shape, *1–4.5 m* (3.2–14.8 ft) *high; leaves* alternate, simple, *deciduous,* broadest near base or middle, sometimes narrowly so, *3–8 cm (1.2–3.2 in) long,* 2–3 cm (0.8–1.2 in) wide, usually entire, greenish-yellow. *Flowers densely clustered,* each tubular to urn-shaped, white to pink, 5–10 mm (0.2–0.4 in) long. *Fruits fleshy berries, rounded, 6–12 mm (0.2–0.5 in) in diameter, dark blue to bluish-black, sweet,* containing many tiny seeds. **Harvest:** Gather ripe fruits in late summer. They can be eaten as trail snack or stored for later use. Fruits ripen as do those of LATE SWEET BLUEBERRY (next), but are easier to gather. Hand pick or shake berries onto blanket or plastic tarp spread beneath bush. **Preparation:** Same as LATE SWEET BLUEBERRY. Also see basic recipes early in book. Add cup dried blueberries to favorite stew recipe. For fritters prepare batter from 1 cup biscuit mix, 3 tbsp sugar, ⅓ cup milk, 1 beaten egg, 1 cup fresh blueberries. Drop spoonfuls into hot cooking oil; brown both sides. Drain; dust with sugar. **Related edible species:** See LATE SWEET BLUEBERRY. **Poisonous look-alikes:** none.

Late sweet blueberry   *Vaccinium angustifolium*

Habitat: dry rocky soils, barrens, mountain slopes, occasionally bogs; northcentral and northeastern North America. **Identification:** *low shrub to 0.3 m* (1 ft), much branched, often forming thickets. *Leaves* alternate, simple, deciduous, *narrow* and broadest at or below middle, 1–3 cm (0.4–1.2 in) long, *finely toothed along margins,* bright green, smooth. *Flowers produced in short tight clusters,* each nearly cylinder-shaped, white to pinkish tinged, 5–6 mm (0.2 in) long. *Fruits* are *fleshy berries 5–12 mm* (0.2–0.5 in) *in diameter,* rounded, *bright blue,* white bloom, sweet. **Harvest:** This and other blueberry species ripen in summer, generally after raspberries (RED RASPBERRY) and before blackberries (COMMON BLACKBERRY) where those berries grow. Pick by hand. **Preparation:** Blueberries were probably the most important fruit to American Indians. Excellent dried like raisins and fresh, both raw and in most berry recipes, especially pies, jams, and breads (see basic recipes early in book). Dry thoroughly in sun or warm attic about 10 days or in 100°C (210°F) oven for 4–5 hr; store in sealed containers. For bannock, blend 2 cups sifted flour, 3 tsp baking powder, ½ tsp

Bog billberry: fruiting plant (Elias).

Highbush blueberry: flowering branch (NYBG). Fruiting branch (Elias).

Late sweet blueberry: flowering and fruiting branches (Speas).

Black huckleberry: fruiting branch (Elias).

Beach plum: fruiting branches (Elias).

salt, 6 tbsp shortening, 4 tbsp powdered milk. Mix in 1 cup blueberries, then ⅓ cup water. Shape into 1 in thick cake, dust with flour, place in heated frying pan. Cook over coals until bottom is crusty. Turn with spatula and bake until done; test with straw or sliver. See HIGHBUSH BLUEBERRY (preceding) for other uses. **Related edible species:** Other *VACCINIUM.* **Poisonous look-alikes:** none.

Black huckleberry *Gaylussacia baccata*

Habitat: woodlands, clearings, dry to moist soils. **Identification:** shrub to 1.2 m (4 ft), often forming low thickets; branches numerous, stiff, resembling blueberry bush. *Leaves* alternate, simple, deciduous, *3–6 cm* (1.2–2.4 in) *long,* uniformly wide to broadest near or below middle, entire, *gland-dotted above and below. Flowers few on short elongated clusters, each white,* small, cone-shaped to almost tubular, 4–7 mm (0.2–0.3 in) long. *Fruits fleshy berries 6–9 mm* (0.2–0.4 in) *in diameter, black at maturity,* containing 10 tiny seeds, sweet. **Harvest and preparation:** Pick berries as they ripen in late June in south to September in far north. Eat as fresh fruit or use in desserts, pancakes, jam, and jelly. For pancakes add 1 cup berries to 3–4 cups batter. To dry, spread berries in single layer on tray, foil, or paper in warm attic; dry about 10 days or until squashed berry releases no juice. Store in sealed container. Use dried berries in baking or pemmican. Or add ½–1 cup dried berries to beef stew. See LATE SWEET BLUEBERRY and HIGHBUSH BLUEBERRY for other recipes. **Related edible species:** Dwarf huckleberry *(G. dumosa),* box huckleberry *(G. brachycera),* and dangleberry *(G. frondosa)* all yield berries edible but inferior to blueberries. **Poisonous look-alikes:** none.

Beach plum *Prunus maritima*
Also edible autumn

Habitat: coastal regions, sandy soils. **Identification:** shrub to 2.5 m (8 ft) or low and straggling; branches hairy when young, smooth later. *Leaves* alternate, simple, deciduous, *3–7 cm* (1.2–2.8 in) *long,* 1.5–3.5 cm (0.6–1.4 in) wide, broadest at or below middle, rarely widest above middle, pointed at tip, *sharply toothed along margin,* dull green and smooth above, softly hairy beneath. *Flowers 2–4 per cluster, each 1–1.5 cm* (0.4–0.6 in) *across,* with 5 *white* petals. *Fruits rounded* or nearly so, *1.5–2.5 cm* (0.6–1 in) *in diameter, deep purple to reddish-black at maturity,* fleshy, sour tasting, enclosing large stone. **Harvest:** Pick fruit from August through October, depending on location. Slightly unripe fruit best for jelly. **Preparation:** similar to AMERICAN PLUM but fruit is more tart. Use jelly and jam recipes early in book. Also, make jellies and jams from blend of plum and other fruits. Combine with peaches or other sweet pulpy fruit for pie filling; see basic plum pie recipe early in book. To dry fruit for later use, slit skin and remove pit. Pits contain toxic hydrocyanic acid. Spread fruit in sun or warm oven until no juice can be squeezed from them, about 4–6 hr. Makes tart trail snack. **Related edible species:** AMERICAN PLUM, FLATWOOD PLUM, and several others. **Poisonous look-alikes:** none.

CURRANT or GOOSEBERRY GENUS   *Ribes*

This large group of about 120 species is centered in western North America and the Andes Mountains of South America. They are shrubs, sometimes armed with spines, with simple, maplelike, alternate leaves, flowers in small clusters, and a 1-celled pulpy berry, sometimes transparent, variously colored, containing several seeds. North American species are sometimes difficult to distinguish. Fortunately, none is known to be poisonous. We recommend 2 common yellow-flowered species with smooth fruits and 2 pink- to purple-flowered species with glandular hairy fruits. **Harvest:** Pick fruits in summer as they ripen. **Preparation:** Sweetness and juiciness vary greatly among species. Some fruits can be eaten fresh. Some are spiny and so require cautious eating. Adapt recipes to berry characteristics. For no-cook currant or gooseberry preserves, wash and mash fruits thoroughly. Slowly mix in sugar equal to volume of crushed fruit. Pour into sterilized jelly glasses and seal. For preserves wash and stem 1 lb currants; add ¾ lb sugar and let stand overnight. Bring slowly to boiling point and boil 3–5 min. Let stand overnight, pour into jelly glasses, and seal. To make

Golden currant: flowers (NYBG). Fruiting branches (USDA).

currant/gooseberry conserve, wash and stem 3 lb berries. Grate rind of 3 oranges and cut up pulp. Mix berries, orange rind and pulp, 1 lb seeded raisins, and 3 lb sugar, cook slowly until thick. Pour into sterilized jars and seal. For simple currant/gooseberry pie wash and stem 1 pt berries. Cook in saucepan with 1 cup sugar and small amount of water about 15 min until berries soften. Pour into pie crust, add top crust, bake at 175°C (350°F) oven until crust is done. Add fresh or dried berries to kuchen dough and muffins. To dry whole or mashed berries spread in thin layer on baking sheet; place in sun or 105°C (220°F) oven until dry. Store in paper bag in dry place. To make pemmican mix 1 lb dried and finely ground or pounded meat with ¼ cup brown sugar and ½ cup dried berries. Add ¾ lb melted suet and blend into paste. Form into bars and store dry. Eat as is, boil, or fry. For pie and cooked jelly see recipes early in book. **Related edible species:** many in addition to the four described; widely distributed. **Poisonous look-alikes:** Sticky currant *(R. viscosissimum)* is reported to be a strong vomitory. It has a sticky substance on the leaves, twigs, and fruit. Some fruits are covered with short, bristly hairs.

Golden currant   *Ribes aureum*

Habitat: along streams, ravines, washes, mountain slopes, mainly between 750–2,380 m (2,460–7,800 ft) elevation. **Identification:** shrub, erect, open, to 2 m (6.6 ft); branches stiff, nearly smooth. *Leaves* alternate, deciduous, 1.2–4.5 cm (0.5–1.8 in) long, 1.5–5 cm (0.6–2 in) wide, *broadly rounded to widest near base, 3-lobed,* rounded at tip, entire to coarsely toothed along margin, *light green,* smooth, stalked. *Flowers* produced in drooping, 5–15-flowered, elongated clusters in late spring, each flower *bright yellow,* 5-parted, 6–10 mm (0.2–0.4 in) long, *smooth. Fruits stalked berries,* rounded, 6–9 mm (0.2–0.4 in) in diameter, *red* or occasionally black, *smooth, beaked* (persistent floral parts), produced in summer. **Harvest and preparation:** See CURRANTS, GOOSEBERRIES (preceding). This species both wild and cultivated was much used by western Indians; one of the best flavored species.

Wax currant *Ribes cereum*

Habitat: canyons, dry ravines, hillsides, prairies, open woodlands. **Identification:** open spreading shrub to 1 m (3.2 ft) high; branches stiff, crooked. *Leaves* alternate, simple, deciduous, 2–2.5 cm (0.8–1 in) long, 2.5–3 cm (1–1.2 in) wide, *broadly rounded, wider than long, shallowly 3-lobed,* rounded at tip, irregularly *round toothed along margin,* yellowish-green, glandular hairy on both surfaces, leafstalk 8–15 mm (0.3–0.6 in) long. *Flowers* in drooping, 1–6-flowered, elongated clusters in late May or June, each flower *white to pinkish,* 5-parted, 6–10 mm (0.2–0.4 in) long. *Fruits stalked berries, globe-shaped,* 8–12 mm (0.3–0.5 in) in diameter, *dull to bright red, with stalked glandular hairs,* beaked (the persistent floral parts), produced in July or August. **Harvest and preparation:** See CURRANTS, GOOSEBERRIES (preceding). Wax currant is native in West, though frequently cultivated in East.

Subalpine prickly currant *Ribes montigenum*

Habitat: along streams, wet forests, ravines, washes, mainly in subalpine zone 2,140–3,800 m (7,000–12,500 ft) elevation. **Identification:** *shrub,* open, spreading, sometimes straggling, to 0.7 m (28 in) high; branches tough, *densely covered with glandular hairs, stiff bristlelike prickles with small spines at leaf bases. Leaves* alternate, deciduous, simple, 0.8–3 cm (0.3–1.2 in) long, as wide or wider, almost circular in outline, *deeply 5-lobed,* pointed at tip, sharply toothed along margin, glandular hairy on both surfaces, stalked. Flowers produced in drooping, few-flowered clusters in late spring or early summer, each *flower* stalked, *purplish,* 5-parted, 4–8 mm (0.2–0.3 in) long, *covered with glandular hairs. Fruits* stalked *berries,* rounded, 4–6 mm (0.2 in) in diameter, *red, covered with glandular hairs,* produced in summer. **Harvest and preparation:** See CURRANTS, GOOSEBERRIES (preceding).

Fragrant golden currant *Ribes odoratum*

Habitat: prairies, open woodlands, bluffs, ledges, ravines. **Identification:** *shrub,* upright, open, to 1.5 m (5 ft); branches tough, reddish-brown, hairy, *spineless. Leaves* alternate, simple, deciduous, 3–6 cm (1.2–2.4 in) long, slightly wider, broadly rounded to widest near base, *3–5-lobed,* pointed to blunt at tip, coarsely toothed along margin, hairy, stalked. *Flowers* produced in drooping, few-flowered clusters from older wood in spring, each flower *pale yellow,* 5-parted, 12–16 mm (0.5–0.6 in) long, smooth. *Fruits, produced in summer, stalked berries, globe-shaped, 9–12 mm* (0.4–0.5 in) *in diameter, purplish-black, smooth,* with beaked persistent floral parts. **Harvest and preparation:** See CURRANTS, GOOSEBERRIES (preceding).

Wax currant: fruiting branches (Ross).

Subalpine prickly currant: fruiting branch (Dykeman).

Fragrant golden currant: fruiting branches (Kavasch).

American hazelnut: fruiting branches (Elias).

Beaked hazelnut: fruits (Speas).

American hazelnut
Corylus americana
Also edible autumn

Habitat: widespread, dry to moist woodlands, thickets. **Identification:** shrub to 5 m (16.4 ft) with rounded head and glandular hairy twigs. *Leaves* alternate, simple, deciduous, 5–15 cm (2–6 in) long, 3–12 cm (1.2–4.7 in), broadest below or above middle, long-pointed at tip, *doubly toothed* along margin, usually hairy beneath. Male flowers in dense slender catkins in early spring. Female flowers usually solitary or paired, tiny, inconspicuous in early spring. *Fruits are hard-shelled nuts, broader than long,* 1–1.5 cm (0.4–0.6 in) across, *partially enclosed by 2 ragged-edged leaflike bracts,* nutmeat sweet. **Harvest:** Nuts mature in late summer or autumn. **Preparation:** Remove husk, shell, and eat as is, or use in any recipe calling for nuts. For no-cook candy, mix 1 egg white with 2 cups confectioner's sugar. Add 2 tsp butter or margarine and blend until smooth. Work in 2 cups chopped hazelnuts and form into balls. Eat and enjoy. For hazelnut hot cakes, finely grind 0.2 kg (½ lb) dried hazelnuts. Boil in 2 cups water until mushy, about 30 min. Add 1 tsp maple syrup and ⅓ cup fine cornmeal, stir well, let stand for 20 min or until thick. Heat ⅓ cup frying oil in skillet. Drop batter by tablespoonfuls into hot oil. Brown on one side, flip, flatten, brown on other side. Drain and serve hot or cold. See also BEAKED HAZELNUT (next). **Related edible species:** BEAKED HAZELNUT. **Poisonous look-alikes:** none.

Beaked hazelnut
Corylus cornuta
Also edible autumn

Habitat: dry or moist woodlands, hills or mountain slopes, absent on Coastal Plain. **Identification:** shrub to 3 m (9.8 ft), often forming thickets; twigs hairy when young. Leaves alternate, simple, deciduous, 3–10 cm (1.2–4 in) long, 2–8 cm (0.8–3.2 in) wide, broadest near base, long-pointed at tip, doubly toothed along margin, hairy beneath. Male flowers in dense, slender catkins in early spring. Female flowers solitary or few per cluster, tiny, inconspicuous. *Fruits* are *thin-shelled nuts,* broadest near base, 1–1.5 cm (0.4–0.6 in) in diameter, *enclosed by 2 bristly leaflike bracts 4–7 cm* (1.6–2.8 in) *long which form narrow beak;* nutmeat sweet. **Harvest:** Nuts mature in late summer or autumn. **Preparation:** Remove husk. Shell and eat as is or use in recipes calling for nuts or grind into meal to use as flour. For hazelnut torte preheat moderate oven 175°C (350°F). Beat 11 egg yolks well, add 0.5 kg (1 lb) confectioner's sugar, continuing to beat. Add 0.5 kg (1 lb) ground hazelnuts and 1 tsp instant coffee. Fold in 11 stiffly beaten egg whites. Bake in 30 cm (12 in) greased and floured spring baking form for 50–60 min. See also AMERICAN HAZELNUT (preceding). **Related edible species:** AMERICAN HAZELNUT. **Poisonous look-alikes:** none.

Sweet fern
Comptonia peregrina

Also edible winter, spring

Habitat: dry rocky, sandy, or gravelly soils of clearings, pastures, poor open woodlands. **Identification:** small shrub 0.4–1.2 m (1.3–4 ft) high, with rounded shape; young branches hairy. *Leaves* in fernlike pattern, alternate, simple, deciduous, *6–14 cm* (2.4–5.5 in) *long, 0.8–1.2 cm* (0.3–0.5 in) *wide,* widest near middle or base, *deeply lobed along margin, fragrant due to numerous resinous glands* on leaves and twigs. Male and female flowers produced in separate small catkins on same bush in spring. *Fruits small, green burrs 1–2 cm* (0.4–0.8 in) *in diameter,* each partially or totally enclosing 1–4 nutlets, maturing in mid to late summer. **Harvest:** leaves any time for fragrant tea. Immature nutlets during June and July while still tender. **Preparation:** For tea add 1 tsp dried or 2 tsp fresh leaves per cup boiling water; steep. When camping, put 8 tsp fresh, chopped leaves per qt of water in glass jar. Cap and place in sun 3 hr or until water is dark. Strain, dilute to taste, sweeten if desired. Not bitter like many brewed teas. Strong tea (infusion) has been used to alleviate dysentery. Using thumbnail, separate nutlets from burrs when immature and eat raw. **Edible related species:** northern bayberry *(Myrica pensylvanica),* SOUTHERN BAYBERRY and SWEET GALE (next). **Poisonous look-alikes:** none.

Southern bayberry, Wax myrtle
Myrica cerifera

Also edible autumn, winter

Habitat: coastal plain, swamps, along ponds and lakes, pine barrens, wet sandy soils. **Identification:** shrub or small tree to 8 m (26 ft) with rounded crown and slender, hairy, *gland-dotted twigs. Leaves* alternate, simple, deciduous but often persisting until second year, *3.5–10 cm* (1.4–4 in) *long,* 0.6–1.2 cm (0.2–0.5 in) wide, *narrow* but broadest near tip, *coarsely toothed along margin, yellow-green, gland-dotted, fragrant when rubbed.* Male and female flowers on separate bushes in spring; male flowers in slender catkins 1.2–1.9 cm (0.5–0.7 in) long; female flowers in broader catkins 0.6–1.2 cm (0.2–0.5 in) long on older twigs. *Fruits few to several clustered on short spikes, each rounded, 2–4 mm (0.1 in) in diameter, covered with light blue waxlike coating.* **Harvest and preparation:** Pick leaves any time available but best in early summer. Wash and spread to dry thoroughly in warm shaded area. Store in sealed jars in dark place. Crumble and blend into stews and sauces for cooking and serving meats. Also use berries picked from late summer into winter as seasoning and to provide wax used in candles. **Related edible species:** northern bayberry *(M. pensylvanica)* and other wax myrtle species are used the same way. Also SWEET GALE (next) is used for seasoning but fruits lack wax. **Poisonous look-alikes:** none.

Sweet fern: mature plant and branch with fruit (Elias).

Southern bayberry: fruiting branches (NYBG).

Sweet gale

Myrica gale

Also edible autumn, winter

Habitat: swamps and shallow water along ponds and streams. **Identification:** shrub 0.3–2 m (1–6.6 ft) tall with upright brown branches. *Leaves* alternate, simple, *deciduous, wedge shaped,* rounded, *broadest near tip,* toothed near tip, *dark green above, pale beneath, downy on veins,* 2–7 cm (0.8–2.8 in) long, *aromatic* when crushed. *Male flowers in spikelike catkins at end of twigs; female flowers usually on separate plants,* about 8 mm (0.3 in) long, *at base of leaves. Fruit small nutlike, not waxy,* resin dotted, aromatic, with 2 winglike scales, *in small conelike clusters.* **Harvest:** Pick leaves as described for SOUTHERN BAYBERRY (preceding) and aromatic nutlets from summer through winter. **Preparation:** Dry and use leaves as described for SOUTHERN BAYBERRY and for making hot tea. Use nutlets like dried leaves for seasoning. **Related edible species:** See SOUTHERN BAYBERRY. **Poisonous look-alikes:** none.

New Jersey tea

Ceanothus americanus

Habitat: open woodlands and prairies, in well-drained rocky, gravelly, or sandy soils. **Identification:** *shrub* to 1 m (3.2 ft) with slender, reddish-brown, densely hairy twigs. *Leaves* alternate, simple, 3-ribbed, deciduous, *4–8 cm* (1.6–3.2 in) *long,* 2–4 cm (0.8 –1.6 in) wide, broadest near base, rounded at tip, *finely toothed along margin,* green above, gray and hairy beneath. *Flowers tiny, white, produced in dense, short cylinder-shaped, branched clusters in spring,* each with 5 white petals shaped like tiny tobacco pipes. Clusters from leaf junctions. *Fruits* produced in rounded clusters in late spring or early summer, each *capsulelike, 5–6 mm* (0.2 in) *long,* splitting open to release tiny, reddish-brown seeds. **Harvest:** Gather fresh leaves in summer, best when bushes are flowering. Dry leaves thoroughly in sun, by fire, or in warm oven. **Preparation:** For tea, steep 1 tbsp fresh or 1 tsp dried leaves in 1 cup boiling water for 15 min. Sweeten to taste. Caffeine free. Dried root bark tea was used as sedative by Indians. **Related edible species:** Red root *(C. ovatus)* is also known as New Jersey tea. *C. americanus* has wider leaves and flower clusters at leaf junctions instead of at end of twig. **Poisonous look-alikes:** none.

Sweet gale: fruiting branch and fruits (Elias).

New Jersey tea: flowers (Mohlenbrock). Flowering branch (NYBG).

Silver buffaloberry: fruiting branches (Elias). Flowering branch (NYBG).

BRAMBLES, BLACKBERRIES, RASPBERRIES   *Rubus*

This is a large and variable group of approximately 300 to 400 species in the temperate regions of the world. Members of this genus are shrubs or trailing, often prickly, vines, collectively known as brambles. Fruits may or may not separate from the spongy core of the fruit base when picked. The genus normally is divided into subcategories; one containing blackberries and dewberries, another containing thimbleberries, another raspberries. Most of the species have edible fruits; many have delicious fruits. Six of the more common species are treated on the following pages. **Harvest and preparation:** Pick fruit as it ripens. Berries of most species are excellent fresh, except for thimbleberries which have a rather dry taste and may require mixing with other berries. The berries are good with cream and sugar, in pancakes, on cereals, and in jams, jellies, and pies. To make berry bannock over campfire, mix 2 cups flour, 3 tsp double-acting baking powder, ½ tsp salt, 6 tbsp margarine or butter, and 4 tbsp powdered milk until uniformly mixed into mealy texture. Add 1 cup washed damp berries; mix gently to coat fruit. Add ⅓ cup water to make workable dough. Shape into 1-in-thick

Silver buffaloberry

Shepherdia argentea

Also edible autumn

Habitat: riverbanks, low meadows, plains, canyons. **Identification:** spreading shrub or small tree to 5 m (16 ft) with dull gray bark shredding in long strips; *branches* stout, *covered with silvery-white scales,* usually *thorny. Leaves opposite,* simple, deciduous, 3–5 cm (1.2–2 in) long, 7–10 mm (0.3–0.4 in) wide, uniformly wide to widest near middle, entire, *leathery, densely covered with silvery scales on both surfaces.* Male and female flowers on separate trees; flowers small, inconspicuous, lacking petals. *Fruits berrylike, rounded,* 6–9 mm (0.2–0.4 in) long, smooth, *bright red,* slightly fleshy, enclosing single flattened seed. **Harvest:** late summer fruits pleasantly tart, better after frost has sweetened them. Shrub is frequently prolific fruit producer. Handpick or spread tarp beneath shrub and shake branches. **Preparation:** Use fruit fresh or dry thoroughly in sun. Use prefrost berries for jelly. Eat ripe fruit fresh or dried; add sugar as desired. Seeds are chewable. For beverage crush 1 cup fresh berries with 1 cup sugar in 3 cups hot water or mash 1 cup dried berries in 1 pt water. Add sugar to taste. Strain and drink. Cook berries with meat or prepare like CRANBERRY sauce for use with meat. For dessert mash fresh fruits and whip or blend into froth. Blend in sugar if needed. **Related edible species:** Canadian buffaloberry *(S. canadensis)* and silverberry *(Elaeagnus argentea)* are edible but less flavorful, and are improved by cooking and adding sugar. **Poisonous look-alikes:** none.

cake, dust with flour, place in warm, greased fry pan. Cook over moderate heat until crust forms on bottom. Turn over with spatula and cook until browned and no dough sticks to fork inserted into center of dough. Adapt other berry recipes from your favorite cookbooks. Tender growth tips of many species are edible, and leaves of many are good for tea. **Related edible species:** See above. **Poisonous look-alikes:** none.

Red raspberry

Rubus idaeus var. *strigosus*
(synonym: *R. strigosus*)

Habitat: margins of woodlands, clearings, roadsides, abandoned fields. **Identification:** subshrub to 2 m (6.6 ft) high; *branches* spreading to trailing along ground, often with a whitish cast, *armed with usually numerous prickles* and stiff hairs. *Leaves* alternate, deciduous, compound on nonflowering canes, *with 3–7 leaflets,* each leaflet broadest near base, 2–10 cm (0.8–4 in) long, long-pointed at tip, coarsely and sharply toothed along margin, *pale green to whitish and hairy beneath.* Flowers white to greenish-white, 1.2–1.8 cm (0.5–0.7 in) across, produced June–July in small clusters of 2–5 flowers along upper part of canes. *Fruits globe-shaped or nearly so, 1.2–2 cm (0.5–0.8 in) in diameter, bright red,* juicy, *separating easily from fruiting stalk and base,* maturing from July–September. **Harvest and preparation:** See BRAMBLES (preceding).

Wineberry

Rubus phoenicolasius

Habitat: introduced from Asia; grows wild in disturbed sites, along streams, rivers, roads, especially in coastal eastern U.S. **Identification:** shrub to 2.5 m (8 ft) high; *branches* spreading, often arching over, *lacking spines but with dense, red, gland-tipped hairs. Leaves* alternate, deciduous, *3-parted* (trifoliolate), *broadest near base and often as broad as long,* 4–10 cm (1.6–4 in) *long and wide,* often lobed, toothed. *Flowers white,* produced in elongate, many-flowered clusters; *each 2–3 cm (0.8–1.2 in) across (including calyx lobes), petals shorter than the narrow, pointed, calyx lobes. Fruits globe-shaped, 0.8–1.2 cm (0.3–0.5 in) in diameter, bright red* at maturity, juicy, maturing from midsummer to early autumn. **Harvest and preparation:** See BRAMBLES (preceding).

Thimbleberry

Rubus parviflorus

Habitat: widespread from sea level to mountains; woodlands, canyons, open areas, along roads, trails, streams. **Identification:** shrub to 2 m (6.6 ft) high with *upright to spreading branches, without spines* but with glandular hairs. *Leaves* alternate, deciduous, *simple, 5-lobed,* 5–15 cm (2–6 in) *long and wide,* sharply toothed along margin. *Flowers* large, *white to pink, 2–5 cm (0.8–2 in) across,* produced in loose, 2–9-flowered, spreading clusters. *Fruits large,* globe-shaped, *1.2–1.8 cm (0.5–0.7 in) across, bright red to scarlet,* sweet, juicy, maturing throughout season. **Harvest and preparation:** See BRAMBLES (preceding).

Red raspberry: fruiting branch (Elias).

Wineberry: fruiting branch (Elias).

Thimbleberry: fruiting branch (McNeal).

Common blackberry: mature fruits (Elias).

Black raspberry: fruiting branch (Elias). Flowering branch (Dykeman).

Common blackberry   *Rubus allegheniensis*

Habitat: margins of woodlands, old fields, fencerows; also roadsides, thickets, mountain slopes. **Identification:** shrub, sometimes to 3 m (9.8 ft), branches upright to spreading, sometimes trailing, with scattered straight spines. *Leaves* alternate, deciduous, palmately compound, ***usually with 5 leaflets,*** sometimes 3, variable, typically broadest near or just below middle, long-pointed at tip, usually 10–18 cm (4–7 in) long, with numerous sharp-pointed teeth along margin, *pale green beneath.* ***Flowers white,*** 1.7–2.5 cm (0.7–1 in) across, produced in May, June, or early July (usually about 2–3 weeks later than black raspberry) *in elongated 6–15-flowered clusters. Fruits globe- to short cylinder-shaped, to 2 cm (0.8 in) long,* juicy, sweet, black at maturity; maturing in late July or August. **Harvest and preparation:** See BRAMBLES (preceding).

Black raspberry   *Rubus occidentalis*

Habitat: disturbed areas, especially margins of woodlands, ravines, fields, thickets; sometimes in full shade. **Identification:** shrub with upright to spreading *branches, sometimes arching to ground; stems with scattered, straight or curved, stout spines. Leaves* alternate, deciduous, compound, each leaf *with 3– 5 leaflets,* terminal leaflets broadest near base, pointed at tip, sharp and irregularly toothed along margin; lateral leaflets smaller, *whitish beneath.* Flowers white, produced in May or June in 3- to 7-flowered nearly flat clusters. *Fruits purplish-black to black, 0.8–1.2 cm (0.3–0.5 in) across,* rounded or nearly so, *easily separated as a unit* from fruiting stalk and base, juicy, sweet, maturing in June or July. **Harvest and preparation:** See BRAMBLES (preceding).

California blackberry: fruits (Ross).

Smooth sumac: fruiting branch (Dykeman). Fruits (Elias).

California blackberry *Rubus ursinus*

Habitat: disturbed sites, along trails, roads, canyons, fields, open woodlands; common at lower elevations, below 1,000 (3,200 ft). **Identification:** *shrub, often low; branches spreading to trailing along ground;* armed with slender, slightly flattened spines. *Leaves* alternate, deciduous, *usually 3-parted (trifoliolate),* sometimes simple; *leaflets broadest near base, 6–12 cm (2.4–4.7 in) long, 4–10 cm (1.6–4 in) wide,* coarsely toothed, occasionally shallowly lobed. Flowers white, produced in elongate, loose, 3–12-flowered clusters; each 1–3 cm (0.4–1.2 in) across. *Fruits short cylinder-shaped to nearly cone-shaped, 1–2 cm (0.4–0.8 in) long, black at maturity,* juicy, sweet. **Harvest and preparation:** See BRAMBLES (preceding).

Smooth sumac *Rhus glabra*

Also edible autumn

Habitat: common and widespread; abandoned farmlands, fields, margins of woodlands, along streams. **Identification:** shrub or small *tree* to 7 m (23 ft) *with smooth stout branches* and open rounded crown. *Leaves* alternate, deciduous, *featherlike (pinnate) compound, with 11–31 leaflets,* leaflets usually lance-shaped, 5–9.5 cm (2–3.7 in) long, 1.2–3 cm (0.5–1.2 in) wide, long pointed at tip, sharply toothed along margin, dark shiny green above, whitish beneath. Male and female flowers on different plants, produced in dense, cone-shaped clusters 10–25 cm (4–10 in) long. *Fruits produced in autumn in large cone-shaped clusters, each fruit berrylike, rounded, 3–5 mm (0.1–0.2 in) in diameter, dark red, fuzzy.* **Harvest:** Pick fruit clusters when glazelike bloom appears on bright red berries. Lick like lollipop for delicious lemony thirst quencher. Flavor is washed out by rains more quickly than in STAGHORN SUMAC. **Preparation:** same as STAGHORN SUMAC. Make delicious jelly from 2 cups sumac extract (see beverage under STAGHORN SUMAC) and 2 cups elderberry juice. Boil juice and extract with 1 pkg powdered pectin. Add 5 cups sugar. Bring to hard boil, boil 1 min, remove from heat, skim, pour into jars, seal. For other recipes, see SQUAW-BUSH and STAGHORN SUMAC (next). See *caution* under STAGHORN SUMAC. **Related edible species:** STAGHORN SUMAC, SQUAWBUSH, plus lemonade sumac *(R. integrifolia)* of southern California and sugar bush *(R. ovata)* of the Southwest. **Poisonous look-alikes:** Poison sumac *(Toxicodendron vernix)* grows in wet areas and has white fruits. Avoid white fruited sumacs. POISON IVY and poison oak *(T. diversiloba)* are in the sumac genus.

Squawbush
Rhus trilobata

Also edible autumn

Habitat: foothills, canyons, slopes, washes, often in dry rocky soils. **Identification:** *shrub* to 2 m (6.6 ft) with numerous spreading branches and *densely hairy twigs, with strong odor when broken.* Leaves alternate, deciduous, *with 3 leaflets* (trifoliolate), occasionally 1 leaflet, leaflets broadest near base or tip, 1–3 cm (0.4–1.2 in) long, nearly as wide, *with large rounded teeth along margin,* rounded at tip, hairy. Flowers yellow, small, densely clustered in short spikes in spring. *Fruits berrylike, rounded, 4–6 mm (0.2 in) in diameter, red, hairy, sticky.* **Harvest:** Gather fruits from end of August. **Preparation:** Suck on fresh fruits for refreshing sour taste. For beverage and jelly see SMOOTH SUMAC (preceding) and STAGHORN SUMAC (next). For syrup combine ½ cup dried, ground, sifted berries with 1⅓ cups water and ¾ cup honey (or 1 cup sugar). Cover, boil mix 30 sec, reduce heat, simmer 15 min. Uncover and boil until mix thickens, stirring constantly. Pour into jar and refrigerate for further thickening. Good dessert topping or spread on bread. If fresh berries are used, crush, simmer, and strain before adding honey or sugar. Then boil and complete process as above. See *caution* under STAGHORN SUMAC. **Related edible species:** See SMOOTH SUMAC. **Poisonous look-alikes:** Leaves resemble those of poison oak *(R. diversiloba)* and POISON IVY, both with white fruits. See also SMOOTH SUMAC.

Staghorn sumac
Rhus typhina

Also edible autumn, winter

Habitat: woodland margins, fencerows, roadsides, old fields, streambanks. **Identification:** shrub or small *tree* to 10 m (33 ft) *with thick densely hairy branches and twigs.* Leaves alternate, deciduous, featherlike (pinnate) compound, 40–60 cm (16–24 in) long, with 11–31 leaflets, leaflets usually lance-shaped, 5–12 cm (2–4.7 in) long, 2–4 cm (0.8–1.6 in) wide, sharply toothed along margin. Male and female flowers on same or separate trees, produced in crowded cone-shaped clusters. *Fruits produced in dense, cone-shaped clusters 10–20 cm (4–8 in) long; each fruit berrylike, rounded, 3–5 mm (0.1–0.2 in) in diameter, densely covered with dark red hairs.* **Harvest:** Pick fruit clusters late summer to autumn when deep red and fruits have developed strong lemony taste. Dense hairs on fruits prevent rain from penetrating cluster and washing out all malic acid flavor so fruits are usable though less potent through winter. Dry some clusters for winter use. **Preparation:** For beverage separate fruits from twigs. Steep in near boiling water (no less than 1 cup fruits to 1 qt water) for at least 15 min. Strain through cloth, dilute, sweeten to taste. Drink hot or cold but in moderation; some people show allergic reaction. Using whole heads of fruits will include small arthropods within them, and twigs may add slight bitterness. See other uses under SMOOTH SUMAC and SQUAWBUSH (preceding). **Related edible species:** SMOOTH SUMAC and SQUAWBUSH, and lemonade berry *(R. integrifolia)*. **Poisonous look-alikes:** See SMOOTH SUMAC.

Squawbush: fruiting branch (Dykeman).

Staghorn sumac: fruiting branch, left (Dykeman). Fruits (Elias).

Screwbean mesquite: fruiting branch (Feldman).

Glandular mesquite: fruiting tree (Feldman). September branches (Hutchins).

Screwbean mesquite

Prosopis pubescens

Also edible autumn

Habitat: gullies, washes, stream banks, riverbottoms, floodplains. **Identification:** shrub or *small spreading tree* to 10 m (33 ft) with slender *branches armed with pair of sharp spines at each leaf base. Leaves* alternate, deciduous, *twice compound and featherlike* (bipinnate), with 1 or 2 pairs of side branches (pinnae), each 3.8–5 cm (1.5–2 in) long, composed of 5–8 pairs of small leaflets. Flowers produced in densely flowered cylinder-shaped spikes 5–7.5 cm (2–3 in) long, each flower greenish-white to yellow, 3–4 mm (0.2 in) long. *Fruits* are *spiral twisted pods 3–5 cm* (1.2–2 in) *long,* brown, hairy, becoming hard and tough at maturity. **Harvest:** Gather and clean immature pods, the younger the tenderer. **Preparation:** Boil until soft or cook with other vegetables. The pods can be boiled down to make a sweet syrup with many uses. **Related edible species:** GLANDULAR MESQUITE (next) and mesquite (*P. veluntina*). **Poisonous lookalikes:** slightly similar to CORALBEAN, which has poisonous seeds.

Glandular mesquite

Prosopis glandulosa

Also edible autumn

Habitat: desert valleys, open range, grazing lands where plant becomes a pest. **Identification:** shrub or small spreading tree to 8 m (26 ft) with slender *branches that have paired, sharp-pointed spines where each leaf is attached. Leaves* alternate, deciduous, *twice compound and featherlike* (bipinnate), with 1 pair of side branches (pinnae), each 12–20 cm (4.7–8 in) long and composed of 7–18 pairs of leaflets. Flowers produced from May to August in densely flowered, narrow, cylinder-shaped clusters; each flower yellow, 3–4 mm (0.2 in) long. *Fruits long, narrow, straight pods 10–25 cm* (4–10 in) *long,* rounded, slightly constricted between seeds. **Harvest:** Gather flower clusters as they open and fruits as they ripen during summer. **Preparation:** Suck sugar-rich nectar from newly open flowers. The yellowish gelatinous to mealy pulp surrounding seeds in mature pods contains up to 30% sugar and can be eaten fresh. Make beverage by boiling clean pods in fresh water and straining off residue. Dry pods, grind, mix with little water to form dry, mealy dough; bake in sun for several hours or over very low heat. Soak seeds in water several hours for lemon-flavored drink or grind dry seeds into meal and use to make porridge. Discard those seeds infested with larvae of bean beetle. **Related edible species:** SCREWBEAN MESQUITE (preceding) and mesquite *(P. veluntina)*. **Poisonous look-alikes:** may resemble CORALBEAN, which has toxic seeds.

American elder, Common elder *(Also edible spring)*   *Sambucus canadensis*

Habitat: rich moist soil of woodland margins, stream and river banks, fencerows and right-of-ways. **Identification:** mainly shrubby, 1–4 m (3–13 ft), with upright to spreading branches and broad rounded crown. *Leaves opposite,* deciduous, featherlike (pinnate) *compound,* 15–25 cm (6–10 in) long, composed of 5–11 *leaflets,* each leaflet broadest near base to uniformly wide, 6–12 cm (2.4–4.7 in) long, 2–4 cm (0.8–1.6 in) wide, pointed, toothed, dark shiny green. *Twigs* with prominent *white pith. Flowers* white, small, in branched, *round or flat-topped showy clusters* in late spring or early summer. *Fruits berrylike,* rounded, 4–6 mm (0.2 in), *deep purple,* juicy, 3-seeded, in large clusters, maturing in mid to late summer. **Harvest:** When flowers are fully open, pick whole clusters or shake petals of old flowers into container. When fruit is deep purple, pick whole clusters or strip berries from bush. **Preparation:** Dip flower cluster in fritter batter and deep fry; dust with sugar and sprinkle with orange juice. Add cup of blossoms to pancake batter. Extract juice from fresh fruit by simmering mix of 1 cup water per 1 qt mashed berries 20–25 min; strain through cloth. Sweetened juice good with tart juices. Use juice with (STAGHORN SUMAC) extract in jelly. Fresh fruit has rank flavor; improves with drying; use dried fruit for pies and breads. Dry fruit in sun or warm attic; before using stew in little water. Flowers and fruit excellent for wine. Fruits high in vitamin C. *Warning:* Roots, stems, leaves, unripe fruits are somewhat toxic. **Related edible species:** BLUE ELDER (next). **Poisonous look-alikes:** See BLUE ELDER.

Blue elder *(Also edible spring)*   *Sambucus cerulea*

Habitat: stream banks, gullies, washes, margins of fields, woodlands, pastures. **Identification:** shrub or small tree with broad rounded crown. Leaves *opposite,* deciduous, featherlike (pinnate) *compound,* 12–18 cm (4.7–7.1 in) long, composed of 5–9 *leaflets,* leaflets broadest at middle to uniformly wide, 5–15 cm (2–6 in) long, 1.2–5 cm (0.5–2 in) wide, long-pointed at tip, coarsely-toothed, bright green above. *Flowers* tiny, yellowish-white, produced in spreading, *many-flowered, flat-topped clusters* in late spring or early summer. *Fruits* in clusters, each *berrylike,* rounded, 6–10 mm (0.2–0.4 in), *dark blue to nearly black,* juicy, maturing in mid to late summer. **Harvest:** Flowers in early summer, fruits in late summer, can be eaten raw or dried like raisins. **Preparation:** Prepare tea from blossoms. For jelly, wash berries, partially crush, cover with water, cook over low heat 10 min. Pour contents into wet jelly bag and collect juice; do not squeeze bag. Add 2 cups elderberry juice to 3 cups apple juice prepared in similar manner. Heat to boil, add 1 pkg pectin; stir until dissolved. Bring to rapid boil, add 6 cups sugar. Stir until rolling boil cannot be stirred down; continue for 1 min. Pour mix into prepared jelly jars; cover with ¼ in paraffin; seal with lid. For other uses see AMERICAN ELDER (preceding). **Related edible species:** AMERICAN ELDER, Mexican elder *(S. mexicana),* and black berried elder *(S. melanocarpa).* **Poisonous look-alikes:** Red fruited elder *(S. pubens)* of East and Midwest somewhat toxic. Pacific elder *(S. callicarpa)* bitter but not poisonous.

American elder: fruiting branches (Elias). Flowers (NYBG).

Blue elder: fruiting bush and fruits (Kavasch).

Singleleaf pinyon pine: branch with immature cone (Dykeman).

Sugar pine: branches with cones (McNeal).

Digger pine: leader and cones (McNeal).

Singleleaf pinyon pine   *Pinus monophylla*

Habitat: lower mountain slopes, foothills, canyons from 650–2,350 m (2,100–7,800 ft) elevation; often growing with junipers. **Identification:** small, spreading tree with rough, irregularly furrowed, dark brown bark. *Leaves (needles) 1 per sheath, 2.5–5 cm (1–2 in) long, sharp-pointed, stiff, often curved toward branches,* yellowish-green to gray-green; only native North American pine with single leaves. Fruits hard, egg-shaped cones 5–7.6 cm (2–3 in) long, composed of thick, stiff, light brown, blunt scales, each scale bearing 2 large, *egg-shaped, brown, wingless seeds 1.8–2 cm* (0.7–0.8 in) *long.* Trees produce moderate to large cone crops every 2–3 yr. Each cone requires 2 growing seasons to mature. **Harvest and preparation:** Gather second year cones in August or September. Oily seeds, rich in protein and oils, have nutty taste and can be eaten fresh. Thin shell can be cracked with teeth. Roast nearly ripe cones to facilitate seed removal and improve flavor. Store cones or seeds for later use, especially after roasting. Several cones tossed into campfire coals 10–20 min yield an excellent snack. Carry roasted cones or seeds in backpack for trail snack. If large numbers of seeds are available, roast and grind into meal and use in breads, soups, or mixed with cornmeal or flour. **Related edible species:** SUGAR PINE, DIGGER PINE, PINYON PINE, Mexican pinyon pine *(P. cembroides).* **Poisonous look-alikes:** none.

Sugar pine   *Pinus lambertiana*

Habitat: mountain slopes from 750–3,000 m (2,500–9,850 ft) elevation. **Identification:** tall trees to 65 m (213 ft) with tall, straight trunk and thick, deeply, irregularly furrowed, dark, reddish-brown to purplish-brown bark. *Leaves (needles) 5 per sheath, 8.8–10 cm (3.5–4 cm) long, stout, stiff, deep bluish-green and marked with silvery lines. Fruits large woody cones, 27–46 cm (10.6–18 in) long,* to 12 cm (4.7 in) in diameter; seeds nearly egg-shaped to football-shaped, 1.2–1.5 cm (0.5–0.6 in) long, dark chocolate-brown, nearly black, winged. **Harvest:** See SINGLELEAF PINYON PINE (preceding). *Note:* Cones with seeds are difficult to obtain because of height of the trees. **Preparation:** same as for SINGLELEAF PINYON PINE. **Related edible species:** Coulter pine *(P. coulteri),* DIGGER PINE (next), and the PINYON PINES. **Poisonous look-alikes:** none.

Digger pine   *Pinus sabiniana*

Habitat: foothills, lower mountain slopes from 20–1,000 m (66–3,300 ft) elevation, often found with BLUE OAK. **Identification:** medium-size spreading tree to 15 m (50 ft) with short, thick trunk, soon branching, with irregular, scaly, dark brown to almost black bark. *Leaves (needles) 3 per sheath, 17–43 cm (6.7–17 in) long, slender, flexible, dull blue-green. Fruits large 15–25 cm (6–10 in) long,* to 18 cm (7 in) broad, light reddish-brown, *scales thick, each armed with clawlike spine;* seeds 1.7–2 cm (0.7–0.8 in) long, egg-shaped, with hard, dark brown to almost black shell. **Harvest and preparation:** same as for SINGLELEAF PINYON PINE. **Related edible species:** PINYON PINES, Coulter pine *(P. coulteri),* SUGAR PINE (preceding). **Poisonous look-alikes:** none.

JUNIPER GENUS   *Juniperus*

The 13 species of junipers native to North America are mostly common widespread trees and shrubs. These evergreen conifers are more abundant in the drier western states, although eastern redcedar and southern redcedar are prevalent in the eastern U.S. All junipers provide excellent cover for small game and food for many birds. Only three species, all western, are recommended for their edible fruits and then primarily as a survival food. The stems, leaves, and fruits contain varying amounts of resins which affect fragrance and taste.

Rocky Mountain juniper   *Juniperus scopulorum*
Also edible autumn, winter

Habitat: bluffs, ridges, cliffs, dry rocky hillsides from sea level to 3,000 m (9,850 ft) elevation. **Identification:** large evergreen shrub or small tree to 15 m (49 ft) with reddish-brown to gray scaly bark separating in long narrow strips. *Leaves tiny, scalelike, opposite each other,* closely pressed against branchlets, 2–4 mm (0.1 in) long with tiny gland on back, *pale green to grayish green,* resinous. Male and female flowers on separate trees in spring, inconspicuous and easily overlooked. *Fruits small, fleshy, sweet, berrylike cones, nearly rounded, 6–9 mm (0.2–4 in) in diameter, bright blue, maturing in 2 seasons,* containing 1–2 seeds. **Harvest:** Gather ripe berries from summer to early winter. Use fresh or dry and store for later use. **Preparation:** Although high in sugars, ripe fruits have an unpleasant resinous taste, so fresh fruits become strictly survival fare. Use a few fresh berries as substitute for sage in flavoring meats. Roast dried fruits, grind, and use as coffee substitute. **Related edible species:** UTAH JUNIPER and CALIFORNIA JUNIPER (next). **Poisonous look-alikes:** Take care in identification of junipers. Fruits of most species have such high resin content that they are unpalatable or may cause stomach upset.

California juniper   *Juniperus californica*
Also edible autumn, winter

Habitat: dry slopes, canyons, desert slopes from 125–1,350 m (410–4,500 ft) elevation. **Identification:** large shrub or small tree with fluted and ridged trunk and reddish-brown to ash-gray bark that splits into long, loose, shredding strips. *Leaves tiny, scalelike, arranged in 3s,* overlapping and closely pressed against branchlets, 2–4 mm (0.1 in) long, with tiny gland on back, light yellowish-green. Male and female flowers on separate trees in spring, inconspicuous and easily overlooked. *Fruits* are *leathery, berrylike cones, almost rounded, 10–16 mm (0.4–0.6 in) in diameter, dry, sweet, not resinous, light reddish-brown,* maturing in 2 seasons, each containing 1–3 seeds. **Harvest and preparation:** same as for ROCKY MOUNTAIN JUNIPER (preceding) except that nonresinous fruits are superior to those of other junipers as wild food source. **Related edible species:** UTAH JUNIPER (next), ROCKY MOUNTAIN JUNIPER. **Poisonous look-alikes:** same as for ROCKY MOUNTAIN JUNIPER.

Rocky mountain juniper: fruiting branch (Dykeman).

California juniper: fruiting branch (Webber, Jepson Herbarium).

Utah juniper: fruiting branch (Pawloski).

Sea grape: fruiting and flowering branches (Elias).

Utah juniper
Also edible autumn, winter

Juniperus osteosperma
(synonym: *J. utahensis*)

Habitat: mesas, mountain slopes, high plains, principally from 1,000–2,650 m (3,300–8,700 ft) elevation in dry rocky or gravelly soils. **Identification:** large *shrub* or small *bushy tree* to 8 m (26 ft) high with *furrowed ash-gray bark that shreds in long, loosely attached strips. Leaves* tiny, *scalelike, opposite and overlapping one another in 2s, closely pressed against branchlets,* 3–4 mm (0.1–0.2 in) long, usually gland-dotted on back, *sharp-pointed at tip, yellowish-green.* Male and female flowering cones usually produced in spring on separate trees, inconspicuous and usually overlooked. *Fruits small, leathery berries 6–9 mm* (0.2–0.4 in) *in diameter, nearly globe-shaped, reddish-brown, resinous, sweet,* with mealy texture, containing 1, rarely 2, seeds. **Harvest and preparation:** same as for ROCKY MOUNTAIN JUNIPER. **Related edible species:** CALIFORNIA JUNIPER and ROCKY MOUNTAIN JUNIPER (preceding). **Poisonous look-alikes:** same as for ROCKY MOUNTAIN JUNIPER.

Sea grape

Coccoloba uvifera

Habitat: beaches, along sea shores; Southern Florida, Bermuda, Bahama Islands, the West Indies. **Identification:** very distinctive large shrub or tree to 15 m (50 ft) with compact rounded crown, trunk short, covered with pale blotchy bark. *Leaves* alternate, simple, *persistent and appearing evergreen, 10–27 cm* (4–10.6 in) *long, 12–25 cm* (4.7–10 in) *wide, almost circular in outline,* rounded at tip, entire, heart-shaped at base, *thick, leathery,* dark shiny green above. Flowering clusters produced along narrow, elongate stalks to 30 cm (12 in) long. *Fruits crowded together in long, hanging clusters,* each fruit nearly rounded, 1.8–2.5 cm (0.7–1 in) long, greenish-white to purple, with thin, juicy flesh; seed hard, nutlike. **Harvest:** Since fruits do not ripen uniformly, spread sheet under bush and shake branches vigorously. Ripe fruits will fall while green ones persist in cluster. **Preparation:** best used for jelly. Partially crush 2 qt clean ripe fruits with ½ cup water and cook for 20 min. Strain juice through jelly bag. Boil juice with equal amount of sugar until jelling point is reached. Skim off foam, pour into sterilized jars, seal with paraffin. **Related edible species:** dove plum *(C. diversifolia)* of coastal southeastern Florida, but not a recommended substitute for sea grape. **Poisonous look-alikes:** none.

California laurel, California bay
Umbellularia californica
Also edible autumn, spring

Habitat: lower mountain slopes, hillsides, flatlands, in variety of soils; Pacific coastal regions and western slopes of Sierra Nevada. **Identification:** small to medium-size tree to 20 m (66 ft) with thin, dark brown bark. *Leaves* alternate, simple, *evergreen,* 8.6–13 cm (3.4–5.1 in) long, lance-shaped to broadest near middle, usually pointed at tip, *entire, dark green and shiny, leathery, with spicy odor when crushed.* Flowering clusters flat-topped, containing 4–9 flowers, each small, 1–1.4 cm (0.4–0.6 in) across, yellow. *Fruits resembling an olive,* globe-shaped to broadest near base, *2–2.6 cm* (0.8–1 in) *long,* slightly fleshy, green turning yellowish-green or purplish-green at maturity, containing single large seed. **Harvest:** Pick young unblemished leaves, wash and leave in sun until thoroughly dry. Store in cool dry place for later use. Pick ripe fruits in late summer or autumn, remove and clean seeds. **Preparation:** Use dried leaves as substitute for bay leaves. California laurel is more potent, so cut recipe amount by ⅓ unless stronger flavoring is desired. Good in stews, chili, spaghetti sauce, soups. Roast seeds in campfire, split open, and eat or grind into flour for bread and other recipes. Indians of California used leaves in lodges to repel fleas. **Related edible species:** none. **Poisonous look-alikes:** none.

Pawpaw, Papaw
Asimina triloba
Also edible autumn

Habitat: river valleys and bottomlands, usually in deep, rich, moist soils; grows in association with sweetgum, swamp chestnut, black gum, cherrybark oak. **Identification:** large shrub or small tree with thin, smooth bark (dark brown with gray blotches) 3–12 m (10–40 ft) tall. Leaves alternate, deciduous, simple, 18–30 cm (7–12 in) long, 8–14 cm (3.2–5.5 in) wide, usually broadest near tip, entire along margin, papery textured, light green. Flowers *green turning deep purple, produced in spring along stems of previous year, bell-shaped,* with 3 sepals, 6 thick, almost rounded petals 2–2.6 cm (0.8–1 in) long. Fruits irregular, cylinder-shaped, 4–10 cm (1.6–4 in) long, aromatic, green turning yellow then black and fleshy at maturity; mature in late summer or early autumn. **Harvest:** when fruits mature or while still green but full size; store in cool place (safe from small animals) until ripe. **Preparation:** Tasty sweet pulp of fruit can be eaten raw. Cook creamy, custardlike pulp, minus seeds and skin, and use in puddings, breads, ice cream. *Caution:* Fruits disagree with some people. **Related edible species:** dwarf pawpaw (*A. parviflora*). **Poisonous look-alikes:** none.

California laurel: flower and fruiting branch (U. of Cal., Davis).

Pawpaw: flowering branch (Folkerts). Fruiting branch (Elias).

White mulberry *(Also edible spring)*   *Morus alba*

Habitat: introduced and cultivated tree that now grows wild along fencerows, roadsides, margins of abandoned fields, and in woodlands. **Identification:** medium-size tree with widespreading, rounded crown and thick, irregularly furrowed, light to dark gray to yellowish-brown bark and *milky sap. Leaves* alternate, deciduous, simple, *6–16 cm (2.4–6.3 in) long, 3–8 cm (1.2–3.2 in) wide, broadest near base,* pointed at tip, *unlobed or 2–3 lobed, sharply toothed along margin.* Male flowers tiny, clustered on short spikes; female flowers tiny, clustered in round heads, both appearing in spring on new growth. *Fruits globe-shaped to short cylindrical, 1–2 cm (0.4–0.8 in) long, blackberrylike, fleshy, white to pinkish at maturity* (June–July). **Harvest and preparation:** Pick fruits as they ripen from late May through July. Fully ripe berries may be shaken from tree onto plastic sheets but tend to be very syrupy and too sweet for most palates. Dry like raisins for breads, cookies, and puddings. Use plastic or aluminum screen supported so air can reach all sides of fruit. If solar drying, protect from dew condensation at night. Dry until crushed fruit lacks any watery juice. Drying time: bright sun, 2 days; warm attic, 4 days; warm oven, 10–15 hr. Store dried berries in sealed containers. Afghans grind dried fruit with almonds for nutritious combination. Substitute any other type of nut, roll small balls of ground mix in confectioner's sugar, eat as candy. Pick shoots and prepare as RED MULBERRY (next). **Related edible species:** RED MULBERRY, Texas mulberry *(M. microphylla),* black mulberry *(M. nigra).* **Poisonous look-alikes:** none; see RED MULBERRY caution.

Red mulberry *(Also edible spring)*   *Morus rubra*

Habitat: river valleys, floodplains, lower slopes of hills, usually in rich, moist soils. **Identification:** small to medium-size tree with broad, rounded crown and irregularly fissured, dark reddish-brown bark and *milky sap. Leaves* alternate, deciduous, simple, *7.5–10 cm (3–4 in) long, 5–5.8 cm (2–2.3 in) wide, broadest near base to almost rounded, unlobed or 1–3-lobed, heart-shaped at base, pointed at tip, with coarse teeth along margin, with whitish hairs on lower surface.* Male flowers tiny, crowded together in slender, hanging clusters; female flowers tiny, crowded in broader, elongated clusters. *Fruits cylinder-shaped, blackberrylike, 2.2–3 cm* (1–1.2 in) *long, fleshy, red turning dark purple to almost black, sweet,* maturing from May to July. **Harvest and preparation:** Pick ripe fruit from ladder, or spread tarps beneath tree and shake limbs. Delicious as picked or with cream. Do not let persistent small stem and axis of fruit bother you. For beverage mash and squeeze fruit through cheesecloth or use electric juicer or blender. Add sweetener and lemon juice to taste. Serve with ice and, if desired, club soda. Also good for pies, jams, jellies. Use like other berries in breads, muffins, cakes. Pick shoots as leaves are beginning to unfold. Boil 20 min, drain, add butter and seasoning. *Caution:* Raw shoots and unripe fruits contain hallucinogens. **Related edible species:** WHITE MULBERRY (preceding), Texas mulberry *(M. microphylla),* black mulberry *(M. nigra).* **Poisonous look-alikes:** none.

White mulberry: flowering branch (NYBG). Fruiting branch (Elias).

Red mulberry: fruiting branch (Elias).

American plum: flowering branch (Weber). Fruiting branch (Elias).

Flatwood plum: flowering and fruiting branches (Anderson).

American plum, Wild plum

Prunus americana

Habitat: common, mixed deciduous woodlands, along streams, fencerows, margins of fields. **Identification:** shrub or small tree to 11 m (36 ft) with spreading crown and *spiny* branches. *Leaves* alternate, simple, deciduous, *6–10 cm* (2.4–4 in) *long, 3.5–4.5 cm* (1.4–1.8 in) *wide, with double row of sharp pointed teeth along margin,* dark green and smooth. *Flowers produced 2–5 per cluster* in early spring, like cherry blossoms, each with 5 rounded, *white* petals 9–12 mm (0.4–0.5 in) long. *Fruits* solitary or 2–4 per cluster, each *rounded or nearly so, 1.8–2.5 cm* (0.7–1 in) *in diameter, orange to red,* juicy. **Harvest:** ripe fruits in mid to late summer. **Preparation:** Boil unripe fruits with sugar for emergency food. Use fresh ripe fruits in any cultivated plum recipes. Especially good in jams and jellies. For plum butter, puree pulp and skins after extracting juice for jelly. Blend with equal amount of maple sugar or honey in crock or bean pot and bake at 165°C (330°F) for 3 hr with occasional stirring. Seal in hot, sterilized jars. For jam add ½ cup water to each 2 cups raw pitted fruit. Boil until skins are tender, 10–15 min. Add 1 cup sugar for each cup of fruit pulp. Mix and cook about 15 min to jelly stage with constant stirring. Pour into sterilized jars and seal. For pie, use plums with equal volume of sweeter fruit such as peaches and use basic pie recipe. **Related edible species:** several throughout the country, including BEACH PLUM, FLATWOOD PLUM (next), and cherries. **Poisonous look-alikes:** none. Pits and seeds contain hydrocyanic acid which can react with stomach acids to release highly poisonous cyanin.

Flatwood plum

Prunus umbellata

Habitat: coastal plain, piedmont; along rivers, in swamps and hammocks. **Identification:** small tree to 6 m (20 ft) with irregular rounded crown and reddish bark. *Leaves* alternate, simple, deciduous, *5–7 cm (2–2.8 in) long, 2.5–4 cm (1–1.6 in) wide, broadest at or above middle,* rounded to slightly heart-shaped at base, *with fine, sharp-pointed teeth along margin,* dark green and smooth. *Flowers 2–4 per cluster* in early spring before leaves appear, each with 5 *white* rounded petals. *Fruits* solitary or in small clusters, *rounded, 1.2–1.5 cm* (0.5 in) *in diameter, dark red to almost black,* sour, containing flattened stone. **Harvest:** Handpick fruits as they mature from June to September. **Preparation:** See AMERICAN PLUM (preceding), but use additional sugar as with BEACH PLUM. **Related edible species:** BEACH PLUM, AMERICAN PLUM, and several other species. **Poisonous look-alikes:** none.

Black cherry   *Prunus serotina*

Habitat: widely distributed; mixed hardwood forests, woodlands. **Identification:** tree to usually 20 m (66 ft), rarely taller, with rounded crown and dark reddish-brown to nearly black bark; inner bark with odor of almond extract. *Leaves* alternate, simple, deciduous, 5–15 cm (2–6 in) long, 2.5–4 cm (1–1.6 in) wide, narrow but widest near base to uniformly wide, *with numerous blunt teeth along margin,* dark green and shiny. *Flowers and fruits produced in narrow elongated clusters 10–15 cm* (4–6 in) *long,* each flower with 5 white rounded petals. *Fruits fleshy, rounded, 8–10 mm* (0.3–0.4 in) *in diameter, dark red to black at maturity* (late summer), juicy, enclosing egg-shaped stone, slightly bitter tasting. **Harvest:** Handpick fruit or if fully ripe shake loose onto tarp August through September. **Preparation:** Eat fresh as trail snack or with sugar and cream as dessert, though pits make eating an effort. Prepare jelly as described under COMMON CHOKECHERRY (next) but use 2 cups each of apple and cherry juice. Also use black cherries for brandied cherries, breads, beverages, pies, wine. For pie add 1½ cups sugar, 2 tbsp cornstarch or flour, and ¼ tsp salt to 1 qt pitted cherries (a pitter makes the task easier). Mix and pour into uncooked 9-in piecrust. Add top crust or lattice of pastry. Bake at 230°C (450°F) for 20 min, then reduce heat to 190°C (375°F) and bake 10 more min. Indians prepared and used dried black cherries as described under COMMON CHOKECHERRY. **Related edible species:** See COMMON CHOKECHERRY. **Poisonous look-alikes:** See COMMON CHOKECHERRY for details.

Common chokecherry   *(Also edible autumn)*   *Prunus virginiana*

Habitat: common and widespread; moist soils of roadsides, fencerows, woodland margins. **Identification:** shrub or small tree to 8 m (26 ft) with smooth usually reddish-brown bark. *Leaves* alternate, simple, deciduous, 5–10 cm (2–4 in) long, 2.5–5 cm (1–2 in) wide, uniformly wide to broadest near base, pointed at tip, *with numerous sharp teeth along margin,* dark green and smooth. *Flowers produced in short cylinder-shaped clusters 8–15 cm* (3.2–6 in) *long,* each with 5 white, rounded petals. *Fruits fleshy, rounded, 8–10 mm* (0.3–0.4 in) *in diameter, usually dark red or black,* juicy, enclosing egg-shaped stone. **Harvest:** Pick fruit from midsummer to October, depending on location. **Preparation:** Best use, aside from trail thirst quencher, is for jelly. Prepare juice by crushing 1 qt unpitted cherries in 1 cup water. Simmer, stirring about 30 min and strain out juice. Quarter several whole apples, cover with water, simmer until tender. Strain off juice. Combine 2 cups apple juice with 1 cup cherry juice. Add 4 cups sugar and stir until dissolved. Boil rapidly until jelly temperature is reached. Pour into sterilized jelly glasses and seal. Or use sour cherry jelly recipe accompanying pectin package. Indians ground whole fruits, leached poison from seeds, formed pulp into cakes, and dried them in sun for sauce and pemmican. **Related edible species:** BLACK CHERRY (preceding) and several other sweet and sour fruited species, with various ranges. **Poisonous look-alikes:** Autumn and wilted leaves and pits of fruits contain hydrocyanic acid. Do not eat them! Also, Carolina laurelcherry *(P. caroliniana)* fruits are somewhat toxic.

Black cherry: flowering branch (Dykeman). Fruiting branch (Elias).

Common chokecherry: fruiting branch (Elias).

Downy serviceberry: fruiting branch (Elias). Flowering branch and tree (Dykeman).

Saskatoon serviceberry: flowering and fruiting branches (Ross).

SERVICEBERRY GENUS
Amelanchier

There are about 25 species of serviceberries native to North America, Europe, Northern Africa, and Asia. In North America, they are small trees or shrubs that occur in deciduous forests and mountains, where their attractive white flowers announce spring. Many birds and wildlife eat the small fruits produced in summer.

Downy serviceberry
Amelanchier arborea
(synonym: *A. laevis*)

Habitat: woodlands, rocky slopes, river banks, and along swamps; often growing with OAK, hickory, tulip tree, SWEET BIRCH. **Identification:** shrub or *small tree* with rounded crown and thick, slightly ridged and furrowed, ash-gray to nearly black bark. *Leaves* alternate, deciduous, simple, 5–9 cm (2–3.5 in) long, 2.5–3.5 cm (1–1.4 in) wide, widest at or near middle, *finely toothed along margin. Flowers white, attractive,* produced in spring (February in South to May in North), each *with 5 strap-shaped petals 1–1.4 cm (0.4–0.6 in) long.* Fruits in clusters, each rounded, 6–10 mm (0.2–0.4 in) in diameter, red to dark purple, fleshy, containing 5–8 black seeds. **Harvest and preparation:** Pick berries when ripe, usually mid to late summer. Eat as picked. Use fresh in recipes for jelly, jam, pie; fresh or dried in breads. For fruit sauce, stew 3 cups berries with 1 cup sugar for about 20 min. Mix dried berries with dried beef and suet to form pemmicanlike product. **Related edible species:** SASKATOON SERVICEBERRY (next) and other less common species. **Poisonous lookalikes:** none.

Saskatoon serviceberry
Amelanchier alnifolia
(synonym: *A. florida*)

Habitat: mountain slopes, moist hillsides, prairies, margins of lakes and streams. **Identification:** shrub or small tree, sometimes forming thickets, with rounded crown and thin, smooth, or finely furrowed, brown bark. *Leaves* alternate, deciduous, simple, 2–6 cm (0.8–2.4 in) long, 2.5–4 cm (1–1.6 in) wide, broadest near base to uniformly wide, *entire near base, sharply and coarsely toothed along upper margin. Flowers showy, white, produced in early spring,* each with 5 *strap-shaped petals 0.9–1.5 cm* (0.4–0.6 in) long. Fruits in clusters, each rounded to egg-shaped, 6–11 mm (0.2–0.4 in) long, dark reddish-purple to almost black. **Harvest and preparation:** Fruits ripen in mid to late summer; eat raw or dried but better cooked. Use fruits in recipes calling for fruit, as in cakes, pies, jellies, puddings. To make jelly, wash fruits thoroughly, drain, partially crush, cover with water, and cook over low to medium heat until soft. Pour contents into wet jelly bag. For clear jelly do not squeeze bag. Simmer juice 5 min, removing any surface foam. Add sugar while stirring (1 cup juice to ⅔ cup sugar). Simmer 10–15 min or until mix shows sign of jelling. Pour mix into properly prepared jelly jars to within ¼ in of top. Cover with ¼ in melted paraffin. **Related edible species:** DOWNY SERVICEBERRY (preceding) and other less common species. **Poisonous look-alikes:** none.

Autumn

Autumn is the season for fruits and nuts. These come mainly from trees and shrubs that require a full growing season before flowers transform into mature seeds and fruits. Oaks, beech, hickories, walnuts, hawthorns, viburnums, and grapes are common sources and easy to identify. In autumn you can gather large quantities of edibles and consume them then or store them. The oaks, beech, walnuts, and hickories are cyclic in nut production, or mast crop. That is, a large mast crop is normally followed by two or three years of smaller crops. So one year you may encounter a large crop of hickory nuts and the next year run into the acorn bounty of oaks instead.

This is also the time to note or even map populations of native edible plants (other than nuts) for harvest the next year. Keep track of the edible populations, especially immature ones; and avoid overharvesting them. Many plant species have been seriously depleted by greedy collectors. On the other hand, if you harvest fruits and nuts, you don't destroy the trees and shrubs. They will live to produce again, and their offspring will eventually be producers too—especially if you plant a fruit or nut now and then.

Additional autumn edibles

Plants listed below have parts that are edible in autumn and at least one additional season. Descriptions and photos of these plants appear in a seasonal section other than "Autumn," as indicated.

Jerusalem artichoke
Also edible winter, spring

Helianthus tuberosus

Habitat: damp or rich thickets, waste areas, roadsides; often cultivated today as by Indians in past. **Identification:** perennial herb to 3 m (9.8 ft) tall, forming colonies; stems upright, rough-hairy, from a root system with elongated, fleshy, edible tubers 7.5–12.5 cm (3–5 in) long. *Leaves opposite or in whorls of 3 on lower part of stems, alternate above,* broadest near base, *to 25 cm* (10 in) *long, 6–15 cm* (2.4–6 in) *wide,* tapered at tip and base, *hairy above, rough, leathery.* *Flower heads yellow* with rounded central disc 1–2.5 cm (0.4–1 in) across, *10–20 ray flowers,* each about 4 cm (1.6 in) long, *several flower heads per plant, on slender stems from leaf bases on upper part of stems.* **Harvest:** Identify colonies in summer when in bloom; dig tubers from first frost through winter. **Preparation:** Peel or scrub tubers before using. Slice raw in salad, make potato salad, boil and mash, roast with meat, slice and fry. For pickles, peel and boil 3–4 min, cover with wine vinegar, age 3–5 weeks. Adapt to many potato and carrot recipes. Food value equal to potato. The carbohydrates are mostly inulin and suitable for low starch diets. **Related edible species:** other SUNFLOWERS (*Helianthus* species) produce edible seeds. **Poisonous look-alikes:** none.

Lotus lily, American lotus
Also edible spring, summer

Nelumbo lutea

Habitat: lakes, ponds, slow-moving streams, bays and tidal waters. **Identification:** *aquatic perennial herb;* roots large, thick with swollen tubers. *Leaves large,* 20–70 cm (8–28 in) across, circular, often *rising above water level, center depressed,* bluish-green; *leafstalk attached at center of blade,* variable in length, strong but flexible. *Flowers* solitary on long stalks, *showy,* 14–26 cm (5.5–10.2 in) across, *with numerous pale yellow petals* or petallike structures. *Fruits produced in large cone-shaped, flat-topped receptacles* raised above water level; each fruit dry, hard, nutlike, globe to egg-shaped, 1–2 cm (0.4–0.8 in) long. **Harvest:** Some part edible most of year. Pick unopened leaves and young stalks in spring. Pick seed receptacle either before or after seeds ripen during summer through autumn. Dig up tuberous root in autumn or early spring if you can overcome the difficulty of its deep water bed. **Preparation:** Leaves and young stalks are edible, but not exceptional, potherbs. Immature seeds are excellent raw, boiled, or roasted. Mature seeds are hard-shelled; crack shells before boiling to soft chestnutlike texture. Or roast *fresh* mature seeds, crack, and remove shells. Eat like nuts, or grind into meal and substitute for part of flour in bread and muffin recipes. Bake or boil tubers like sweet potatoes until tender. Peel and mash. To every cup add 1 tbsp butter, ¼ tsp salt, and a little hot milk. Beat to smooth texture. **Related edible species:** various species of YELLOW POND LILY (next) and water lily *(Nymphaea).* **Poisonous look-alikes:** none.

Jerusalem artichoke: flowers and tubers (Elias).

Lotus lily: receptacle with protruding fruits and flower (Feldman).

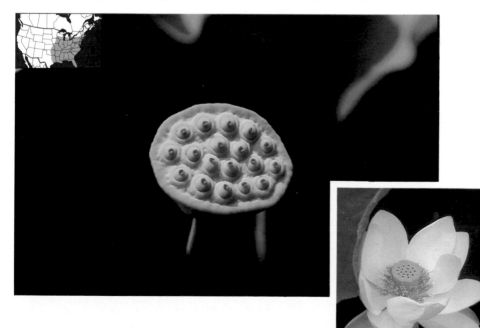

Yellow pond lily: flower prior to seed development (Elias).

Arrowhead: flower and whole plant (NYBG).

Yellow pond lily, Spatterdock
Also edible winter, spring, summer

Nuphar advena

Habitat: lakes, ponds, slow streams, swamps, tidal waters. **Identification:** *aquatic perennial herb;* roots (actually stems or rhizomes) large, thick, to 13 cm (5 in) in diameter, elongate, branching, covered with leaf scars. *Leaves large,* 10–40 cm (4–16 in) long, 5–16 cm (2–6.3 in) wide, broadest below middle, *deeply lobed at base to form U- or V-shaped cleft,* shiny green, *usually raised above water level,* sometimes floating; leafstalk thick, stout, attached at base of cleft. *Flowers* solitary on long stalks, *showy,* 3–10 cm (1–4 in) across, *with numerous yellow, green-tipped petals. Fruits broadly urn-shaped,* 2–5 cm (0.8–2 in) long, with short thick neck and flattened top, *ribbed,* green, containing numerous, yellowish-brown, small, egg-shaped seeds. **Harvest:** Cut fruits free of stalk as they ripen (late summer or fall). Air-dry until fruits pull apart to separate seeds. Dump seeds in bucket of water. After 5–6 hr good ones sink; dry in sun or warm oven. Loosen tuberous roots from mud in bottom of pond from autumn to spring. Indians used their toes. **Preparation:** Seeds store well. Pop seeds like popcorn or remove shells by parching over coals or in oven, pounding lightly to crack shells, and winnowing. Then boil nutmeats like rice or grind and use like cornmeal. Peel, slice, and boil roots in 2 water changes. Mash, season, and serve like potatoes or dry and use like flour. **Related edible species:** several other species of yellow pond lilies *(Nuphar)*, most important is cow lily *(N. polysepalum)* in West. **Poisonous look-alikes:** none.

Arrowhead, Duck potato, Wapato
Also edible winter, spring, summer

Sagittaria latifolia

Habitat: shores of lakes, ponds, streams, ditches, bogs, wet meadows; common and widespread. **Identification:** *perennial herb* 0.6–1.2 m (2–4 ft) high, with fibrous roots developing small tubers (potatolike) 0.5–5 cm (0.2–2 in) in diameter. *Leaves all at base,* blades 10–25 cm (4–10 in) long, 1–25 cm (0.4–10 in) wide, *arrowhead-shaped with long pointed lobes at base, leaf shape highly variable* from extremely narrow to very broad, smooth or hairy; leafstalks flexible, to 1 m (3.2 ft) long. Flowering stalk taller than leaves; *flowers in clusters of 3s along upper part of spike, each flower with 3 delicate, white petals.* Fruiting heads globe-shaped or nearly so, containing numerous flat, winged seeds. **Harvest:** Collect tubers from late summer through early spring, whenever there is no ice. Dislodge tubers from roots in mud beneath water with rake or hoe, or wade in as the Indians did and loosen them with your toes. Tubers will float to surface and are easily collected. **Preparation:** Tubers are edible but not always tasty raw; better cooked like potatoes. Bake or boil about 30 min until tender; peel after cooking. Serve topped with mixture of butter and lemon juice or STAGHORN SUMAC extract. Use in potato recipes. To dry tubers for storage, boil until tender, drain, slice about ½-in thick, dry thoroughly in sun or warm oven. Store in warm dry place. Before using soak 20 min; allow 20 min cooking time. **Related edible species:** several other arrowhead species *(Sagittaria)*; all have arrowhead leaves; PICKERELWEED has similar leaves but lacks tubers. **Poisonous look-alikes:** none.

WILD GRAPES   *Vitis*

North America has about 50 native species of grapes along with several introduced ones that now grow wild. While it is easy to identify a grape vine, determining grape species can be challenging. It is best to familiarize yourself with the grapes in your region and the variation in fruit quality. Grapes are climbing vines with large lobed or toothed leaves, numerous small flowers in elongate clusters, and then fruit bunches. Three of the more common grapes are described here. **Harvest:** Gather leaves in spring when young and tender but full grown. Collect fruits between August and October, depending upon species and region. **Preparation:** Boil leaves until tender, and serve with other vegetables. Check cookbook recipes for stuffed grape leaves. Most fresh grapes are too acid to eat in quantity. Best to make juice, jelly, preserves, pie, and wine. For jelly, use mixture of ripe and unripe (for pectin) fruits. Wash, drain, remove stems, and mash in kettle. Add small amount of water and cook until fruit comes apart, about 15–20 min. Strain juice through jelly bag. Prevent crystallization in jelly by letting juice sit overnight or cooking 1 cup tart apples with each 4 cups of grapes. Boil 4

Riverside grape   *Vitis riparia*
Also edible spring, summer

Habitat: stream and river banks, margins of woodlands, thickets. **Identification:** *large vine,* usually climbing; branches tough, rounded, becoming smooth, pith chambered. *Leaves* alternate, simple, deciduous, *12–20 cm* (4.7–8 in) *long,* 8–16 cm (3–6 in) wide, nearly circular in outline to broadest near base, *usually 3-lobed, long-pointed at tip,* coarsely toothed along margin, heart-shaped at base, smooth above, *hairy beneath.* Flowers tiny, produced in many-flowered, elongate clusters to 10 cm (4 in) long. Fruits are dense bunches of *berries,* each *rounded, 8–14 mm* (0.3–0.6 in) *in diameter, black with whitish bloom,* sour tasting. **Harvest and preparation:** See WILD GRAPES (preceding).

Frost grape   *Vitis vulpina*
Also edible spring, summer

Habitat: streams and river banks, low wetlands, thickets. **Identification:** *large vine,* often climbing; branches stout, rounded, becoming smooth, pith chambered. *Leaves* alternate, simple, deciduous, *10–18 cm* (4–7 in) *long, almost as wide,* very broad, widest near base to almost round, *usually unlobed or slightly 3-lobed,* pointed at tip, coarsely toothed along margins, heart-shaped at base, smooth above, smooth below except for junctions of major veins. Flowers tiny, produced in many-flowered, elongated clusters to 18 cm (7 in) long. Fruits are clusters of *berries,* each *rounded, 4–10 mm* (0.2–0.4 in) *in diameter, black,* sour tasting until frost, then sweet. **Harvest and preparation:** See WILD GRAPES (preceding).

cups juice with 4 cups sugar until jelling point is reached. Skim off foam, pour into sterilized jars, seal with paraffin. For pie, squeeze skins from 4 cups ripe grapes. Simmer pulp until it comes apart; sieve to remove seeds. Chop skins and combine with strained pulp, 1½ cups sugar, 2 tbsp flour, ¼ tsp salt, 1 tbsp lemon juice, 2 tbsp melted butter. Mix well and pour into unbaked pie shell. Fit and slit top crust. Bake at 205°C (400°F) for 30–40 min until crust is browned. For juice, use ripe fruit. Crush in kettle, heat and simmer for 30 min, but do not boil. Press through sieve and strain through jelly bag. Sweeten to taste. For wild grape butter, puree remaining pulp. Add equal amount to maple sugar or honey and blend in bean pot. Bake in preheated 160°C (320°F) oven, stirring occasionally, for 3 hr. Seal in sterilized jars. For emergency water source, cut off large vine and drain sap. **Poisonous look-alikes:** moonseed *(Memispermum canadense)* is a vine with simple entire or shallowly lobed leaves and clusters of black fruits resembling a bunch of grapes. The leafstalk is attached on the lower surface of the blade above the base (peltate) and the leaves are not coarsely toothed as those of most grapes. Single seed a flat crescent.

Riverside grape: fruiting branch (Elias).   **Frost grape:** fruiting branch (Elias).

California grape
Vitis californica

Also edible spring, summer

Habitat: stream and river banks, moist canyons, margins or clearings of forests. **Identification:** large *woody vine,* climbing; branches stout, rounded, with shredding bark, pith chambered. *Leaves* alternate, simple, deciduous, *6–14 cm* (2.4–5.5 in) *long,* nearly as wide, *circular in outline, nearly unlobed to 3-lobed,* short-pointed at tip, coarsely toothed along margin, deeply lobed at base, hairy above, dense cobweblike hairs beneath. Flowers tiny, produced in many-flowered, branched, elongated clusters. *Fruits* are dense bunches of *berries,* each rounded, *6–10 mm* (0.2–0.4 in) *in diameter, dark purple and covered with whitish bloom.* **Harvest and preparation:** See WILD GRAPES (preceding).

Wild potato vine
Ipomoea pandurata

Also edible spring, summer

Habitat: fields, fencerows, roadsides; dry, open or partly shaded areas. **Identification:** *perennial* trailing or slightly twining *vine,* 0.9–3.6 m (3–12 ft) long, *often purplish along stem,* branching, *from a large tuberous root to 9 kg* (20 lbs), *vertical, deep, slightly milky,* resemble a yam. *Leaves 4–8 cm* (1.6–3.2 in) *long, 3–8 cm* (1.2–3.2 in) *wide, heart-shaped, pointed at the tip, entire along the margins. Flowers* to 7.5 cm (3 in) across, with a *white* (sometimes purple-centered), *funnel-shaped* corolla, like a morning glory flower. Fruit a 2-chambered capsule 0.8–1.2 cm (0.3–0.5 in) long, broadest near the base and tapering to a tip. **Harvest:** Dig deep root any time when ground is not frozen, but best not in summer when starch level is low. Young roots are preferred to older, woody ones. **Preparation:** Boil or bake roots like sweet potatoes. When boiling, change water 2 or 3 times for bitter ones; others will not need changing. All roots have tough outer skins and require peeling. Serve with butter and seasonings. Some older roots may be too woody to use. Dry peeled slices of root for later use. **Related edible species:** Bush morning glory *(I. leptophylla)* of the West is variously described from excellent to nearly inedible. Edibility of other species has not been reported. **Poisonous look-alikes:** Flowers may resemble those of JIMSON WEED; however, JIMSON WEED is an upright herb with large, coarsely toothed leaves.

California grape: fruiting branch (Ornduff).

Wild potato vine: flower (Mohlenbeck).

Common barberry: fruiting branch (Dykeman).

Spice bush: fruiting branch (Elias). Flowers (NYBG).

Common barberry

Berberis vulgaris

Habitat: widely planted European shrub; also grows wild, the seeds spread by birds; disturbed woodlands, fencerows, fields, roadsides. **Identification:** shrub 1–3 m (3–10 ft) high, with rounded crown. Branches grooved, yellowish-red, turning gray by second season, with *3-forked sharp-spines*. *Leaves* alternate, simple, deciduous, *often crowded together on short shoots,* 2–4.8 cm (0.8–2 in) long, 0.8–2.4 cm (0.3–1 in) wide, *broadest above middle, rounded at tip, finely sharp-toothed along margin*. Flowers produced in spring, stalked, in 10–20-flowered, elongated, narrow clusters, each flower greenish-yellow. *Fruits in drooping clusters* in late summer or early autumn, *berries 8–12 mm* (0.3–0.5 in) *long, orange-red to scarlet*. **Harvest and preparation:** Pick fruits in autumn when full color has developed. For jelly, 4 cups crushed barberries, 2 whole oranges, chopped, 2 cups water, 1½ cups sugar, 1 pkg pectin. Combine berries, oranges, and water. Bring to boil, simmer until tender, about 20 min. Strain juice through cloth or jelly bag. Combine juice and sugar; bring to rolling boil. Add pectin; bring to boil. Pour into hot, sterilized jars; seal. Yields 3 pt. For straight barberry jelly, cook berries and extract juice. Boil juice to 105°C (200°F); pour into hot, sterilized jars; seal. Needs no pectin, very tart. Juice also good in sauces and beverages where tartness is needed. To relieve thirst, chew a few leaves. **Related edible species:** red-fruited barberry *(B. haematocarpa),* southwestern U.S.; American barberry *(B. canadensis)*, southeastern U.S.; and other species. **Poisonous look-alikes:** none.

Spice bush

Lindera benzoin

Also edible winter, spring, summer

Habitat: rich woodlands, stream banks, especially in moist soils. **Identification:** shrub to 5 m (16.4 ft) high, with numerous, spreading to upright, smooth *branches, with spicy fragrance when broken*. Leaves alternate, simple, deciduous, 6–14 cm (2.4–5.5 in) long, 3–6 cm (1.2–2.4 in) wide, broadest near or above middle, long-pointed at tip, entire along margin, thin, smooth, bright green, stalked. *Flowers in early spring before leaves appear, yellow, small, produced in dense clusters along previous year's twigs. Fruits* produced in clusters, each *a berry,* widest at middle, rounded at end, *6–10 mm (0.2–0.4 in) long,* green turning *bright red at maturity*. **Harvest:** young leaves in spring; bark and twigs all year; fruits in late autumn before migrating flocks of birds eat them all. **Preparation:** For tea steep 15 leaves or handful of fresh twigs and bark in 4 cups boiling water for 15 min. Strain if necessary; serve with honey and milk for best flavor. Dry fruits thoroughly in warm oven. Grind and use as substitute for allspice. **Related edible species:** none. **Poisonous look-alikes:** none.

Desert hackberry, Spiny hackberry   *Celtis pallida*

Habitat: desert foothills and mesas at 450–1,050 m (1,500–3,500 ft). **Identification:** *shrub or small tree,* to 5 m (16 ft) tall, single or in thickets, *densely branched, twigs with many single or paired spines at base of leaves.* Leaves *simple, alternate, evergreen, broadest near or below the middle,* 2.5–7.5 cm (1–3 in) long, *unequal at base, toothed from mid margin to tip, rough upper surface.* Flowers in spring, small, greenish white, in long clusters at base of younger leaves. *Fruits single, fleshy,* 6–8 mm (0.2–0.3 in) diameter, *yellow to red-orange, sweet, containing 1 large seed.* **Harvest:** fruits in late September and October; crop frequently abundant if rain was sufficient. **Preparation:** Eat fresh or dried as snack. Dry whole or mashed and formed into small cakes; dry in sun or 100°C (212°F) oven. Store in dry place. For seedy jam, mash 6 cups fresh berries in saucepan with 2 cups sugar, 3 tbsp lemon juice, and ½ cup water. Bring to boil; reduce heat and simmer with stirring until thick. Ladle into sterilized jars and seal with paraffin. If seeds are annoying, grind fruit fine before cooking. Use fresh or dried fruits in baking. **Related edible species:** American hackberry *(C. occidentalis)* and several other species are edible; palatability depends on species and weather. **Poisonous look-alikes:** none.

ROSES   *Rosa*

There are about 35 species of roses native to North America and several introduced species that now grow wild on roadsides and disturbed sites. While it's easy to distinguish roses from other groups of plants, the distinctions among individual species are often difficult. Fortunately, all roses have edible parts although quality and size vary greatly. Roses are shrubs normally with spiny branches, and alternate featherlike (pinnate) compound leaves. The large attractive flowers have 5 petals, and many stamens and pistils. Four of the more common species are treated on upcoming pages. **Harvest and preparation:** Gather fruits (hips)

California rose   *Rosa californica*
Also edible winter, summer

Habitat: along streams, rivers, washes, and in moist canyons. **Identification:** shrub to 3 m (9.8 ft) tall with coarse, erect to nearly erect branches, armed with stiff, flattened, usually curved spines. Leaves alternate, deciduous, compound, each with 5–7 leaflets, leaflets broadest near base and gradually tapering to a pointed to blunt tip, 1.2–3.6 cm (0.5–1.4 in) long, about half as wide, with 1 or 2 rows of sharp teeth along margin, hairy. *Flowers in few-flowered clusters* in spring or summer, each with green smooth floral tube (hypanthium), narrow lance-shaped sepals, *5 white or pink petals 1.2–2.5 cm* (0.5–1 in) *long. Fruits* (hips), fleshy, *egg- to globe-shaped, 1.2–1.8 cm* (0.5–0.7 in) *in diameter, with distinct neck,* red, smooth. **Harvest and preparation:** See preceding. **Related edible species:** all native roses. **Poisonous look-alikes:** none.

Desert hackberry: fruiting branch (Cramer).

as they ripen in autumn (after frost) or during winter, wash and remove dried persistent flower parts from top of hips, then split open and remove seeds. Eat pulpy portion fresh or in jellies or sauces. Dry whole or halved cleaned fruits for later use (soak overnight in warm water) or finely grate or grind dried hips to yield a slightly fragrant powder rich in vitamin C and essential minerals. Sprinkle on hot breakfast cereals or use to make hot tea. Also wash young leaves, cut into small pieces, and dry for hot rose tea. Flower petals can be used in candy, tea, and jellies, but fruits are more nutritious.

California rose: fruits and flower (McNeal).

Wild rose: flowers (NYBG).

Sweetbrier rose: flower (Speas).

Wrinkled rose: fruits (Crow). Flower (Hardin).

Wild rose, Pasture rose *(Also edible winter, summer)* *Rosa carolina*

Habitat: open woodlands, margins of woodlands, fields, pastures, rocky outcrops. **Identification:** low shrub to 1.5 m (5 ft) high, with slender arching branches, with stiff hairs and armed with broad-based straight or curved spines, especially on lower half. Leaves alternate, deciduous, compound, each with 3–7, rarely 9, leaflets, leaflets usually broadest near middle to almost rounded, 1.6–3.8 cm (0.6–1.5 in) long, about half as wide, pointed to blunt at tip, *coarsely sharp-toothed along margin. Flowers* usually solitary and produced in spring or early summer, each *with glandular-hairy floral tube* (hypanthium), narrow lance-shaped sepals, and 5 *pink petals* 2–3.2 cm (0.8–1.3 in) long. *Fruits (hips)* fleshy, *nearly globe-shaped, 6–10 mm* (0.2–0.4 in) *in diameter,* red, containing several seeds. **Harvest and preparation:** See ROSES. **Related edible species:** all native roses. **Poisonous look-alikes:** none.

Sweetbrier rose *(Also edible winter, summer)* *Rosa eglanteria*

Habitat: disturbed sites such as roadsides, abandoned pastures and fields, edges of woodlands, fencerows. **Identification:** shrub to 3 m (9.8 ft) high, with large arching coarse branches, new branches with laterally flattened, broad-based, spines curved or straight. Leaves alternate, deciduous, compound, apple odor when crushed, each leaf with 7–9 leaflets, *leaflets* broadest near or above middle, 1–4 cm (0.4–1.6 in) long, pointed or blunt at tip, *doubly toothed and glandular along margin,* hairy. *Flowers* solitary or in few-flowered clusters from May to July, each with green, *smooth or sparsely hairy floral tube* (hypanthium), *featherlike* (pinnate) *glandular sepals,* and 5 pink petals 1.4–2.4 cm (0.6–1 in) long. *Fruits* (hips) fleshy, *elongate and broadest near middle, 1.5–2 cm* (0.6–8 in) *long,* red, containing several seeds. **Harvest and preparation:** See ROSES. **Related edible species:** all native roses. **Poisonous look-alikes:** none.

Wrinkled rose *(Also edible winter, summer)* *Rosa rugosa*

Habitat: introduced from Asia; grows wild along roadsides, in dunes, and near seashores. **Identification:** shrub to 2 m (6.6 m) tall, with coarse, arching *branches, densely covered with stiff hairs and stiff needle-shaped spines.* Plants forming dense clumps. *Leaves* alternate, deciduous, compound, each leaf with 5–9 leaflets, leaflets widest near or above middle, 2–5 cm (0.8–2 in) long, about half as wide, pointed to rounded at tip, with teeth curving downward (recurved) along margin, *dark green, deeply furrowed or wrinkled. Flowers* solitary or in few-flowered clusters in spring, summer, or early fall, each *with green, smooth floral tube* (hypanthium), *narrow spoon-shaped sepals, and 5 rose-purple to white petals* 2.5–5 cm (1–2 in) long. *Fruits* (hips) fleshy, *globe-shaped but depressed at top and bottom, 2–2.5 cm* (0.8–1 in) *in diameter,* red, *smooth,* containing many seeds. **Harvest and preparation:** See ROSES. **Related edible species:** all native roses. **Poisonous look-alikes:** none.

Highbush cranberry

Viburnum trilobum

Also edible winter

Habitat: stream banks, wet thickets, moist woodlands. **Identification:** Not a real cranberry, this is a *shrub,* upright, to 5 m (16.4 ft) high; branches upright to spreading, ash-gray with age. *Leaves* opposite, simple, deciduous, *6–12 cm* (2.4–4.7 in) *long, almost as wide,* broadest near base, *deeply 3-lobed,* long pointed at tip, coarsely toothed along margin, rounded to squared at base, dark green and sparsely hairy above, hairy beneath; *leafstalks with 1 or 2 small glands. Flowers produced in dense, many-flowered, round-topped clusters, with showy white sterile flowers on margin of flower cluster;* small sterile flowers in center. *Fruits berrylike,* rounded to egg-shaped, 8–14 mm (0.3–0.6 in) long, *bright red, translucent* when ripe, juicy, containing single flattened stone. **Harvest:** Fruits ripen in late summer but persist on shrub and become less sour through winter. To make sure your shrub is highbush cranberry and not its bitter look-alike, the introduced guelder rose *(V. opulus),* make a harmless taste test. Pick in fall and winter. **Preparation:** much the same as CRANBERRY except large seeds must be removed. While cooking add lemon or orange peel shavings to eliminate bad odor of berries. For sauce, cover several quarts of berries with water in kettle. Add outer peels of 2 lemons or oranges. Bring to boil and simmer 5 min. Mash thoroughly and simmer another minute or two. Force juice and pulp through coarse strainer to remove seeds. Add 1 pkg pectin to 4 cups strained fruit, bring to boil, and add 5 cups sugar. Boil again for 1 min and seal in sterile jars or refrigerate. If fruits are picked before first frost, pectin may not be needed. For juice and jelly, cook berries as above but strain through jelly bag. For juice, dilute and sweeten to taste. For jelly, proceed with 4 cups juice as for sauce. **Related edible species:** HOBBLEBUSH, NANNYBERRY, and SQUASHBERRY (next), and in the Pacific Northwest the cranberry tree *(V. pauciflorum).* **Poisonous look-alikes:** none.

Hobblebush

Viburnum alnifolium

Habitat: stream banks, moist woodlands, ravines. **Identification:** *shrub,* often spreading, to 3 m (9.8 ft) high, *branches spreading, some drooping and rooting in ground. Leaves* opposite, simple, deciduous, 10–24 cm (4–9.4 in) long, almost as wide, *broadest near base,* short-pointed at tip, heart-shaped at base, finely double toothed along margin, hairy beneath. *Flowers produced in many-flowered, round-topped clusters, with sterile flowers, each with showy pink or white petals 2–3.8 cm (0.8–1.5 in) wide on margin of flower cluster;* tiny fertile flowers in center. *Fruits berrylike, slightly flattened,* egg-shaped, 6–12 mm (0.2–0.5 in) long, *black,* containing single flattened stone. **Harvest:** fruits in autumn, generally only on shrubs in open area, not in dense woods. **Preparation:** same as NANNYBERRY (next). **Related edible species:** See NANNYBERRY. **Poisonous look-alikes:** none.

Highbush cranberry: fruiting branches (Elias). Flower cluster (Stevenson).

Hobblebush: flower cluster (NYBG). Fruiting branch (Elias).

Nannyberry: fruits and flower cluster (Dykeman).

Squashberry: fruiting branch (Clawson).

Nannyberry   *Viburnum lentago*

Habitat: swamps, stream banks, rocky hillsides, margins of woodlands. **Identification:** *shrub* or small tree to 10 m (33 ft) with short branching trunk and slender tough, dark reddish-brown branches. *Leaves opposite,* simple, deciduous, 5– 10 cm (2–4 in) long, 2.5–4 cm (1–1.6 in) wide, *broadest near base or middle,* occasionally rounded, with many fine, sharp teeth along margin, bright shiny green and smooth. *Flowers produced in dense, many-flowered, rounded heads to 12 cm (4.7 in) in diameter,* each flower white to cream, 5-lobed. *Fruits berrylike, rounded,* 8–12 mm (0.3–0.5 in) in diameter, *dark blue to black,* sweet, juicy, containing single flattened seed. **Harvest:** fruits when ripe in autumn as leaves are falling. **Preparation:** fruits good for trail snacks; flavor excellent, seeds a nuisance. For pudding add 1½ cups water to 1 qt fruits, boil for 5 min. Mash and work pulp through food mill. If pulp remains with seeds, scrape residue into small pan and add ½ cup water. Stir, mash, mill again. Yields about 1 cup pulpy syrup. Add 1 tbsp lemon rind, juice of ½ lemon, 1 cup sugar, ⅛ tsp cinnamon, ¾ cup water. Bring to boil and simmer 15 min. In separate pan combine ⅓ cup cornstarch with 1 cup cold water. Blend into fruit mixture. Cook slowly 15 min, pour into mold, and cool. Serve plain or with whipped cream. **Related edible species:** black haw *(V. prunifolium)*, northern wild raisin *(V. cassinoides)*, and HOBBLEBUSH (preceding); use fruits in same ways as for nannyberry. **Poisonous look-alikes:** none.

Squashberry   *Viburnum edule*
Also edible winter, summer

Habitat: stream banks, wet thickets, margins of woodlands, moist low woodlands. **Identification:** *shrub,* often sprawling, to 2.5 m (8 ft) high; stems usually spreading, smooth. Leaves opposite, simple, deciduous, 4–11 cm (1.6–4.3 in) long and wide, *broadly circular in outline, with 3 shallow lobes,* sharply and irregularly toothed along margin, squared to slightly heart-shaped at base, sometimes hairy beneath. *Flowers produced in loose, round-headed clusters 4–6 cm (1.6–2.4 in) across,* each flower milky white, 5-lobed. *Fruits berrylike, rounded,* 6–10 mm (0.2–0.4 in) in diameter, *red,* containing single flattened seed. **Harvest:** fruits similar to HIGHBUSH CRANBERRY but smaller and less acid. Pick in late summer through winter. **Preparation:** same as HIGHBUSH CRANBERRY, except juice does not require dilution for use as beverage. **Related edible species:** See HIGHBUSH CRANBERRY. **Poisonous look-alikes:** none.

Pinyon pine   *Pinus edulis*

Habitat: mesas, plateaus, lower mountain slopes, and foothills from 825–2,350 m (2,700–7,700 ft) elevation. Often occurs with JUNIPERS, GAMBEL'S OAK, and ponderosa pine. **Identification:** small, spreading, bushy tree with thin, irregularly furrowed, scaly ridged, gray to reddish-brown bark. *Leaves (needles) 2 per bundle* (rarely 1 or 3), *1.2–5 cm* (0.6–2 in) *long,* stiff, sharp-pointed, curved inward toward branches, bluish-green when young, turning yellowish-green with age. Fruits hard, short, egg-shaped cones 3.8–5 cm (1.5–2 in) long, composed of thick, blunt, yellowish-brown scales, each scale with 2 seeds. *Seeds egg-shaped, 1.2–1.4 cm* (0.5–0.6 in) *long, wingless,* pale yellow with reddish-brown markings, oily, sweet. **Harvest and preparation:** large cone crops produced every 3–4 yr. Gather ripe, almost open, cones in autumn. Store dry so that scales will separate to release seeds. Eat seeds fresh or after roasting 20–30 min. Roasting dries cones, facilitates seed removal, improves nutty flavor of seeds, and permits longer storage. Grind roasted nuts into meal. Seeds are rich in protein (14.5%) and fats and have high caloric content. **Related edible pines:** SINGLELEAF PINYON PINE, Mexican pinyon *(P. cembroides),* Parry pinyon *(P. quadrifolia).* **Poisonous look-alikes:** none.

OAKS   *Quercus*

This large genus of about 55 native trees and shrubs north of Mexico offers important food sources to wildlife and provides nuts edible to people as well. North American oaks are divided into two subgenera: the white oak group and the red/black oak group.

White Oak Group   *Quercus* subgenus *Quercus*

This large group of related oaks occurs in the Americas, Europe, and Asia. There are 32 native species north of Mexico. They are distinguished from other oaks by a combination of characteristics: leaves entire, toothed, or lobed but never bristle-tipped; acorns maturing at end of first growing season on current year's twigs, and inner surface of acorn shell lacking hairs. Four of the most common species are discussed on upcoming pages. **Harvest and preparation:** Gather acorns in autumn as they turn brown and fall. They are usually sweet and need no leaching to remove tannins (if any bitterness exists, process as NORTHERN RED OAK acorns). Store nuts in cool dry place or shell for immediate use. For grits, dry nutmeats in air or warm oven and grind coarsely. Use like chopped nuts. For meal, regrind grits to finer texture and redry in warm oven, stirring occasionally. Use in recipes under RED OAK group. For candy combine 2 cups sugar, 1 cup water, 1/8 tsp cream of tartar, and pinch of salt in small pan and boil until carmelization begins. Maintain liquid by placing in larger pan of boiling water. Dip dried whole nutmeats in syrup and place on wax paper to harden.

White oak   *Quercus alba*

Habitat: mixed deciduous forest in sandy, gravelly, loamy soils; widespread, often growing with hickories or other oaks. **Identification:** medium-size to tall

Pinyon pine: immature cones (Pawloski).

White oak: immature acorns (Elias).

Chestnut oak: immature acorn and flowering branch (Elias).

Gambel's oak: fruiting branch and tree (Dykeman).

Blue oak: mature acorns with dried leaves (Dykeman). Normal blue oak form foreground; weeping form background (Kruckeberg).

tree with broad round crown and thick, shallow to deeply furrowed, light ash-gray bark. *Leaves* alternate, deciduous, simple, *12–22 cm (4.7–8.7 in) long, 5–10 cm (2–4 in) wide, with 7–10 shallow to deeply rounded lobes along margin, bright green,* smooth. Fruits are *acorns* on current year's twigs, *1.2–2 cm (0.5–0.8 in) long,* widest near middle or base, light brown at maturity, *acorn cup bowlshaped, 8–12 mm (0.3–0.5 mm) deep, enclosing about ¼ of nut,* cup scales thick, warty; nutmeat sweet. **Harvest and preparation:** See WHITE OAK GROUP (preceding).

Chestnut oak
Quercus prinus

Habitat: mixed deciduous woodlands, especially dry to moist well-drained slopes and ridges. **Identification:** medium-size tree with broad, open, rounded crown and thick, *deeply furrowed,* dark brown to reddish-brown *bark. Leaves* alternate, deciduous, simple, *12–25 cm* (5–10 in) *long, 3.6–7.5 cm* (1.4–3 in) *wide,* broadest above middle, *coarsely and irregularly round-toothed along margin,* greenish-yellow. Fruits are *acorns 2.5–3.8 cm* (1–1.5 in) *long,* uniformly wide to broadest near base, acorn *cup deeply bowl-shaped to top-shaped, enclosing about half of nut;* cups scales thick, warty; nutmeat sweet. **Harvest and preparation:** See WHITE OAK GROUP (preceding).

Gambel's oak
Quercus gambelii

Habitat: dry foothills, canyons, lower mountain slopes, usually from 1,350–2,800 m (4,400–9,200 ft) elevation. **Identification:** shrub or small tree with rounded crown and thin, light gray to grayish-brown, rough, scaly bark. *Leaves* alternate, deciduous, simple, *8–16 cm* (3.2–6.3 in) *long,* 4.5–7.6 cm (1.8–3 in) wide, broadest above middle to uniformly wide, *with 5–9 moderately deep to deep lobes along margin,* leathery, *yellowish-green.* Fruits are *acorns* on current year's twigs, *2–2.5 cm* (0.8–1 in) *long,* nearly globe-shaped, *acorn cup* shallow to deeply bowl-shaped, *enclosing ¼ to ⅓ of nut,* scales thick; nutmeat sweet. **Harvest and preparation:** See WHITE OAK GROUP (preceding).

Blue oak
Quercus douglasii

Habitat: interior valleys, rolling hills, lower mountain slopes to 1,350 m (4,400 ft) elevation. **Identification:** small to medium-size tree with rounded crown and thick, checkered, light gray bark. *Leaves* alternate, deciduous, simple, 3.8–10 cm (1.5–4 in) long, 1.9–5 cm (0.7–2 in) wide, uniformly wide to broadest above middle, *entire to shallowly and irregularly lobed along margin, bluish-green.* Fruits are acorns on current year's branches, 1.6–3.1 cm (0.6–1.2 in) long, broadest near base; *acorn cup saucer-shaped, enclosing only base of nut,* cup scales small, warty; nutmeat somewhat sweet. **Harvest and preparation:** See WHITE OAK GROUP (preceding).

Northern red oak: acorn with cap and without. Summer branch. (Elias photos)

American beech: fruiting branch (Elias).

Red/Black Oak Group   *Quercus* subgenus *Erythrobalanus*

The red oak species and black oak species and the numerous relatives in this subgenus occur only in the Americas. This group is characterized by leaves entire, toothed, or lobed and always with bristlelike tips extending beyond the margin of the leaf; acorns maturing at end of second year on the previous year's twigs, and the inner surface of the acorn shell hairy. Acorn nutmeats are nearly always bitter. Because of this, only 1 species is discussed here as edible, although most species can be utilized after the bitter properties have been removed.

Northern red oak   *Quercus rubra*

Habitat: valleys, ravines, lower and mid slopes of hills and mountains. **Identification:** medium-size tree to 20 m (66 ft), rarely taller, with open, irregular crown and shallowly furrowed, checkered bark. *Leaves* alternate, deciduous, simple, *10–22 cm* (4–8.7 in) *long,* 6–12 cm (2.4–5 in) wide, widest above middle, *with 7–9 moderately deep lobes,* dull green and smooth above, paler beneath and with occasional tufts of hairs in junction of principal veins. Fruits are *acorns on previous year's twigs, 1.2–2.5 cm (0.5–1 in) long, acorn cup* saucer-shaped, *enclosing about 1/4 of nut,* cup scales thin, overlapping; nutmeat bitter. **Harvest and preparation:** Gather acorns in autumn as they turn brown and fall. Store in cool dry place or shell for immediate use. Place whole, chopped, or coarsely ground nutmeats in cloth (clean T-shirt will do) and tie with string. Place in boiling water until water turns brown, drain, add more boiling water. Repeat many times until water remains clear. In the field, place bag filled with nutmeats in clear running stream until nutmeats are no longer bitter, from 1 to several days. Spread leached acorns in pan and dry in sun or warm oven. Use whole nutmeats or prepare and use as grits or meal as described under WHITE OAK GROUP. For acorn muffins, cream ¼ cup butter with ½ cup sugar or molasses. Add alternately and blend 2 eggs, 1 cup milk, and dry mix of 1 cup acorn meal or grits, 2 cups flour, 4 tsp baking powder, ¾ tsp salt. Beat thoroughly. Bake in greased muffin pan at 200°C (390°F) for about 20 min. For pancake batter, repeat muffin recipe but add 1 more egg plus milk. For acorn coffee, roast acorn meal at 175°C (350°F) until dark and crisp, about 30 min. Use ½ cup roasted meal to 4 cups water. Combine, boil 15 min, strain, and serve.

American beech   *Fagus grandifolia*

Habitat: river valleys, lower mountain slopes, mixed deciduous forests, usually in rich, moist soils. **Identification:** medium-size to tall tree with narrow to spreading, rounded crown and *thin, smooth, light gray to bluish-gray bark.* Leaves alternate, deciduous, simple, 6–14 cm (2.4–5.5 in) long, 2.5–7.2 cm (1–3 in) wide, broadest just below middle, sharply toothed along margin, leathery texture at maturity. Male flowers tiny, in globe-shaped, hanging heads; female flowers tiny, usually paired at or near tips of branches. *Fruits consist of 2 triangular nuts enclosed in 2 spiny bracts, bracts 1.6–2.2 cm (0.6–1.9 in) long,* *opening in late summer to release oily nuts.* **Harvest and preparation:** Gather nuts as they drop from trees following hard frost. Separate burrs from nuts by shaking and winnowing or singly by hand. Dry in open, warm area. Crack brown shells by heating in oven; remove shells by beating or rubbing in hands and winnowing. Nutmeats are edible raw. Grind and air dry nutmeats for flour; crush and boil in water; skim off excellent oil for cooking. Roast nutmeats at 160°C (320°F) 30–40 min and grind for coffee substitute. For beechnut pie, substitute 1½ cups beechnuts for pecans in PECAN pie recipe. Thoroughly whip 3 eggs. Slowly beat into them ½ cup melted butter or margarine, 1 cup white corn syrup, and ¾ cup sugar. Turn into unbaked 9-in pie shell and bake at 150°C (300°F) 35 min. Remove pie long enough to cover quickly with nuts. Return to oven, turn up heat to 175°C (350°F), and bake another 15 min. **Edible related species:** none. **Poisonous look-alikes:** none.

Allegheny chinkapin

Castanea pumila

Also edible summer

Habitat: widespread; dry woodlands and mountain slopes or along coast in dry sandy soils. **Identification:** shrub or small tree to 8 m (26 ft) with a rounded crown and light reddish-brown bark. Twigs densely hairy when young. *Leaves* alternate, simple, deciduous, *6.8–16 cm* (2.7–6.3 in) *long, 3.8–5 cm* (1.5–2 in) wide, *broadest near middle, with numerous large teeth along the margin,* whitish and hairy beneath. Male flowers numerous on the upper ⅔ of semi-erect spikes; female flowers fewer on the lower ⅓ of flowering spike. *Fruits are spiny burrs 3–4 cm (1.4 in) in diameter, enclosing 1, rarely 2, nuts;* nuts broadest near the base and pointed at tip, nutmeat sweet. **Harvest and preparation:** Gather nuts as they ripen in late summer or early autumn. Separate nuts from burs and store whole, or shell, blanch, and dry nutmeats. To shell and blanch the nuts, cover with boiling water and boil until shell and skin can be easily removed. Then place nutmeats in shady place about 1 week until dry and shriveled. Store shelled and dried or unshelled nuts in porous bag in dry place. Before using nuts, soak in water for 30 min. Use chestnuts in stuffings, soups, desserts, as a vegetable, and as a coffee substitute. Nuts can be eaten directly by slitting shells and roasting over coals or in hot oven. For soup, combine 1½ cups dried ground chestnuts, 2 sliced carrots, 1 cup sliced acorn or butternut squash, 2 tbsp chopped fresh parsley, ½ tsp oregano or native plant seasonings, and 5 cups water. Cook until tender, about 40–50 min. For coffee, chop freshly shelled chestnuts, spread on foil, and roast at 190°C (375°F) until dark and dry. Grind to a powder as needed. Boil gently 28 grams (1 oz) powder per cup of water for 15 min. Strain and serve. **Related edible species:** American chestnut (*C. dentata*) produces large sweet nuts but the persistent chestnut blight has literally eliminated it from its native range. **Poisonous look-alikes:** Do not confuse poisonous horsechestnuts with true chestnuts. Horsechestnuts (*Aesculus* species) have compound (palmate) leaves and nuts with a large circular scar, and belong to the family Hippocastanaceae. Allegheny chinkapin and true chestnuts have simple leaves and belong to the beech family (Fagaceae).

Allegheny chinkapin: fruiting branch (Elias). Flowering branch (NYBG).

Washington hawthorn: unripe fruits (Elias). Flower clusters (Feldman).

Downy hawthorn: fruiting branch (Speas).

HAWTHORNS   *Crataegus*

This large group of trees and shrubs contains highly variable species that are often difficult to distinguish. Nearly all of the 26 distinguishable North American species of hawthorns have edible fruits. They are mostly small spreading trees with dense branches often armed with long sharp spines. The toothed leaves may be entire, shallowly or deeply lobed. Bisexual flowers are generally white, with 5 petals and the rounded to pear-shaped fruits yellow, green, red, orange, or nearly black at maturity. Four common species are discussed on upcoming pages. **Harvest:** Most fruit ripens in autumn and may persist for several months, but some southern species, including May hawthorn *(C. aestivalis)*, have fruit ripening in late spring. The fruits vary greatly in flavor from sweet to bitter. Sample the fruits from each plant and harvest the best, but be careful of the vicious thorns. **Preparation:** Eat sweetest fruits fresh. For jelly, crush 1.4 kg (3 lb) fruit or 1 kg (2 lb) if a juicy type, cover with water, and cook until soft. Add more water if necessary. Strain juice through jelly bag. Bring 4 cups juice to boil. Unless fruits are unripe, add 1 pkg pectin, stir, add 6–7 cups sugar, stir, and bring to rolling boil. If no pectin is added, boil to 115°C (239°F). Remove from heat, skim, pour into sterilized jelly glasses, and seal. If fruits do not seem acid enough, add juice of 1 or 2 lemons. For tea, steep 2–3 tbsp crushed fruits and sprig of mint in cup of boiling water for 5–10 min. Fruits can be dried and stored for winter use. Substitute hawthorn fruits in recipes calling for rose hips. The fruits were used by Indians to some extent in pemmican. **Related edible species:** many *Crataegus* species. **Poisonous look-alikes:** none.

Washington hawthorn   *Crataegus phaenopyrum*

Habitat: stream banks, old fields, openings in woodlands. **Identification:** small tree to 12 m (40 ft), with rounded, spreading crown; branches dark reddish-brown, zigzagging, *armed with slender sharp-pointed spines 3–5 cm* (1.2–2 in) *long. Leaves* alternate, simple, deciduous, 2–6 cm (0.8–2.4 in) long, 2–5 cm (0.8–2 in) wide, broadest near base, *with 1–4 pairs of shallow lobes,* pointed at tip, broadly rounded at base, sharply toothed along margin, dark green, shiny, smooth. *Flowers white, attractive,* produced in branched, spreading many-flowered clusters. *Fruits* are *dry, berrylike, globe-shaped,* 5–8 mm (0.3 in) in diameter, *bright red.* Harvest and preparation: See HAWTHORNS (preceding).

Downy hawthorn   *Crataegus mollis* (syn.: *C. arnoldiana, C. canadensis, C. submollis*)

Habitat: along streams and rivers, bottomlands, lowland fields, clearings. **Identification:** small tree to 12 m (40 ft) high, with dense, wide-spreading crown; *branches* covered with dense white hairs when young, *almost thornless,* occasionally with sharp, slender dark reddish-brown spines to 5 cm (2 in) long. *Leaves* alternate, simple, deciduous, 3.5–10 cm (1.4–4 in) long, 3–8 cm (1.2–3.2 in) wide, usually broadest near base, sharp-pointed along margin, *dark yellowish-green, hairy on lower surface.* Flowers white, attractive, produced in branched, spreading clusters in spring. Fruits stalked, dry, berrylike, globe-shaped, 9–16 mm (0.4–0.6 in) in diameter, red. **Harvest and preparation:** See HAWTHORNS (preceding).

Fleshy hawthorn
Crataegus succulenta

Habitat: along coast, hillsides, abandoned fields, usually in rocky or gravelly soils. **Identification:** shrub or small tree to 8 m (26 ft) high, with irregular, usually rounded, crown; branches stout, slightly zigzagging, gray, *armed with frequent, stiff, slightly curving, dark reddish-brown spines* 3–4.5 cm (1.2–1.8 in) long. *Leaves* alternate, simple, *3–7 cm* (1.2–2.8 in) *long, 2–5.2 cm* (0.8–2 in) *wide,* broadest above or below middle, *shallowly lobed near tip, pointed* at tip, tapering at base, *sharply pointed* and *double-toothed along margin,* dark green, shiny. Flowers white, attractive, produced in branched, spreading clusters in spring. *Fruits* stalked, dry, berrylike, *globe-shaped, 0.8–1.6 cm* (0.3–0.6 in) *in diameter, bright red.* **Harvest and preparation:** See HAWTHORNS (preceding).

Cockspur hawthorn
Crataegus crus-galli

(synonyms: *C. acutifolia, C. canbyi, C. regalis, C. pyracanthoides*)

Habitat: hillsides, lower mountain slopes, river valleys, abandoned fields. **Identification:** small tree to 8 m (26 ft) high, with broad spreading, *nearly flat-topped crown;* branches stiff, light brown to gray, armed with stout, slender, straight to slightly curved, sharp-pointed spines. *Leaves* alternate, simple, deciduous, *2–6 cm* (0.8–2.4 in) *long, 1–3.2 cm* (0.4–1.3 in) *wide, usually broadest above middle* or near middle, *unlobed,* rounded to pointed at tip, gradually tapering at base, sharply toothed along upper ⅔ of margin, *glossy, dark green. Flowers white, pink, or red,* attractive, produced in branched, spreading clusters in spring. *Fruits* stalked, *dry, berrylike,* globe-shaped, *0.7–1 cm* (0.4 in) *in diameter, dull red to green.* **Harvest and preparation:** See HAWTHORNS (preceding).

Common persimmon
Diospyros virginiana

Also edible winter

Habitat: rich bottomlands, especially Mississippi River Valley, margins of woodlands and fields, rocky hillsides, along fencerows and highways. **Identification:** large shrub or small to medium-size tree with thick dark gray to grayish-brown bark that forms small square blocks. *Leaves* alternate, deciduous, *7–13 cm* (2.8–5.1 in) *long, 3.5–8 cm* (1.4–3.2 in) *wide,* broadest near base or middle, entire, dark green and shiny. *Male and female flowers on separate trees,* produced at bases of leaves along younger branches, *each flower tubular or urn-shaped,* greenish-yellow to cream-white. *Fruits are globe-shaped, 2–6 cm* (0.8–2.4 in) *in diameter, orange to orange-purple, fleshy,* containing a few flattened seeds 1.2–2 cm (0.5–0.8 in) long. **Harvest:** Fruits mature in early autumn and persist on trees into early winter. Best collected after first frost when soft and skin becomes slightly wrinkled. Prior to that fruits will be very sour. To obtain many fruits, shake branches. **Preparation:** Delicious as fresh fruit. The pulp, strained to remove seeds and skin, can be used to make bread, pie, pudding, jam, even frozen for later use. See jam recipe early in book. A tea can be made from clean dried leaves. **Related edible species:** Texas persimmon *(D. texana).* **Poisonous look-alikes:** none.

Fleshy hawthorn: fruiting branch (Elias).

Cockspur hawthorn: fruiting branch (Elias).

Common persimmon: fruiting and flowering branches (Speas).

American mountain ash   *Sorbus americana*
Also edible winter

Habitat: rocky slopes, seepage areas along ridges, at higher elevations. **Identification:** shrub or small tree to 9 m (30 ft) with open, rounded crown and thin, light gray smooth bark. *Leaves alternate,* deciduous, *featherlike (pinnate) compound, 12–25 cm (5–10 in) long, with 9–17 leaflets, each leaflet* 3–8 cm (1.2–3.2 in) long, lance-shaped to uniformly wide, *finely toothed along margin,* dull green. *Flowers in dense, many-flowered, flat-topped clusters* to 15 cm (6 in) across, each flower tiny, with 5 white petals. *Fruits in large, dense clusters, persisting into winter, each fruit* 4–8 mm (0.2–0.3 in) in diameter, *bright orange-red, shiny,* slightly fleshy, containing 1 or 2 seeds. **Harvest and preparation:** Fruits become palatable in winter after 1 or more freezings and are easily stripped from twigs. Edible raw but better cooked. For sauce, stew like CRANBERRIES; bring to boil 2 lb fruits and 2 cups sugar in 1 cup water, or berries plus 1 cup maple sugar (SUGAR MAPLE) and 1 cup cider. Reduce heat and simmer until berries mash easily and a drop of the sauce gels on cold plate. Pour into mold or storage jars. For pie, to sauce (above) add rind of ½ lemon and ⅛ tsp cinnamon. Line pie plate with crust, put in sauce, cover with crisscross strips of crust, leaving spaces between. Bake at 230°C (450°F) 20 min. Try basic jelly recipe with vinegar replacing about ¼ of water for sauce to serve with game. Also use regular jelly recipe. Berries keep well but must be dry for prolonged storage. **Related edible species:** European mountain ash *(S. aucuparia)*, Greene mountain ash *(S. scopulina)*, Sitka mountain ash *(S. sitchensis)*. **Poisonous look-alikes:** none.

Pecan   *Carya illinoensis*

Habitat: bottomlands, rich moist soils; also extensively cultivated. **Identification:** tall tree with open round crown and thick, irregularly furrowed, dark reddish-brown bark. *Leaves* alternate, deciduous, *featherlike (pinnate) compound, 32–52 cm (13–21 in) long with 9–17 leaflets; leaflets* 8–20 cm (3.2–8 in) long, 2.5–7.5 cm (1–3 in) wide, *lance-shaped,* coarsely toothed along margins. Male flowers in slender hanging catkins; female flowers short, inconspicuous, at tips of branches; flowers occur in early spring as leaves unfold. *Fruits* in clusters of 3–6, each large, uniformly wide, 3.5–5 cm (1.4–2 in) long, *husk splitting into 4 thin sections to expose nut.* Nuts cylinder-shaped to broadest near base, pointed at tip, light brown to reddish-brown, shell thin, meat oily, sweet. **Harvest:** Gather nuts in autumn as leaves turn and begin to fall. **Preparation:** Excellent eaten directly from shell, or use in any recipes calling for nuts. For pecan pie filling, beat 3 eggs, add ½ cup sugar, 1 cup dark corn syrup or molasses, ¼ tsp salt, 1 tsp vanilla, ⅓ cup melted butter. Spread 1 cup pecans over bottom of 9-in pie shell. Pour above ingredients over pecans and bake 10 min in 230°C (450°F) oven, then reduce heat to 175°C (350°F) and bake 35 min longer. **Related edible species:** BIG SHELLBARK HICKORY, SHAGBARK HICKORY, and MOCKERNUT HICKORY (following). **Poisonous look-alikes:** none.

American mountain ash: fruiting and flowering branches (Elias).

Pecan: summer branches and nuts with splitting husks (Elias/Dykeman).

Big shellbark hickory: immature fruits (Clawson).

Shagbark hickory: flowering and fruiting branch (Elias). Bark (Dykeman).

Big shellbark hickory   *Carya laciniosa*

Habitat: deep rich soils of floodplains and bottomlands, especially of Ohio and Mississippi River valleys. **Identification:** large tree with rounded crown and *light gray, somewhat shaggy bark.* *Leaves* alternate, deciduous, featherlike (pinnate) compound, 25–60 cm (10–24 in) long, *with 5–9 leaflets, usually 7;* leaflets 6–25 cm (2.4–10 in) long, 3.7–12.5 cm (1.5–5 in) wide, lance-shaped to broadest near base, sharp-pointed at tip, with numerous tiny teeth along margin. Male flowers in slender hanging catkins; female flowers short, inconspicuous, at ends of branches; both produced in early spring as leaves unfold. Fruits solitary or in pairs, globe- to egg-shaped, 3.5–7 cm (1.4–2.8 in) long, thick husk splitting lengthwise into 4 parts to expose nut. *Nut egg-shaped,* usually ridged, *shell thick, hard, nutmeat sweet.* **Harvest:** Gather nuts in autumn as leaves turn and fall; PECAN (preceding) and SHAGBARK (next) nuts are superior because they have thinner shells. **Preparation:** Remove nutmeats from shells; see SHAGBARK HICKORY. Use in any nut recipes. For nut-corn pudding, combine thoroughly 1½ cups cooked corn, ½ cup shelled, dried hickory nuts, 2 tbsp nut butter or oil, 1 cup boiling water, 2 beaten eggs, 2 tbsp honey, 2 tbsp fine cornmeal, ¼ cup seeds, raisins, or edible blossoms. Pour into well-greased casserole. Sprinkle top with more hickory nutmeats. Bake in preheated 175°C (350°F) oven for 1 hr. Serve hot. See other hickory species for additional uses. Trees can be tapped in late winter for sap. Prepare syrup as with SUGAR MAPLE. **Related edible species:** PECAN, SHAGBARK HICKORY, MOCKERNUT HICKORY. **Poisonous look-alikes:** none.

Shagbark hickory   *Carya ovata* (synonym: *C. carolinae-septentrionalis*)

Habitat: dry upland slopes, well-drained soils of lowlands and valleys. **Identification:** medium-size to tall tree with open rounded crown and *light to dark gray, shaggy bark.* Leaves alternate, deciduous, featherlike (pinnate) compound, 20–36 cm (8–14.2 in) long, *usually with 5,* sometimes 7, *leaflets;* leaflets broadest near middle or tip, 8–18 cm (3–7 in) long, 1.5–6 cm (0.6–2.4 in) wide, *with fine, sharp-pointed teeth along margin.* Male flowers in slender, hairy catkins 10–13 cm (4–5.1 in) long; female flowers short, inconspicuous, at tips of branches; flowers occur in spring as leaves unfold. Fruits produced singly or in 2s, egg- to globe-shaped, 3–5 cm (1.2–2 in) long, husk thick, splitting lengthwise into 4 equal parts to expose the egg-shaped, *4-sided nuts.* Nuts with thin shell and sweet nutmeat. **Harvest and preparation:** Gather nuts in early autumn as they fall with leaves. Crack nuts with hammer and remove meats with nutpick. For efficient extraction, crack nuts enough to identify and eliminate wormy ones. Then smash enough to loosen meats. Place pounded nutmeats in pot, cover with water, and bring to boil. Most of meats will rise and can be skimmed off if desired. Indians boiled mix slowly and skimmed oil from surface to use as butter; then meats were skimmed and mixed with potatoes or meal, or dried into cakes. Boiled mix separated from shells is nutritious soup Indians called *powcohicora.* For hickory pie, use PECAN pie recipe, but increase amount of nuts to 1½ cups. See other hickory recipes. **Related edible species:** PECAN, BIG SHELLBARK HICKORY (preceding), MOCKERNUT HICKORY (next). **Poisonous look-alikes:** none.

Mockernut hickory

Carya tomentosa (synonym: *C. alba*)

Habitat: ridges, hills, slopes, river valleys. **Identification:** large tree with rounded crown and dark gray, shallowly furrowed bark. *Leaves* alternate, deciduous, featherlike (pinnate) compound, 14–32 cm (5.5–12.6 in) long, *with 5 or 7 leaflets; leaflets 8–22 cm (3–9 in) long, 6–12.5 cm (2.4–5 in) wide, narrow, broadest above middle,* pointed at tip, toothed along margin. Male flowers in slender, stalked, 3-clustered catkins; female flowers small, 2–5 at tips of branches. Fruits solitary or few-clustered, globe- to egg-shaped, 4–8 cm (1.6–3.2 in) long, almost as wide, husk splitting lengthwise to expose nutmeat. *Nut nearly rounded, often 4-sided, shell thick, hard, nutmeat sweet.* **Harvest:** Gather nuts in autumn as leaves turn; PECAN and SHAGBARK HICKORY (preceding) are superior because of thin shells. **Preparation:** Remove nutmeats from shell; see SHAGBARK HICKORY instructions. Use any nut recipe including those for other hickories. For salad dressing, combine ½ cup ground hickory nuts, 1¼ cups vegetable oil, 3 tbsp lemon juice or STAGHORN SUMAC extract, 2 tbsp vinegar, ¼ tsp pepper, 1 chopped clove garlic. Shake well and use on salads. Tap trees in late winter for sap and prepare syrup as with SUGAR MAPLE. **Related edible species:** PECAN, SHAGBARK HICKORY, BIG SHELLBARK HICKORY. **Poisonous look-alikes:** none.

Black walnut

Juglans nigra

Habitat: bottomlands, floodplains, rich low mixed deciduous forest, especially in well-drained soils. **Identification:** large tree with open rounded crown and thick, deeply furrowed, light to grayish-brown to almost black bark. *Leaves* alternate, deciduous, *featherlike* (pinnate) *compound, 20–60 cm (8–24 in) long, with 15–23 leaflets;* leaflets 4–9 cm (1.6–3.5 in) long, 2–3.5 cm (0.7–1.4 in) wide, broadest near base to broadly lance-shaped, with numerous fine, sharp-pointed teeth along margin. Male and female flowers separate, appearing in spring. *Fruits large, rounded, 4–6 cm (1.6–2.4 in) in diameter, with thick husk enclosing globe-shaped nut,* nut 3–4 cm (1.2–1.6 in) in diameter, *shell irregularly and deeply furrowed,* thick, nutmeat 4-lobed at base, sweet. **Harvest:** Gather nuts in autumn as they fall from trees. Remove thick brown-staining husks immediately by partially crushing, then rubbing with gloved hands or scrubbing with stiff brush to remove all remaining husk material. (Indians first suspended nuts in mesh bag in running water for several days.) Allow hulled nuts to dry thoroughly before using. **Preparation:** Crack shell with hammer, rock, or vise, applying blow or pressure at right angles to seam. Use nutpick. Indians crushed shells well to obtain oil and meats. See SHAGBARK HICKORY. After boiling crushed nuts for 30 min or more, allow shells and nutmeats to settle; then skim off oil. Boil again and use sieve to skim nutmeats as they rise above shells. Remove coarse shell pieces, dry and grind nutmeats. Use oil like that of hickories. Use nutmeats in baking or grind with honey or herbs to make nut butter. Use sap under SUGAR MAPLE. For other uses, see BUTTERNUT, hickory species, and book's Introduction. **Related edible species:** BUTTERNUT, CALIFORNIA WALNUT (next), Texas black walnut (*J. microcarpa*), Arizona walnut (*J. major*), Hinds walnut (*J. hindsii*). **Poisonous look-alikes:** none.

Mockernut hickory: immature fruits, male flowers, bark (Eye).

Black walnut: nearly mature fruits (Elias).

California walnut: male flowers and immature fruits (Shevock).

Butternut: nearly mature fruits (Elias).

California walnut
Juglans californica

Habitat: stream and river banks, bottomlands, often in gravelly soils at lower elevation, usually below 1,000 m (3,200 ft). **Identification:** small to medium-size tree with open rounded crown and thick deeply furrowed dark brown to almost black bark. _Leaves_ alternate, deciduous, _featherlike (pinnately) compound, 15–25 cm_ (6–10 in) _long, normally with 9–15 leaflets;_ leaflets 2.5–7.5 cm (1–3 in) long, 1–2 cm (0.4–0.8 in) broad, lance-shaped to uniformly wide, with fine sharp-pointed teeth along margin. Male flowers in slender, hanging catkins; female flowers small, 1–4 at tips of new branches, both produced in early spring as leaves unfold. _Fruits small, globe-shaped, 1–2 cm (0.4–0.8 in) in diameter, with thin husk surrounding nut; nuts rounded, with few shallow grooves,_ shell thin, nutmeat large, sweet. **Harvest:** Gather ripe nuts in autumn as they fall from tree. Remove brown-staining hulls immediately as described for BLACK WALNUT (preceding). Air dry before using. **Preparation:** Crack shells of dried nuts and remove meats with nutpick; easier to extract than some other walnuts. For Indian method, see BLACK WALNUT instructions. For uses, see other walnuts, hickories, and the book's introductory section. **Related edible species:** BLACK WALNUT. **Poisonous look-alikes:** none.

Butternut (Also edible summer)
Juglans cinerea

Habitat: bottomlands, floodplains, mixed deciduous forests. **Identification:** medium-size tree with open, broadly rounded crown and thick, deeply furrowed, light gray to light brown bark. _Leaves_ alternate, deciduous, _featherlike_ (pinnate) _compound,_ 30–60 cm (12–24 in) long, _with 11–17 leaflets;_ leaflets 5–11 cm (2–4.3 in) long, 2–6 cm (0.8–2.4 in) wide, lance-shaped to widest above middle, finely toothed along margin. Male and female flowers separate, both appearing in early spring. _Fruits large, egg-shaped, 5–8 cm_ (2–3.2 in) _in diameter,_ often 4-sided, husk not splitting open at maturity. Nut egg-shaped, 3–6 cm (1.2–2.4 in) in diameter, 4-ribbed, shell deeply furrowed, thick, nutmeat sweet. **Harvest:** Pick partly grown nuts in summer for pickling when needle will penetrate husk. Gather ripe nuts in autumn as they fall from trees. Remove brown-staining hulls immediately as described for BLACK WALNUTS. Dry thoroughly before using. **Preparation:** Crack like BLACK WALNUTS or hold nut in vertical position and hammer on end until well cracked. Remove nutmeats with nutpick or use Indian method described under BLACK WALNUT to prepare oil and nut butter. For pickling, scald immature nut and remove all outer fuzz. Place nuts in kettle; cover with water and boil until water discolors. Change water and continue boiling. Repeat water changing and boiling until water remains clear. Pack nuts in canning jars with 1 dill flower, 3 walnut leaflets, 1 heaping tsp pickling spices, 1 tsp salt, ¼ tsp alum. Fill jar with boiling cider vinegar and seal. Age at least 1 month. For other uses see BLACK WALNUT, hickories, and book's introductory section. **Related edible species:** BLACK WALNUT, CALIFORNIA WALNUT (preceding), Arizona walnut (_J. major_), Hinds walnut (_J. hindsii_), and Texas black walnut (_J. microcarpa_). **Poisonous look-alikes:** none.

Winter

Winter is hardly the season for wild plant foraging—especially in colder climates. Aboveground, edibles are basically limited to berries that persist into winter, twig bark for tea, and the inner bark of some trees. The most nutritious plant parts are underground; these are the starch-rich roots and tubers of perennials and biennials. But, in winter, roots and tubers are difficult to locate and identify, even if there's no snow cover. Besides, digging them in frozen ground would cost you more calories than the plants would return.

What about survival foods? You can survive many days without food, provided you stay warm and reasonably dry, and drink sufficient water to prevent dehydration. If you decide to stay put until help arrives, choose or fashion a shelter you can heat with a reflected campfire. In selecting a site, consider access to firewood, water, and an open area for distress signalling. Expend as little energy as possible. If you expect a long wait, consider passive means of obtaining meat: fishing with set lines or setting snares on small-game trails. If you have a firearm, you could

watch game trails from your shelter or attempt to call predators to you by imitating the squeal of an injured rabbit.

In winter, Indians sometimes raided the nut caches of squirrels and arrowhead tubers cached by muskrats. But such raids are strenuous. Besides, getting into a muskrat's house can be a wet, cold ordeal.

Some northern Indians made the inner bark of trees their major winter food staple. Since bark stripping kills trees, today it should be done only for survival.

You can also partake of wild edibles in winter by manipulating the seasons. That is, you can feast on wild preserves you harvested earlier. Or, if you are highly dedicated, you can in autumn dig up the whole roots of dandelion, chicory, dock, and pokeweed. Then plant the roots in a deep, soil-filled container until after a hard freeze. Bring the container into a dark cellar. Watered and kept at 13°C (55°F), the roots will produce several crops of blanched, tender, and mild leaves for salads or cooking.

The plant species shown in upcoming pages provide berries you can eat raw, berries and twigs for beverage flavoring, inner bark for gruel and flour, and sap for pure water or boiling down to syrup and sugar. These plants are shown as they look in winter, though most of them are also shown elsewhere in this book. Many other winter-edible plants are difficult to locate and identify in winter and so are not described in this winter section. In some regions, edible plants normally harvested in autumn may also be gathered in early winter.

(Dykeman)

Staghorn sumac   *Rhus typhina*
Also edible summer, autumn

Habitat: common; woodland margins, fencerows, roadsides, and along streams. **Identification:** shrub or small tree to 10 m (33 ft) with thick, *densely hairy branches and twigs with large orange to olive pith.* Leaf scars C-shaped, nearly surrounding *bluntly conical, hairy buds.* No end bud. *Fruits persist into winter in dense, cone-shaped clusters 10–20 cm (4–8 in) long; each fruit berrylike, rounded, 3–5 mm (0.1–0.2 in) in diameter, densely covered with dark red hairs.* See also p. 186. **Harvest:** Fruits ripen in late summer to autumn and have strong lemony taste. Dense hairs on fruits prevent rain from penetrating cluster and washing out all flavor, so fruits are edible although less potent in winter. **Preparation:** For beverage, steep berries, with all twigs removed, in near boiling water for at least 15 min (at least 1 cup fruit to 1 qt water). Strain through cloth, dilute and sweeten to taste. Drink hot or cold but in moderation; some people show allergic reactions such as hives and cramps. To make jelly prepare extract as for beverage. Bring to boil 4 cups extract with 1 pkg powdered pectin. Add 5 cups sugar, boil hard 1 min, remove from heat, skim, pour into sterilized jars and seal with paraffin. **Related edible species:** SMOOTH SUMAC and SQUAWBUSH, and lemonade berry *(R. integrifolia)*. **Poisonous look-alikes:** Poison sumac *(R. vernix)* has white fruits and grows in swampy areas.

Highbush cranberry   *Viburnum trilobum*
Also edible autumn

Habitat: along streams, wet thickets, moist woodlands. **Identification:** *shrub, upright, to 5 m (16.5 ft) high;* branches upright to spreading. Twigs light reddish-brown turning ash-gray with age. Buds opposite; no end bud. *Fruits berrylike, in clusters of 10 or more, rounded to egg-shaped, 8–14 mm (0.3–0.5 in) long, bright red, translucent* when ripe, juicy, sour, containing a single flattened stone. See also HIGHBUSH CRANBERRY on page 224. **Harvest:** Fruits ripen in late summer but persist on shrub and become less sour in winter. Make sure your shrub is highbush cranberry and not its bitter look-alike, the introduced guelder rose, *V. opulus.* Tasting will tell you. Best to pick in fall and winter. **Preparation:** much the same as CRANBERRY *(Vaccinium macrocarpon)*, except large seeds must be removed. While cooking add lemon or orange peel shavings to eliminate bad odor of berries. For sauce cover several quarts of berries with water in a kettle. Add outer peels of 2 lemons or oranges. Bring to boil and simmer 5 min. Mash thoroughly and simmer another minute or two. Force juice and pulp through coarse strainer to remove seeds. Add 1 pkg pectin to 4 cups strained fruit, bring to boil, and add 5 cups sugar. Boil again for 1 min and seal in sterile jars or refrigerate. Before first frost, pectin may not be needed. For juice and jelly, cook as for sauce above but strain through jelly bag. For juice, dilute and sweeten to taste. For jelly, proceed with 4 cups juice as for sauce. **Related edible species:** SQUASHBERRY (next), HOBBLEBUSH, NANNYBERRY, and the cranberry tree *(V. pauciflorum)*, of Pacific Northwest. **Poisonous look-alikes:** none, but the guelder rose *(V. opulus)* has bitter fruits.

Staghorn sumac: winter fruit cluster and fruiting branches (Dykeman).

Highbush cranberry: early autumn branches (Elias). In winter berries look like this and are sweeter, though leaves will have fallen.

Squashberry: early autumn branch (Clawson). In winter, berries look like this and are sweeter, though leaves will have fallen.

Sweet birch: winter treetop, trunk bark, and immature male catkins (Dykeman).

Squashberry
Viburnum edule

Also edible summer, autumn

Habitat: along streams, wet thickets, margin of woodlands, moist low woodlands. **Identification:** *shrub,* often sprawling, to 2.5 m (8.1 ft) high; stems usually spreading, smooth. New branches reddish brown, older ones gray. *Buds opposite, dark red, shiny, 2-scaled;* both *side and end buds present. Fruits in small clusters, berrylike, rounded,* 6–10 mm (0.2–0.4 in) in diameter, *red, containing a single flattened seed.* See also SQUASHBERRY on page 226. **Harvest:** Fruits are similar to HIGHBUSH CRANBERRY but smaller and less sour. They ripen in August but persist through winter so are listed here. **Preparation:** See HIGHBUSH CRANBERRY (preceding), except juice does not require dilution for use as beverage. Makes excellent jelly. **Related edible species:** HIGHBUSH CRANBERRY. **Poisonous look-alikes:** none; the introduced guelder rose *(V. opulus)* is bitter but not toxic.

Sweet birch, Black birch
Betula lenta

Also edible spring, summer, autumn

Habitat: forest or open woods, especially moist, north facing, protected slopes; in deep, rich, well-drained soils. **Identification:** medium-size tree with rounded crown and smooth, dark red to almost black bark. *Broken twigs have wintergreen fragrance.* Buds alternate, both side and end buds present, 5–7 mm (0.2–0.3 in) long, light brown, broadest near base and tapering to a point. Fruits in erect, *brown cones, 2.5–3 cm (1–1.2 in) long, containing many tiny, winged seeds.* Fruits mature in late summer and early fall. Cones persist into winter. *New male flower catkins 2–3 cm (0.8–1.2 in) long at tips of twigs in winter.* See also p. 122. **Harvest:** twigs, red inner bark, and bark of larger roots year round but best in late winter and spring. Sap in early spring, 3–4 weeks later than SUGAR MAPLE. **Preparation:** Eat inner bark fresh as emergency food, boiled like noodles, or dried and ground into flour. Dry inner bark at room temperature; store in sealed jars for later use. For tea, steep (do not boil) twigs or fresh or dried inner bark in water or, preferably, birch sap. Boiling removes volatile wintergreen oil. Sweeten to taste. For birch beer pour solution of 4 gal birch sap and 1 gal honey (or 5 gal sap and 3 lb sugar), which has been boiled 10 min, over 4 qt fine twigs in a crock. Cool, strain to remove twigs, add 1 cake yeast. Cover, ferment about 1 week, until cloudiness starts to settle. Bottle and cap tightly. For birch syrup, see instructions under YELLOW BIRCH (next). **Related edible species:** YELLOW BIRCH. **Poisonous look-alikes:** none.

Yellow birch
Also edible spring, autumn

Betula alleghaniensis
(synonym: *B. lutea*)

Habitat: rich woodlands, lower slopes and occasionally cool marshlands, usually below 1,000 m (3,300 ft) elevation. **Identification:** medium-size tree with rounded crown and peeling, ragged-edged, reddish-brown bark turning *grayish dull yellow or yellowish-brown.* Buds alternate, end bud absent, side buds 5–7 mm (0.2–0.3 in) long, brown, broadest near base and tapering to sharp point, somewhat sticky, with several scales. *New male flower catkins 2–3 cm (0.8–1.2 in) long at tips of twigs.* See also YELLOW BIRCH on page 122. **Harvest:** For syrup, tap as with SUGAR MAPLE beginning 3–4 weeks after maple sap flow begins. Drill $^7/_{16}$-in hole (just over 11 mm) slightly upward about 7 cm (3 in) into a mature tree. Hammer in metal or wood spile only until firmly anchored; driving spile too far may split wood. Hang bucket and wait. Flow of sap copious but sugar content lower than from maple. For use of twigs and inner bark, see SWEET BIRCH (preceding); wintergreen flavor is milder in yellow birch. **Preparation:** Boil sap in open container, outdoors, adding more as volume decreases, until evaporation leaves a viscous, molasses flavored syrup with boiling temperature of about 104°C (220°F). Store in sterilized, completely filled, sealed jars. **Related edible species:** SWEET BIRCH. **Poisonous look-alikes:** none.

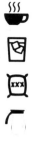

American mountain ash
Also edible autumn

Sorbus americana

Habitat: rocky slopes, seepage areas along ridges at higher elevations. **Identification:** shrub or small tree to 9 m (30 ft) with open, rounded crown and thin, light-gray smooth bark. *Leaf scars alternate, slightly raised on twig surface.* Buds rather conical, *end bud 6–12 mm (0.2–0.5 in) long, curved and gummy;* side buds smaller, flattened and pressed against twig. *Fruits in large, dense clusters, persisting into winter,* each fruit 4–8 mm (0.2–0.3 in) in diameter, *bright orange-red, shiny, slightly fleshy, containing 1 or 2 seeds.* See also AMERICAN MOUNTAIN ASH on page 240. **Harvest and preparation:** Fruits become palatable in winter after one or more freezings and become easy to strip from twigs. Edible raw but better cooked. For sauce, stew like CRANBERRIES; bring to boil 4 cups berries and 2 cups sugar in 1 cup water (or berries plus 1 cup maple sugar and 1 cup cider). Reduce heat and simmer until berries mash easily and a drop of sauce gels on a cold plate. Pour into mold or storage jars. For pie, add to sauce (above) a rind of ½ lemon and ⅛ tsp cinnamon. Line pie plate with crust, put in sauce, cover with crisscross strips of crust leaving spaces between them. Bake at 230°C (450°F) for 20 min. For jelly, see the book's introductory section. For meat sauce substitute 1 cup vinegar for 1 cup water in jelly recipe. Berries keep well; but for prolonged storage, dry them to prevent mold. **Related edible species:** European mountain ash *(S. aucuparia)*, Greene mountain ash *(S. scopulina)*, and Sitka mountain ash *(S. sitchensis).* **Poisonous look-alikes:** none.

Yellow birch: winter immature male catkins, trunk bark, and tree (Dykeman).

American mountain ash: ripening autumn fruits (Elias). In winter, berries are brighter orange-red, and leaves will have fallen.

Sugar maple: trunk bark, winter twigs and tree. Metal spile with sap dripping into bucket. (Dykeman photos)

Sugar maple
Acer saccharum

Also edible spring, summer

Habitat: eastern deciduous forest, common and widespread, especially at lower elevations. **Identification:** medium-size to tall *trees* to 30 m (98 ft) with a rounded crown, slightly *fissured to furrowed dark-gray bark. Buds opposite,* end and side buds present, *light brown,* scaly; *end bud 6–12 mm (0.2–0.5 in) long,* cone shaped; side buds smaller. See also SUGAR MAPLE on page 256. **Harvest:** Obtain sap from first spring flow until buds swell. Good sap flow requires freezing nights and warm days. Drill $^7/_{16}$-in hole (just over 11 mm) for commercial spile, slightly upward and 5–8 cm (2–3 in) into trunk. Drive spile just far enough to hold bucket, not so hard that you split wood. Collect sap and store cold until you have 25–30 gal. Collect winged seeds before fully ripe, usually from June to September. **Preparation:** Boil sap outdoors, indoors only if you like sticky walls. Use large surfaced, open pan, adding sap as water boils away. When 25 gal or so of sap has been added, continue to boil liquid until temperature is 4°C (7°F) above that of boiling water on that particular day. You may wish to boil for the last two degrees on a regulated stove. Filter syrup through milk filter into sterilized canning jars. Fill jars completely and seal. Yields about 3 qt. For maple sugar, boil 1 pt of syrup in saucepan with frequent stirring until temperature is at least 110°C (230°F). Remove from heat, cool, and stir until surface loses sheen. Pour quickly onto foil or waxed paper. When partially hardened, score into pieces with knife. Use sap fresh as a beverage, fermented to form a mild vinegar, or reduced by boiling to 25% its original volume as a base for teas. Soak seeds and remove wings. Boil until tender, drain, season, and roast for 10–15 min. **Related edible species:** Red maple *(A. rubrum)*; sap of all native maples may be used for syrup but sugar maple is best. **Poisonous look-alikes:** none; but avoid Norway maple *(A. platanoides)*, which has milky sap.

Poisonous plants

Plants that are inedible and even poisonous to varying degrees grow among the edible ones. So it's wise to learn to recognize poisonous plants, especially those that may resemble the edibles. In this section, you'll find full coverage of 20 plants that are particularly toxic, and you'll also find mention of many more related toxic species. To learn more about poisonous plants not fully covered here, consult a guidebook for your region.

Unfortunately, there are no general rules for recognition of poisonous plants. Even though birds or mammals eat a particular plant, that plant may still be poisonous to humans. For example, birds readily consume the fruits of poison ivy with no ill effects. But if you tried this, you'd be in serious trouble. Ironically, sometimes the most toxic plants are among the most beautiful. Some toxic beauties include blue flag, yellow flag, star of Bethlehem, and butterfly weed.

The more field experience you gain identifying plants, the easier you'll sort the edibles from the inedibles. Try to identify at least a few new poisonous plants each season.

Star of Bethlehem   *Ornithogalum umbellatum*

Habitat: fields, grassy areas, roadsides, and open woodlands. **Identification:** *small perennial herb* to 35 cm (13.8 in) high, from an egg-shaped bulb 3–4 cm (1.2–1.6 in) long. *Leaves mainly basal, long, narrow, 15–40 cm (5.9–15.7 in) long, 3–6 mm (0.1–0.2 in) wide, channeled, main vein almost white.* Flowering stem erect, bearing several, short- to long-stalked flowers at the tip; *each flower showy, bisexual, with 6 spreading petallike segments, white with a green stripe on lower side, each segment 1.5–2.5 cm (0.6–1 in) long.* Fruits are a 3-lobed, egg-shaped capsule 5–10 mm (0.2–0.4 in) long containing a few, nearly globe-shaped, black seeds. **Poisonous constituents:** Bulbs contain one or more alkaloids that have killed grazing animals. **Related poisonous species:** An introduced species, *O. nutans*, also has poisonous bulbs.

Death camass   *Zigadenus venenosus*

Habitat: meadows, fields, scrubby woodlands along coast, in foothills, and coniferous forests. **Identification:** *perennial herb from an egg-shaped bulb 1.2–2.5 cm (0.5–1 in) long, with dark outer scales;* stems upright, 24–60 cm (9.4–24 in) high, slender, smooth. *Leaves around base and on lower stem; basal leaves very narrow (linear), 15–30 cm (6–12 in) long, 5–10 mm (0.2–0.4 in) wide;* stem leaves usually shorter and sheathing the stem. *Stalked flowers numerous along an upright, unbranched, elongate cluster (lower-most flowers opening* *first), each flower with 6 petals or petallike structures, whitish,* broadest near base, pointed at tip, bisexual. Fruit a small, egg-shaped capsule 1–1.5 cm (0.4–0.6 in) long, splitting open at maturity to release tiny, brown seeds. **Poisonous constituents:** All plant parts, especially the bulbs, contain alkaloids that can cause gastrointestinal distress, weakness, loss of motor function, and death. This plant and its relatives have killed many horses and cattle. **Related poisonous species:** All 12 native *Zigadenus* species should be considered *extremely* poisonous.

Star of Bethlehem: flowering plants (NYBG).

Death camass: flowering plant (NYBG).

Atamasco lily: flowering plants (Speas).

Blue flag: flower (Elias).

Yellow flag: flowers (Elias).

Atamasco lily
Zephyranthes atamasco

Habitat: floodplain and low wet woodlands, wet fields and meadows, coastal plain and lower piedmont. **Identification:** perennial herb to 30 cm (12 in) high, from a small onionlike bulb 2–3 cm (0.8–1.2 in) in diameter. *Leaves all basal, long, narrow (linear), 20–40 cm (8–16 in) long, 4–8 mm (0.15–0.3 in) wide,* channeled, bright-green to bluish-green, shiny. *Flowering stalk upright, to 30 cm (12 in) high, bearing a single flower at the tip; flowers white, rarely pink, showy, 6–10 cm (2.4–3.9 in) long, funnel-shaped with the 6 lobes spreading.* Fruits are papery to leathery, nearly globe-shaped capsules, each 3-lobed and splitting open at maturity to release the shiny, black seeds. **Poisonous constituents:** Toxic compounds in the bulbs have produced staggering, collapse, and death in grazing animals. Thus, they should be regarded as *extremely* poisonous. **Related poisonous species:** All 12 native species of *Zephyranthes* should be considered extremely poisonous.

Yellow flag
Iris pseudoacorus

Habitat: swamps, ditches, borders of ponds, lakes, and streams; common, introduced from Europe. **Identification:** large perennial herb 0.6–1.2 m (2–3.9 ft) high, from spreading, underground stems (rhizomes). *Leaves long,* narrow, *sword-shaped,* 0.4–0.8 m (1.3–2.7 ft) long, 2–4 cm (0.8–1.6 in) wide, flattened, erect, pale green, sheathing the flowering stalks. Flowering stalks usually shorter than the leaves, bearing a *large, showy flower;* flowers usually **bright yellow,** with 3 spreading, petallike sepals each crested with brownish, irregular spots and 3 narrower, upright petals. Fruits are elongate, slightly angled capsules 5–10 cm (2–4 in) long, splitting open lengthwise to release the seeds. **Poisonous constituents:** leaves and roots; see BLUE FLAG (next). **Related poisonous species:** All native and introduced species of irises should be considered poisonous.

Blue flag
Iris versicolor

Habitat: wet meadows, ditches, swamps, marshes, along ponds and streams, native. **Identification:** *large perennial herb* to 1 m (3.3 ft) high, *from thick, spreading, underground stems* (rhizomes). *Leaves long, narrow, sword-shaped,* 0.4–1 m (1.4–3.3 ft) long, 1–3 cm (0.4–1.2 in) wide, flattened, erect, pale green to grayish-green, sheathing the stalks. Flowering stalks with 1 to 3 large, showy flowers; *flowers bluish-purple to violet,* with 3 broadly spreading, petallike sepals with conspicuous white veins and yellowish near base, petals 3, erect, narrow, ¼ to ½ as long as sepals. *Fruits are elongate, 3-angled capsules 3.4–5.6 cm (1.4–2.2 in) long.* **Poisonous constituents:** Leaves and roots are toxic and can cause an inflammation of the mucous membrane of the stomach and intestine. Most grazing animals avoid wild irises, but calves have been fatally poisoned by them. **Related poisonous species:** All native and introduced species of irises should be considered poisonous.

Common buttercup
Ranunculus acris

Habitat: yards, fields, clearings, and other disturbed sites. **Identification:** *slender perennial herb* to 1 m (3.3 ft) high, from a short, thick underground stem (rhizome); stem upright, branched, usually with spreading hairs. *Basal leaves rounded in outline, 4–10 cm (1.6–3.9 in) across, deeply 5–7 lobed,* each lobe coarsely toothed or with narrow lobes, softly hairy, with long leafstalks; stem leaves similar to other leaves except smaller and gradually becoming stalkless. Flowers several in a branched, open, spreading cluster; *each flower with 5 bright glossy, yellow to whitish petals* 7–14 mm (0.25–0.5 in) long, broadest near the tip. Fruits are clusters of flattened, broad, beaked, thin-walled nuts about 2–3 mm (about 0.1 in) long. **Poisonous constituents:** Leaves and stems are bitter tasting, possibly due to oils. These oils can cause abdominal pains from an irritated stomach and intestines. Fresh buttercups have caused diarrhea and blindness in grazing animals. **Related poisonous species:** All native species of buttercups contain toxic or otherwise irritating oils and should not be eaten.

Jimson weed
Datura stramonium

Habitat: disturbed sites and waste grounds, old fields, roadsides, barnyards. **Identification:** *coarse annual herb* to 1.5 m (5 ft) high, from a short taproot; stems upright, branched, usually smooth. *Leaves broadest near the base, 8–16 cm (3.2–6.4 in) long, 4–12 cm (1.6–4.7 in) wide, coarsely and irregularly large-toothed along the margin. Flowers large, 5–8 cm (2–3.1 in) long, showy, white to light purple, upright,* produced singly on upper stem; petals fused and narrowly funnel-shaped, the lobes spreading, with a heavy fragrance. *Fruits upright, egg-shaped capsules 3–5 cm (1.2–2 in) long, usually with short spines,* splitting open along 4 valves to release dark pitted seeds. **Poisonous constituents:** All plant parts, including seeds, are poisonous. Alkaloids will cause impaired vision, thirst, delirium, unpredictable movements, possibly coma and death. **Related poisonous species:** All *Datura* species.

May apple
Podophyllum peltatum

Habitat: rich and open woodlands, wet fields and meadows, pastures, occasionally roadsides. **Identification:** attractive perennial herb to 50 cm (20 in) tall, from a fleshy, spreading, underground stem (rhizome); stem single, short, producing single or paired leaves and single blossom between. *Leaves large, nearly circular in outline, 15–40 cm (5.9–15.7 in) in diameter, deeply 5–9 parted, margins with a few coarse teeth or lobes; leafstalk attached to center of blade.* Flower somewhat showy, cup-shaped, with 6–9 white petals, each 3–5 cm (1.2–2 in) wide, produced on a nodding stalk. *Fruit an egg-shaped, fleshy, yellow (rarely red) berry 2.5–5 cm (1–2 in) long,* containing several seeds. **Poisonous constituents:** Leaves and particularly the roots contain a resinous compound known as podophyllin that can cause violent cathartic reactions. Consumption of small quantities will produce severe gastric upset and vomiting. Death may occur from larger quantities. The fleshy pulp of the fruit is edible, although the seeds should not be eaten. See MAY APPLE on page 140. **Related poisonous species:** none in North America.

Common buttercup: flowering plants (NYBG).

Jimson weed: fruiting branch after frost (Dykeman).

May apple: plants in early spring and flowering plant in May (NYBG).

Horse nettle: flower and immature fruits, above (NYBG).

White hellebore: young plant, upper left (Elias). Top half of flowering plant, left (NYBG).

Yellow sweetclover: flower clusters, bottom left. Flower stalk, below. (NYBG photos)

Horse nettle
Solanum carolinense

Habitat: disturbed sites, fields, vacant lots, roadsides, and sandy waste areas. **Identification:** coarse perennial herb to 1 m (3.3 ft) high, from spreading underground stems (rhizomes); *stem and leaves with branched hairs and slender spines.* Leaves alternate, simple, broadest near base, 6–12 cm (2.4–4.7 in) long, 3–6 cm (1.2–2.4 in) wide, *coarsely and irregularly large-toothed along margin, rough to touch.* Flowers few on elongated terminal cluster; *each flower white to light purple, 2–3 cm (0.8–1.2 in) across,* five-parted petals spreading and even bending backward, broadest near base. *Fruit a yellow fleshy berry* 1–1.6 cm (0.4–0.6 in) in diameter, smooth. **Poisonous constituents:** Leaves and fruits contain the alkaloid solanine, which can cause vomiting, nausea, abdominal pains, and other gastrointestinal problems. **Related poisonous species:** Many species of the genus *Solanum* contain the solanine alkaloid in varying amounts. Among species to avoid are European nightshade *(S. dulcamara)*, black or deadly nightshade *(S. nigrum)*, and silverleaf nightshade *(S. elaeagnifolium)*.

White hellebore, False hellebore
Veratrum viride

Habitat: wetlands, swamps, floodplains, near streams and rivers, low wet sites in woodlands. **Identification:** *large perennial herb* to 2 m (6.6 ft) high, from thick, fibrous roots; stems upright, stout, unbranched. *Leaves* numerous along stem, *broadest near base or middle, 15–32 cm (5.9–12.6 in) long, about half as wide,* entire along margin and pointed at tip, nearly stalkless and almost clasping stem, with conspicuous, slightly sunken ribs. *Flowers numerous in large, erect, branched clusters* 20–50 cm (7.8–19.7 in) high, hairy; each flower yellowish-green, with 6 spreading, petallike segments. Fruits are egg-shaped capsules 1.8–2.6 cm (0.7–1 in) long, containing numerous seeds. **Poisonous constituents:** Several alkaloids from white and other hellebores have been used in medicines and insecticides. While all plant parts contain alkaloids, the roots concentrate them. Eating this plant can cause depressed heart activity, headaches, a burning sensation in the mouth and throat, and prostration. **Related poisonous species:** All 12 native *Veratrum* species should be considered poisonous.

Yellow sweetclover
Melilotus officinalis

Habitat: disturbed sites and waste areas, roadsides, fencerows, old fields; introduced weed from Europe and Asia. **Identification:** biennial herb to 2 m (6.6 ft) high, stems sparingly branched and weakly upright, usually smooth. *Leaves compound, composed of three leaflets (trifoliolate);* leaflets broadest near or above middle, 1.2–2.5 cm (0.5–1 in) long, 5–15 mm (0.2–0.6 in) wide, finely toothed along margin, greenish-yellow, usually smooth; leafstalks with conspicuous leaflike bract (stipule) at junction of stalk and stem. *Flowers numerous on slender, elongated clusters 4–12 cm (1.6–4.7 in) long, each flower yellow, resembling tiny pea blossom.* Fruits are egg-shaped pods 2–4 mm (0.1–0.2 in) long, smooth, stalked. **Poisonous constituents:** Improperly dried sweetclover will easily mold and in the process produce coumarin, an anticoagulant that can cause severe internal bleeding and death. Moldy sweetclover mixed in hay has killed many cattle. Thus, avoid this plant when gathering green leafy edibles. **Related**

Pokeweed: flower cluster (NYBG). Fruit cluster with immature fruits at tip, bottom third; ripe fruits, middle; and stalks after fruits have fallen, upper third (Crow).

Dogbane: flowering branch (NYBG).

Butterfly weed: flowering plant top and fruit capsules (NYBG).

poisonous species: Also introduced from Europe, white sweetclover *(M. alba)* is equally dangerous.

Pokeweed   *Phytolacca americana*

Habitat: woodland margins, disturbed sites, waste ground, roadsides, fencerows. **Identification:** *large, perennial herb* to 3 m (9.8 ft) tall with thick, fleshy roots; stems branched, upright, smooth, *with disagreeable odor when broken.* Leaves alternate, 9–30 cm (3.5–11.8 in) long, 3–12 cm (1.2–4.7 in) wide, broadest near base, pointed at tip, entire along margin; leafstalks to 5 cm (2 in) long. *Flowers greenish to white, produced in narrow, elongate clusters* (racemes); each flower 2–4 mm (0.1 in) long, petals absent. *Fruits are 5–12-parted berries, wider than long, 6–10 mm (0.2–0.4 in) in diameter, green turning purplish-black at maturity.* **Poisonous constituents:** Toxins are more prevalent in mature leaves, stems, and particularly in roots than in young growth and berries. Diarrhea, vomiting, cramps, sweating, reduced breathing capacity, or even death can occur from eating this plant. You can eat young cooked shoots if you discard the cooking water. See also POKEWEED on page 96. **Related poisonous species:** none. There is only one species of pokeweed in North America.

Dogbane   *Apocynum androsaemifolium*

Habitat: open woodlands, margins of woodlands, fields, roadsides, usually drier sites. **Identification:** *perennial herb* to 50 cm (19.7 in) high; stems upright, branching, *with milky juice in all parts. Leaves opposite, broadest near base to almost uniformly wide, 4–8 cm (1.6–3.2 in) long, 2–4.5 cm (0.8–1.8 in) wide,* entire along margin, pointed at tip, dark green above, hairy beneath, sometimes drooping, with slender leafstalk. Flowers several in branched, round-topped clusters at top or upper part of stems; each flower bell-shaped, 5–10 mm (0.2–0.4 in) long, white to pink, 5-parted, spreading to drooping. *Fruits are narrow, cylindrical, capsulelike pods 6–18 cm (2.4–7 in) long, slender pointed at tip, containing numerous small seeds, each tipped with long silky hairs.* **Poisonous constituents:** All plant parts contain resins and glycosides capable of affecting the cardiovascular system of mammals. **Related poisonous species:** All of the 6 or 7 native species of dogbane *(Apocynum)* contain milky sap and probably the glycosides. Thus, all should be considered poisonous.

Butterfly weed   *Asclepias tuberosa*

Habitat: fields, meadows, prairies, open woodlands, margins of woodlands. **Identification:** perennial herb, upright, 30–80 cm (11.8–31.5 in) tall; stems single or branched, stout, hairy. *Sap not milky, leaves alternate on stems and opposite on branches,* variable in shape but often very narrow and widest near base or tip, 5–10 cm (2–4 in) long, 0.4–2.5 cm (0.1–1 in) wide, pointed at tip, *usually without leafstalk,* hairy, especially beneath. *Flowers produced in showy, branched, flat-topped clusters;* each flower *orange to red or yellow,* 5-parted, petals (corolla) deeply lobed. Fruit a dry, narrowly egg-shaped capsule 8–14 cm (3.1–5.5 in) long, splitting open only along 1 side to release tiny, flattened seeds tipped with numerous, long, silky hairs. **Poisonous constituents:** Plant parts contain some glycosides, alkaloids, and resinoids that can cause weakness, staggering, and even seizures. The various species of *Asclepias* have killed sheep, cattle, horses, and goats. **Related poisonous species:** All 30 native species should be considered potentially poisonous.

Poison hemlock   *Conium maculatum*

Habitat: disturbed sites such as fencerows, roadsides, stream and river banks, old fields and vacant lands; introduced from Europe. **Identification:** *large, biennial herb* to 3 m (9.9 ft) high, from large, white, carrotlike taproot; *stems* upright, branching, purple-spotted, hollow, *smooth. Leaves basal,* repeatedly branched, irregularly divided and highly dissected, *resembling parsley leaves,* broadly triangular in outline, smooth, dark green, *with odor of parsnips when crushed.* Tiny *white flowers* produced *in* compound, *flat-topped clusters (umbels)* 4–8 cm (1.6–3.1 in) wide; flower cluster stalks 4–10 cm (1.6–3.9 in) long. Fruits dry, egg-shaped, 3–4 mm (0.1 in) long, flattened on inner surface, conspicuously ribbed, grayish-green. **Poisonous constituents:** All plant parts, especially the stem, leaves, fruits, and root are extremely poisonous. The toxic alkaloids cause nervousness, trembling, reduced heartbeat, coma, and even respiratory failure. **Related poisonous species:** A related genus, *Cicuta,* contains several species, commonly called WATER HEMLOCK (next), which are also extremely poisonous.

Water hemlock   *Cicuta maculata*

Habitat: wet sites such as swamps, stream and river banks, ditches and bottomlands. **Identification:** *large biennial or perennial herb* to 2 m (6.6 ft) high, from one to a cluster of several, thick, fleshy, tuberlike roots; stems upright, branched, often purple spotted, smooth, exuding yellow liquid when cut. *Leaves large,* bi- or tripinnately compound on lower stem, upper stem leaves less dissected, leaf segments usually 4–8 cm (1.6–3.1 in) long, 0.5–3 cm (0.2–1.2 in) wide, toothed, smooth, *with odor of raw parsnips when crushed. Small white flowers numerous in large, compound, flat-topped clusters (umbels).* Fruits brown, dry, egg-shaped, 3–4 mm (0.15 in) long, with conspicuous ribs. **Poisonous constituents:** All parts of this plant are extremely poisonous. A resinlike cicutoxin causes severe abdominal pains, excessive salivation, vomiting within minutes of consumption, and can cause death. One of the most deadly poisonous North American plants! **Related poisonous species:** All 10 native species of *Cicuta* are extremely poisonous. Also see POISON HEMLOCK (preceding).

Poison hemlock: flowering stalks (Speas).

Water hemlock: flowering stalk (NYBG).

Introduced and grows wild. Widespread.

Southwestern coral bean: seeds and dried pods, flower cluster, and fruiting plant (Bernard).

American yew: mature fruits (Bogel). Fruiting branches (NYBG).

Southwestern coral bean   *Erythrina flabelliformis*

Habitat: canyons, washes, desert grasslands, open oak woodlands. **Identification:** large spiny shrub or small tree to 5 m (16.4 ft); *stems leafless except in summer,* thick, brittle, armed with short spines. *Leaves alternate, featherlike (pinnately) compound with 3 leaflets, the leaflets broadly triangular* and tapering to a point, 2.5–7.5 cm (1–3 in) long, 4–8.7 cm (1.5–3.5 in) wide, grayish green; main leafstalk long, armed with several short, hooked spines. *Flowers in large, showy clusters usually in spring, each narrow, elongated, pea-shaped, with 5 bright red to scarlet petals.* Fruits are long, leathery pods 10–25 cm (4–10 in) long, constricted between the seeds; seeds hard, bright red, 1–2 cm (0.4–0.8 in) long. **Poisonous constituents:** Seed wall contains highly poisonous alkaloids that can cause death, even when consumed in small amounts. The seeds are sometimes used to make necklaces, which some wearers unfortunately have played with between their teeth. **Related Poisonous Species:** All species of *Erythrina* are poisonous. Eastern coral bean *(E. herbacea)* is native to the Coastal Plain from North Carolina to Texas.

American yew   *Taxus canadensis*

Habitat: rich woodlands, pine forests, bogs, thickets. **Identification:** *shrub, usually low, spreading and straggly,* occasionally upright, up to 2 m (6.6 ft) high, branches turning reddish-brown with age. *Leaves spirally arranged and spreading in 2 ranks along stems, narrow (linear), 1–2 cm (0.4–0.8 in) long, about 2 mm (0.1 in) wide, abruptly fine-pointed at tip, dark yellowish-green above, with 2 pale-green bands beneath,* leafstalk short. Flowers tiny cones, either male or female. *Fruits consist of a hard, dark, egg-shaped seed about 1 cm (0.4 in) long, enclosed in bright red to reddish-orange, fleshy disc.* **Poisonous constituents:** Leaves and seeds contain one or more alkaloids called taxine, which can cause sudden death in people as well as horses and cattle. The fleshy red disc around the seed is edible but is better avoided because of the highly toxic seeds. **Related poisonous species:** Leaves and seeds of all species of yew *(Taxus)* are extremely poisonous. The introduced English yew *(T. baccata)* and the Japanese yew *(T. cuspidata)* are widely planted as ornamentals.

Poison ivy

Toxicodendron radicans
(synonym: *Rhus radicans*)

Habitat: woodland margins, pastures, streams and river banks, fencerows, and disturbed sites. **Identification:** low shrub or vine, often climbing, with hairy, light-brown twigs. *Leaves* alternate, deciduous, *compound of three leaflets* (trifoliolate), leaflets broadest near base, 10–16 cm (3.9–6.3 in) long, 5–10 cm (2–3.9 in) wide, pointed at tip, *entire or with a few coarse teeth along margin,* yellowish-green, dull, often smooth, *leafstalks reddish near junction with blade.* Plants either male or female. Tiny male flowers produced in elongated, branched clusters 5–10 cm (2–3.9 in) long on new growth; small female flowers produced in smaller branched clusters 4–6 cm (1.6–2.4 in) long. *Fruits are rounded,* 4–6 mm (0.1 in) in diameter, *creamy white,* smooth, *produced in clusters like grapes.* **Poisonous constituents:** All parts of the plant have an oily resin containing urushiol. Contact with urushiol can cause minor to severe dermatitis, consisting of a rash and blisters. This affliction can be serious and most uncomfortable in the mouth, throat, and nasal passages as a result of eating berries or breathing smoke produced from burning plants. **Related poisonous species:** Poison oak *(Rhus toxicodendron),* of sandy soils, pine forest, or barrens in the eastern U.S., and *Rhus diversiloba,* also called poison oak, of the Pacific coastal states, both contain oily resin capable of producing dermatitis like that caused by poison ivy.

Ohio buckeye, Horsechestnut

Aesculus glabra

Habitat: woodlands, hillsides, especially riverbottoms and stream banks. **Identification:** broad spreading tree with open, rounded crown and dark-brown, deeply furrowed bark. *Leaves opposite,* deciduous, *hand-shaped compound* (palmate) *with 5 or 7 leaflets,* leaflets usually widest near middle, 10–15 cm (4–6 in) long, 3.5–6 cm (1.4–2.4 in) wide, pointed at tip, finely toothed along margin, yellowish-green, leafstalks long. Flowers produced in large, erect clusters 12.5–15 cm (5–6 in) long, pale yellowish green, with 5-lobed calyx, 4 petals sometimes with red stripes. *Fruits a leathery, 3-parted capsule 2.5–5 cm* (1–2 in) *long, with short blunt spines on outer surface* of husk, *containing 1 or 2 large, shiny, dark reddish-brown seeds.* **Poisonous constituents:** All plant parts, especially the large seeds, contain aesculin, a glycoside. If ingested, this toxin can cause vomiting, stupor, twitching, paralysis, and possibly even death. Seeds of buckeyes or horsechestnuts resemble those of edible chestnuts. **Related poisonous species:** All native species of the buckeye genus *(Aesculus)* should be considered poisonous. Compounds from some species have been used medicinally. A coumarin glycoside, esculoside, obtained from the European horse chestnut *(A. hippcastanum),* has been used to treat hemorrhoids.

Poison ivy: immature plant with bronze leaves and fruiting branch with shiny green leaves and light-green female flower clusters (NYBG).

Ohio buckeye: Fruiting branch (Clawson).

Nutritional Contents of Selected Foods

Per 100 gram portion (about 3.5 ounces)

Food	ENERGY BUILDING BLOCKS				MINERALS					VITAMINS				
	Calories	Protein (g)	Fat (g)	Carbohydrates (g)	Calcium (mg)	Phosphorus (mg)	Iron (mg)	Sodium (mg)	Potassium (mg)	Vitamin A (IU)	Thiamine (mg)	Riboflavin (mg)	Niacin (mg)	Ascorbic acid (mg)
Apples, raw	58	0.2	0.6	14.5	7	10	0.3	1	110	90	.03	.02	.1	4
Asparagus, raw	26	2.5	0.2	5.0	22	62	1.0	2	278	900	.18	.20	1.5	33
Bananas, raw	85	1.1	0.2	22.2	8	26	0.7	1	370	190	.05	.06	.7	10
Beans, lima, boiled, and drained	111	7.6	0.5	19.8	47	121	2.5	1	422	280	.18	.10	1.3	17
Beef, broiled	207	32.2	7.7	0.0	13	261	3.9	60	370	10	.09	.25	6.4	0
Beverages: Beer	42	0.3	0.0	3.8	5	30	tr	7	25	0	tr	.03	.6	0
Wine	85	0.1	0.0	4.2	9	10	0.4	5	92	0	tr	.01	.1	0
Blackberries, raw	58	1.2	0.9	12.9	32	19	0.9	1	170	200	.03	.04	.4	21
Bread, whole wheat	243	10.5	3.0	48.0	99	228	2.3	527	273	tr	.26	.12	2.8	tr
Broccoli, raw	32	3.6	0.3	5.9	103	78	1.1	15	382	2,500	.10	.23	.9	113
Carrots, raw	42	1.1	0.2	9.7	37	36	0.7	47	341	11,000	.06	.05	.6	8
Cauliflower, raw	27	2.7	0.2	5.2	25	56	1.1	13	295	60	.11	.10	.7	78
Chicken, white meat, roasted	182	32.3	4.9	0.0	11	272	1.3	66	422	110	.08	.10	11.8	0
Chicory greens, raw	20	1.8	0.3	3.8	86	40	0.9	0	420	4,000	.06	.10	.5	22
Cucumbers, raw	15	0.9	0.1	3.4	25	27	1.1	6	160	250	.03	.04	.2	11
Dandelion greens, raw	45	2.7	0.7	9.2	187	66	3.1	76	397	14,000	.19	.26	.0	35
Dock & sheep sorrel, raw	28	2.1	0.3	5.6	66	41	1.6	5	338	12,900	.09	.22	.5	119
Eggs, raw or boiled	163	12.9	11.5	0.9	54	205	2.3	122	129	1,180	.11	.30	.1	0
Grapes, raw	69	1.3	1.0	15.7	16	12	0.4	3	158	100	.05	.03	.3	4
Hazelnuts	634	12.6	62.4	16.7	209	337	3.4	2	704	0	.46	.00	.9	tr
Hickorynuts	673	13.2	68.7	12.8	tr	360	2.4	0	0	0	.00	.00	.0	0
Jerusalem artichoke, raw, fresh	7	2.3	0.1	16.7	14	78	3.4	0	0	20	.20	.06	1.3	4

Nutritional Contents of Selected Foods (continued)

Food	Calories	Protein (g)	Fat (g)	Carbohydrates (g)	Calcium (mg)	Phosphorus (mg)	Iron (mg)	Sodium (mg)	Potassium (mg)	Vitamin A (IU)	Thiamine (mg)	Riboflavin (mg)	Niacin (mg)	Ascorbic acid (mg)
Lamb's-quarters (Pigweed), raw	43	4.2	0.8	7.3	309	72	1.2	0	0	11,600	.16	.44	1.2	80
Leeks, bulb & lower leaf, raw	52	2.2	0.3	11.2	52	50	1.1	5	347	40	.11	.06	.5	17
Lettuce, raw	14	1.0	0.2	2.9	35	26	2.0	9	264	970	.06	.06	.3	8
Milk, cows, whole	65	3.5	3.5	4.9	118	93	tr	50	144	140	.03	.17	.1	1
Mustard greens, raw	31	3.0	0.5	5.6	183	50	3.0	32	377	7,000	.11	.22	.8	97
Onions, bulb, raw	38	1.5	0.1	8.7	27	36	0.5	10	157	tr	.03	.04	.2	10
Papaw, raw	85	5.2	0.9	16.8	0	0	0.0	0	0	0	.00	.00	.0	0
Parsnips, raw	76	1.7	0.5	17.5	50	77	0.7	12	541	30	.08	.09	.2	16
Peanuts, with skins	564	26.0	47.5	18.6	69	401	2.1	5	674	0	1.14	.13	17.2	0
Pears, raw	61	0.7	0.4	15.3	8	11	0.3	2	130	20	.02	.04	.1	4
Peas, green, immature, raw	84	6.3	0.4	14.4	26	116	1.9	2	316	640	.35	.14	2.9	27
Pecans	687	9.2	71.2	14.6	73	289	2.4	tr	603	130	.86	.13	.9	2
Persimmons, raw	127	0.8	0.4	33.5	27	26	2.5	1	310	0	.00	.00	.0	66
Plums, raw	66	0.5	0.0	17.8	18	17	0.5	2	299	300	.08	.03	.5	0
Potatoes, raw	76	2.1	0.1	17.1	7	153	0.6	3	407	tr	.10	.04	1.5	20
Prickly-pears, raw	42	0.5	0.1	10.9	20	28	0.3	2	166	60	.01	.03	.4	22
Purslane, leaves & stems, raw	21	1.7	0.4	3.8	103	39	3.5	0	0	2,500	.03	.10	.5	25
Raspberries, raw	57	1.2	0.5	13.6	22	22	0.9	1	168	130	.03	.09	.9	25
Rice, brown, raw	360	7.5	1.9	77.4	32	221	1.6	9	214	0	.34	.05	4.7	0
Salsify, fresh, raw	13	2.9	0.6	18.0	47	66	1.5	0	380	10	.04	.04	.3	11
Strawberries, raw	37	0.7	0.5	8.4	21	21	1.0	1	164	60	.03	.07	.6	59
Sunflower seed kernels, dry	560	24.0	47.3	19.9	120	837	7.1	30	920	50	1.96	.23	5.4	0
Walnuts, black	628	20.5	59.3	14.8	tr	570	6.0	3	460	300	.22	.11	.7	0
Watercress, leaves & stems, raw	19	2.2	0.3	3.0	151	54	1.7	52	282	4,900	.08	.16	.9	79

Source: *Handbook of the Nutritional Contents of Foods*, U.S. Department of Agriculture, Dover Publications Inc., New York 1975.

g = grams, mg = milligrams, IU = international units, tr = trace

General Index

Index to plant names

Bold face type is used for common names and pages where you'll find plants both described and illustrated. *Bold face italic* is used for scientific names of described and illustrated plants. The thinner typeface (normal and *italic*) is used for plants mentioned incidentally, for example, when they resemble a plant covered in full detail.